Presented to:

Rina

From:

Johan + Betsie

Date:

7 January 2008

The Glory of God's Grace

366 Devotions to comfort and encourage

SOLLY OZROVECH

CHRISTIAN ART PUBLISHERS

Originally published by Christelike Uitgewersmaatskappy
under the title *Die Rykdom van Sy Genade*

© 1993

English edition © 1995
Christian Art Publishers
PO Box 1599, Vereeniging, 1930
First edition 1995
Second edition 2006

Translated by Linda van Tonder
Cover designed by Christian Art Publishers

Scripture taken from the *Holy Bible*, New International Version
Copyright © 1973, 1978, 1984 by International Bible Society.
Used with permission.

Set in 13 on 16 pt Palatino Linotype by Christian Art Publishers

Printed in China

ISBN 978-1-86829-591-3

© All rights reserved. No part of this book may be reproduced in any
form without permission in writing from the publisher, except in the
case of brief quotations embodied in critical articles or reviews.

07 08 09 10 11 12 13 14 15 16 – 11 10 9 8 7 6 5 4 3 2

Dedicated to:

Professor Dawid de Villiers and Mrs. Anna de Villiers with appreciation for a long-standing friendship of more than forty years.

"The greatest gift you can give

your friend is something of yourself."

– Ralph Waldo Emerson

JANUARY

A New Life for a New Year

JANUARY 1

Trust in the LORD with all your heart and lean not on your own understanding; in all your ways acknowledge Him, and He will make your paths straight (Proverbs 3:5-6).

Today is the first day of a new year – it is also the first day of the rest of your life. Whatever decisions you make today may have far-reaching consequences on your future.

Spend some constructive time in God's presence. Review the past under the scrutinizing eye of the Holy Spirit. Bring into the open and confess those hidden sins and weaknesses that, up to now, you have either accepted, refused to acknowledge or felt you could do nothing about. Start the new year confessing your sins because this will prepare you for the wonderful experience of God's forgiveness. By doing this, you are wiping the slate clean and enabling yourself to start a new life.

The foundation of this new life is total and complete faith in the living Christ. He will never disappoint you, as thousands of His followers will confirm. Through His indwelling Holy Spirit He will broaden your horizons about what life can offer you. Your outlook on life will change completely as you start looking at life through His eyes ... the more closely you walk with Him, the more clearly you will understand what He can do in your life.

As you develop a steadfast and positive faith in the Master you will find His Spirit working in you to the extent that you live in such harmony with Him that your only desire is to do His will. Reflecting His Spirit in your life is the ultimate Christian experience. As you enter into the new year, be sure to strengthen and enrich your relationship with Christ so that your spiritual life can flourish and bear the fruit of the Spirit.

Loving Master, I come to You in earnest prayer that my imperfect life might reflect something of Your holiness this year. Amen.

THE ROAD TO REAL GREATNESS

"For even the Son of Man did not come to be served, but to serve, and to give His life as a ransom for many" (Mark 10:45).

JANUARY 2

The depth and quality of your spiritual life depend entirely on your relationship with God. If this relationship is weak and restricted only to the purely religious areas of your life, you are in danger of becoming spiritually stunted.

True spirituality involves your whole life and can only be effective if practiced in every area of your life: where you live, work and relax. It is to be practiced where you come into contact with others. Spirituality in confinement is not the religion preached or exercised by Jesus Christ.

One undeniable fact about the life of Christ is that He was a servant. He came to serve those who were willing to accept His labor of love, and He calls on those who wish to follow Him to do the same. Although this is not a very popular calling today, Jesus taught that it is through service, inspired by His Holy Spirit, that we rise to spiritual greatness and find fulfillment in our calling.

It is not spiritual rituals and traditions that result in inspired and practical service, but only a life surrendered completely to Christ.

True spiritual growth and maturity flow from a spirit and pattern of thought that are in total harmony with Jesus Christ. If you belong to Him unconditionally there is no space for superficiality, pettiness or fanaticism. May this be your spiritual goal for the new year and may the Holy Spirit accompany you and assist you in obtaining this worthy goal.

Dear Redeemer and Lord, I dedicate my life to You and to Your work so that Your Spirit can lead me to be of service to others. Amen.

RENEW YOUR FAITH

JANUARY 3

Examine yourselves to see whether you are in the faith; test yourselves. Do you not realize that Christ Jesus is in you – unless, of course, you fail the test (2 Corinthians 13:5).

Mediocrity is one of the greatest threats to our spiritual lives. Perhaps once you had an unforgettable experience with the living Redeemer. He was such a living reality to you that you were positive that nothing could ever separate you from "the love of God that is in Christ Jesus our Lord" (Rom. 8:39).

You might find it difficult to determine what went wrong. At what stage did the relationship between you and your Lord lose its warmth and became cold and formal? It might be that your relationship with Him is not as vital and exciting as it used to be.

Somewhere along your spiritual pilgrimage you might have loosened your grip on Jesus. Other loyalties became stronger than your dedication to Him and gradually your life lost direction. On the outside, everything seemed fine, but deep down you knew that the light and power of Christ was not such an integral part of your life any more.

It is good to realize that a lukewarm and ineffective faith is your fault and not God's. He still offers you the richness of His love and the power of His Holy Spirit. Get your spiritual life in order now, at the beginning of this new year. Do not allow the opportunity to slip through your fingers.

It is possible to drastically renew your faith by fixing your thoughts on Christ instead of on yourself. Your faith will revive through total commitment to Jesus and His plan for your life. Do it now – it is only a prayer away.

Lord, I commit myself to You afresh today so that, through the guidance of Your Holy Spirit, my faith can grow again and be effective. Amen.

LOOK BACK AND BE GRATEFUL

We give thanks to You, O God, we give thanks, for Your Name is near; men tell of Your wonderful deeds (Psalm 75:1).

Perhaps you sometimes ask in pain and confusion, "Where is God? Why does He allow these things to happen to me?" You experience the unbearable pressure of the moment; trivial and destructive forces shatter your most precious dreams; nothing that you do ends successfully. You question the goodness and the very existence of God.

If, at this moment, your faith has reached the low-level mark and doubt is gnawing at your heart, it will be wise to spend time with God, praying for spiritual renewal. From time to time it is necessary for God's children to put everything else aside to revive the glory and power of their faith. It is a spiritual impossibility to be constantly busy (no matter how worthy the cause) without drawing from the Well of faith and inspiration, our Triune God. You cannot carry on giving of yourself indefinitely without being renewed by the Holy Spirit from day to day.

There are various ways of doing this. One very fruitful method is to recall those times when God was such a living reality to you; when you tangibly experienced the revelation of His love for you. At those times you never doubted His existence or His presence in your life. You just knew: "God is with us."

At that stage you were convinced that you would never forget that awe-inspiring experience and that your life would never again lose its sparkle. But it did! Now is the time to recall those precious moments and once again draw power and inspiration from them for the unknown road that lies ahead. "Give thanks to the LORD, for He is good, His love endures forever" (Ps. 106:1).

Lord, You have done so much for me in the past, but I forget so easily. Thank You for being with me every moment of my life. Amen.

ON THE WAY WITH CHRIST

JANUARY 5

"They asked each other, 'Were not our hearts burning within us while He talked with us on the road and opened the Scriptures to us?'" (Luke 24:32).

You might be familiar with the teachings of Jesus Christ and interested in an in-depth study of the Scriptures, but it is only when the living Christ becomes your constant companion that your faith becomes a living reality.

Quiet moments spent in the presence of God are precious. During these moments you draw inner strength from Him and your spirit is united with His.

As times goes by, this relationship grows and intensifies, becoming more meaningful and enriching. But unfortunately you can't spend all your time alone with the Lord. You have to earn a living and go about your day's work whether it be at home or at work.

At times when you are so busy that you are sapped of energy and concentration, it can easily happen that you neglect your quiet times. It is important to never neglect to spend time alone with God.

When you have met with God you will find it easier to concentrate on Him during those busy times when your thoughts are in turmoil and storms rage around you.

Use such moments to confirm His presence and acknowledge His authority in your life. You will then experience the joy of His closeness and Christ will be your Companion and Leader every day that you walk life's road.

Please help me, O Lord, to be aware of Your presence every moment of the day, and in this way strengthen the bond between us. Amen.

A LIFE DIRECTED BY THE SPIRIT

"Man does not live on bread alone, but on every word that comes from the mouth of God" (Matthew 4:4).

So many people today live unbalanced lives without even being aware of it. They experience frustrations, jealousy, dissatisfaction and covetousness – things that can never bring satisfaction.

They react by becoming busier, rushing on in even greater haste searching for wealth in earthly possessions. They harbor the vain hope that material possessions will bring peace of mind and security.

One of the basic truths of Christianity is that man is a spiritual being created as God's representative on earth and destined for continued fellowship with our heavenly Father.

It is when we ignore this spiritual dimension of our lives that life becomes distorted and unfocused. Our priorities become distorted and we experience an insatiable hunger and longing that only Christ can satisfy.

To be spiritually minded does not imply being fanatical about some or other religious doctrine. What it does mean is that you will recognize the spiritual foundation of life and allow your life to be ruled by Christ's principles.

To live a spirit-orientated life means that you have a balanced attitude towards life; it means that you handle the adversities of life with dignity, and meet with God daily, seeking His will for your life.

Once you have learnt to live according to God's will instead of your own, you have discovered the secret of true life.

Thank You, gracious God, that Your will becomes clear in Your Word. Grant me the wisdom to live my life accordingly. Amen.

When Things Go Wrong

JANUARY 7

Let us examine our ways and test them, and let us return to the LORD (Lamentations 3:40).

For a while everything in your life might run smoothly and your faith in Jesus Christ might be strong and true. Life is wonderful and you are convinced that nothing could possibly shake your spiritual balance and that you will stand strong in prayer and always be an effective witness.

Then suddenly, for no obvious reason, things start to go wrong. At first the change is so slight that you hardly notice it. However, small irritations soon grow into mountains of discontent.

When you realize that something is wrong and you are willing to confess, praise God for that, for then you can at least do something about it. If you set time aside for self-evaluation, make sure you do it in partnership with God. Humbly ask His Holy Spirit to assist you in examining your heart honestly and purposefully.

Through the teachings and guidance of the Holy Spirit, you will also receive the grace and courage to identify the cause of your failure and spiritual breakdown and also to cope with it. As the Holy Spirit reveals to you your true self, He will also lovingly guide you back to the Source of all true life: Jesus Christ!

Returning to the Father always results in feasting and festive joy in the Father's house. Your experience will confirm the Scripture verses, "Every valley shall be filled in, every mountain and hill made low. The crooked roads shall become straight, the rough ways smooth. And all mankind will see God's salvation" (Luke 3:5-6).

Search me, O God, and know my heart, test me and see if there is any offensive way in me and lead me in the way everlasting. Amen.

WHEN A DIFFICULT TASK AWAITS YOU

And who is equal to such a task (2 Corinthians 2:16).

The new year brings with it new challenges. There will be times when you will wrestle with difficult decisions or tasks that will test your mind, strength and abilities to the limit.

When you have accepted Jesus Christ as Lord of your life and have given your life to Him, you've submitted yourself to a totally new approach to life. You did not know exactly what He would expect from you or which task He would assign to you. It could be that the Master has already confronted you with a task that you feel totally inadequate to do. Perhaps you shied away from it, offering the excuse that God would not have called someone as poorly suited to the task as you.

Many followers of Christ become frustrated when they work for God because of their own inabilities, instead of looking beyond themselves at the wisdom, power and ability that God provides. God never calls you to do something that He knows you cannot do, even if you feel inadequate. He does not necessarily call the person skilled for the task, but rather supplies the person that He calls with the necessary skills.

When you have a difficult task to complete pray that the Holy Spirit will give you wisdom and insight to handle the problem in the right way. In the power of Jesus Christ, through the inspiration of the Holy Spirit you will overcome discouragement and complete the task in a way that pleases Him. In this way you will be able to start every day of this new year in His strength – praying, deeply dependent on the One who strengthens you.

Holy Master, through the power of Your Holy Spirit I will tackle every task that comes my way and complete it in Your name. Amen.

THE PRIVILEGE OF STARTING OVER

Therefore, if anyone is in Christ, he is a new creation; the old has gone, the new has come! (2 Corinthians 5:17).

It is exciting to start over because there are endless opportunities in life. Even if there is a possibility of failure, don't let it stop you from trying, trusting that you will complete what you started in faith.

We all wonder what the new year has in store for us, and fortunately we do not know. Not knowing should never cause you to fear or hesitate, but rather to grab hold of every opportunity and consider it a practical exercise in faith.

There is satisfaction in facing the unknown with a deep sense of trust that your love for God, and your unwavering faith in Him will make all things work together for your good. Positive spiritual thinking produces positive spiritual results.

So enter this new period with an awareness of the presence of God in your life. Expect only what is best for you from His loving hand. Work and pray for it faithfully, convinced that God's love is at work in your life every day. "Give thanks to the LORD, for He is good; His love endures forever" (Ps. 106:1).

The icy winds of unbelief may blow around you. You may sometimes find yourself in the suffocating grip of despondency, but never allow your awareness of God's presence to fade.

Should you be fearful, sorrowful or unhappy – bring it to the Father in prayer, through Jesus Christ. Then you will experience a continual strengthening of your spirit.

Lord, I will meet the future with the joyful assurance that it is in Your hands. Thank You for the privilege of a new beginning. Amen.

INNER STRENGTH

I pray that out of His glorious riches He may strengthen you with power through His Spirit in your inner being ... so that you may be rooted and established in love (Ephesians 3:16-17).

Are you perhaps one of those people who pretend to be courageous, but deep down you feel insecure and uncertain? If so, there is nothing to be ashamed of. You are only hiding your true feelings from others who expect you to be strong and unruffled at all times.

The only problem with this pretence is that at a given moment your hidden nature will show. Life has a way of stripping us of our masks in a very cruel and unexpected way. Make use of discipline and prayer so that your character will become a true image of your inner strength.

It is the privilege of each of Jesus' disciples to possess this inner strength that becomes the driving force of a dynamic life. It is very tender in its formative influence: it re-creates your character; creates an awareness of God's presence and makes you realize what an important role you have to play in God's master plan.

Inner strength can only materialize if you are willing to make your commitment to God so real and practical that the Holy Spirit can work freely in your life. This requires prayer; regular time spent with God's Word, meditating on God's grandeur and omnipotence and reading constructive Christian literature. Then you will become aware of your unity with God and appreciate it.

You need the power and guidance of the Holy Spirit if you want to build inner strength. Then your feelings of fear and insecurity will vanish and you will approach the future courageously, knowing God, the Almighty, is holding your hand.

Lord, I know that it's not only what I do that matters but what You do through me. Please make me a useful instrument. Amen.

OVERCOME YOUR FEARS

The LORD replied, "My Presence will go with you, and I will give you rest." Then Moses said to Him, "If Your Presence does not go with us, do not send us up from here" (Exodus 33:14-15).

Many noble plans have been dashed because people lacked the confidence to tackle problems, or failed to see things through after a convincing start. Man must place a sword in the hand of his dreams in defense of both his physical and spiritual life. We dare not allow the work of the Lord to suffer loss due to our lack of courage and confidence.

One of life's basic principles is that you will never achieve anything of value, or undertake anything worthwhile, unless you do it in honor of God, and in His strength. You might experience short-lived joy, but lasting satisfaction will always evade you. The assurance that your attempts are worthwhile depends on the position that you give to God in your life. Your plans and intentions must be central to His holy will.

Experience teaches us that nothing worthwhile comes easily. You will have to overcome obstacles, temptations and disappointments that will threaten your plans. You will feel like making compromises that will force you to lower your standards.

During these times it is important for you to realize that Jesus must form an integral part of your plans, intentions and dreams. Make Him your Partner in everything you do. Allow Him to set the standards. Then you can depend on the guidance of His Spirit to be successful in every undertaking and eventually you will deserve a "well done" from the Master.

Faithful Guide, I lay all my plans and dreams at Your feet. Help me to be faithful to Your call even for the noblest cause. Amen.

MEMORIES OR HOPE?

But one thing I do: Forgetting what is behind and straining toward what is ahead (Philippians 3:13).

We find people who constantly live in the past, remembering the "good old days". The present is then always compared to the past, and the present is always found wanting. This is a sure sign of old age or of dreams and ideals that have died – it is a syndrome that makes you old and indifferent long before your time.

The person who scans the horizon, who looks ahead and believes, is the one who maintains his youthful spirit and adventurous life. If you have already traveled far on life's road, you might think you have no grounds for hope. But remember, you are alive today and this is God's most precious gift to you. Make optimal use of every hour of every day of this year and don't spoil it by fretting about the transience of life.

Pour out all the love and understanding that you can muster on those who are struggling to survive. You will be rewarded, knowing that you are following in the footsteps of the Master.

As a child of God you have the hope of eternal life. Even if your life is a struggle, even though memories of a beautiful yesterday seem to pull you back into the past, grasp this golden day that God grants you and live it to the full and to the glory of God.

Keep hope burning in your heart and remember that the future has many opportunities because your God is in the future as well. If it had not been for this hope, we all would have suffered broken hearts.

O Lord, let Your Holy Spirit keep the flame of hope burning in my heart. Amen.

Never in Your Own Strength

I can do everything through Him who gives me strength (Philippians 4:13).

As a Christian you have spiritual reserves at your disposal. Because this source is invisible it is not appreciated properly. Instead of using and enjoying the dynamics of our faith, we waste energy in a losing battle against frustration, failure and defeat.

Guard against pretending to be a strong Christian while you are actually being destroyed by the knowledge of your insufficiency and failure. Acknowledging and confessing your spiritual need is the first step to recovery and power.

When you realize that it is only through the power of the indwelling Christ that you can lead a real and true Christian life, you will become totally dependent on Him. Unless the Holy Spirit completely inhabits your spirit, all your efforts will be in vain.

The Christian life is not about a personal struggle for victory, but about claiming the victory we have in Christ. He has already fought the battle and won it for you. You just have to accept it in faith and practice it.

Once this truth has become an integral part of your thoughts, your attitude toward life will change radically. You will no longer expect defeat and failure, but will be victorious. The essence of Christianity is not so much what you can do for Christ, but what you allow Christ to do through you in the power of the Holy Spirit. Then your primary reaction won't be: "Lord, what do You want me to do?" but "Lord, what do You want me to be?"

Almighty Father, I humbly confess that my power comes not from me, but is the result of Your Holy Spirit working through me. Amen.

THE CHOICE IS YOURS

"I have set before you life and death, blessings and curses. Now choose life, so that you and your children may live" (Deuteronomy 30:19).

God gets wrongfully blamed for many things that man is responsible for. He gets blamed for adversity and disaster; for problems and troubles; for unfulfilled goals and shattered dreams. In many of these cases the fault lies with man and not with God.

In His wisdom and omnipotence God gave each man the freedom of choice. He has to choose between right and wrong; joy or sadness; success or failure. Where you find yourself today is the direct result of the choices you made yesterday and the day before. As soon as you stop blaming God, others and your circumstances and start owning up to your own mistakes, you will be able to live life to the full.

Spiritual recovery and growth are a matter of choice. You can, in your own power, try boosting your diminishing ego with weak excuses. However, you are only bluffing yourself by believing that you are not to be blamed for the pitiful position you are in.

On the other hand, you can evaluate yourself in the light of the Holy Spirit and see yourself as you really are. After such an honest evaluation you have to make a conscious decision to accept God as your Re-creator and Guide. The choice is yours, but you will have to bear the consequences of whatever you decide.

Pray for God's grace to pursue your objectives this year. Don't blame others for your failures, but live purposefully and accept responsibility for your decisions. Then you can live a life that glorifies God.

Grant me wisdom and insight, dear Lord, to choose to go the way You show me. Amen.

REALIZE WHO YOU ARE FOR A CHANGE!

So God created man in His own image, in the image of God He created him; male and female He created them (Genesis 1:27).

In every person's life there are times when he feels that everything is going wrong and nothing seems to be working out. A sense of infinite loneliness and despondency descends. This is the time to use the spiritual reserves that are at your disposal.

You were created as God's representative. It is true that His image in you has been marred by sin and it may even happen that you scorn your spiritual inheritance. The fact remains, however, that you are a spiritual being and because of this, new hope and inspiration should permeate your spirit and your mind.

You have been created in the image of your Holy Father and you are destined for spiritual greatness. You will never know real peace or fulfillment until you develop a strong spiritual life. This includes prayer, reading your Bible, meditation and commitment – resources you can make use of by the grace of God.

If you feel inferior, it will be of tremendous help to remember your origins: you are a spiritual being who lives and moves in the presence of God. If your life is subjected to stress and tension, you will find indescribable relief in the abundance of grace from God's hand. And this is not nearly as theoretical as it may sound because an experience with God is always very real.

As His representative you can approach life fearlessly, guided by His Holy Spirit and safe in the knowledge that I am God's unique, individual creation.

Creator Father, help me to look away from myself and focus on my spiritual inheritance so that I can live with confidence. Amen.

ENTHUSIASM OR FAITH?

In the same way faith by itself, if it is not accompanied by action, is dead (James 2:17).

There are few things in life as encouraging as an enthusiastic Christian whose faith is practical and alive. When the winds of unbelief start raging around him, when darkness envelops his soul, he remains steadfast, clinging to the essence of his faith.

The Christian who relies on the emotional boost he receives from a loaded church service and who cannot survive on his own inner strength, lacks the firm foundation that is required to remain standing in stormy weather. Enthusiasm without a living faith is insufficient. Nevertheless, positive, practical faith supplies real enthusiasm, enabling the believer to reflect his faith with joy.

Faith and not emotions determines the quality of your Christian life. Faith in the living Christ always brings about new life and growth, spiritual strength, a constructive and consistent goal in life and love for God that makes obedience to Him a joy and a privilege.

Living faith fills every void that may exist in your life with the wonderful assurance that your heavenly Father desires to be totally and completely united with you. Through Christ He revealed how this unity is possible.

Accepting Christ and His principles in your life and in your mind are usually a deeply emotional experience. However, the emotion is always secondary to your faith in Christ Jesus your Redeemer. Once you have accepted Him as your Savior; your emotions will also fall into place.

Creator Spirit, please bring into my life a sound balance between faith and emotions so that my enthusiasm can develop into practical faith. Amen.

THE LIGHT STILL SHINES BRIGHTLY

Though I sit in darkness, the Lord will be my light (Micah 7:8).

Through the ages history has proved that there have been times when everything was dark and the future seemed bleak and grim. At times this was the result of plagues and disasters; drought and famine; economic recessions that created turmoil and blurred visions of the future and wars that left millions dead and just as many maimed.

With unrest, anarchy and crime the order of the day; with people being retrenched, living in fear and insecurity; with peace glimmering like a mirage in the desert; with farmers being ruined by ongoing droughts, it appears as if we are once again entering a dark period.

Yet above our pessimism and our oppressive, terrifying circumstances, above the clamor of demonic forces, the voice of Jesus is heard – clear, triumphant and liberating, "Take heart! I have overcome the world" (John 16:33).

No matter how hopeless circumstances may seem, the Christian always sets his hope in Christ. In spite of all the evil powers joining forces against Him, in spite of the brutality of unbelievers, Jesus triumphed over death in the darkest hour in the history of mankind. He conquered death when He transformed the darkness of Golgotha into the light of the Resurrection.

What God the Father did in Jesus, He has done repeatedly since then, and He will carry on doing. Let us trust in the Lord to the very end and "declare the praises of Him who called you out of darkness into His wonderful light" (1 Pet. 2:9).

Eternal God and Father, no matter how dark my circumstances may seem, I put my hope and trust in You. Amen.

KEEP GROWING SPIRITUALLY

Your faith is growing more and more, and the love every one of you has for each other is increasing (2 Thessalonians 1:3).

If your spiritual experiences no longer satisfy you it is possibly because you have stagnated and lost your spiritual zest. Perhaps your prayer life has deteriorated and you have neglected your Bible study and quiet times. This always has unfortunate results and you dare not take on the new year like this.

A vibrant and powerful spiritual life requires constant attention. You may never reach a point where you feel that nothing is required from you any longer or that you don't have to put in an effort. On the contrary, the longer you walk with the Spirit, the greater your enthusiasm should be and any tendency to relax should be resisted with all your might.

Your quiet time in the presence of God sustains and nurtures your spirit. When you become aware of spiritual decline in your life, don't look for excuses. Ask God for the wisdom and the courage to confess your negligence and weakness and do something constructive about this attitude that makes you spiritually barren and unhappy.

In order to grow spiritually you have to become increasingly aware of the presence of the living Christ in your life. This awareness is not restricted to a few religious fanatics who live in seclusion. It can be experienced daily, with power and glory, by present-day disciples. It will be spring again in your spiritual life.

Lord, You who are the True Vine, let me grow in You so that I can bear fruit that will please You. Amen.

COURAGE AND FAITH

I know whom I have believed, and am convinced that He is able to guard what I have entrusted to Him for that day (2 Timothy 1:12).

In our everyday conversations we so easily say, "I believe." We use the phrase to express passing opinions of little or no value. Yet a statement like this should be confirmation of a firm conviction we arrived at after serious thought or experience.

To say "I believe" as a Christian is to make one of the strongest statements known to man. It can revolutionize your thoughts, transform your life and revive your daily existence. How can you obtain such a strong faith that can transform your life?

A sound Christian faith should have a fixed intellectual basis, founded on the Scriptures. If this is lacking it could mean that your faith is influenced by every passing emotion or imaginary whim that is accepted as dogma. It is important that you should be able to account for your faith, "so that you may know how to answer every one" (Col. 4:6).

To have firm intellectual convictions is commendable, but it is only when these convictions are established in deep emotional experience that they become invincible.

It is possible to be very knowledgeable about theological doctrines and yet be spiritually stagnant. It is only when the Holy Spirit inspires your convictions, that you possess the fundamentals of a vital faith.

This kind of faith creates trust and trust in turn creates a type of calculated courage that every Christian needs in his life. In all circumstances this courage will stem from the certainty of what you believe.

Thank You, Almighty Savior, that I may know You and love You and because of this my faith is a living reality. Amen.

CHRIST UNDERSTANDS

Because He Himself suffered when He was tempted, He is able to help those who are being tempted (Hebrews 2:18).

There is no substitute for experience. If you can say to a despondent person, "I know exactly how you feel because I went through a similar experience," it would mean more than merely saying, "I'm thinking of you."

The perfect holiness of Jesus is something readily accepted by His followers. However, His total humanity is something we find more difficult to grasp. People are inclined to think that even though He was human, He was not as fallible as we are. Yet unless Jesus became completely human, His incarnation was of no value. Because He was totally human, He experienced temptation, hunger and misunderstanding in the same way that you and I do. The difference is that He triumphed over every hardship so that He could fulfill His task of salvation for us all.

He understands our temptations, trials and tribulations and human weaknesses. If you ever feel like a failure, don't despair! Don't let go of Jesus. Remember that He will restore your trust and courage with His love and understanding. He understands us and knows what is best for each one of us at all times. He is not only our Savior, but also our Friend.

The wonder of God's grace is that Christ not only understands our needs, He also intercedes for us with the Father so that our faith may endure. Remember this when Satan launches his sifting process in your life: Christ understands and He prays for you (see Luke 22:31-32).

Thank You, Lord Jesus, for Your love and understanding and the restorative power of Your endless grace. Amen.

PRAYER EXPRESSES OUR NEEDS

Be faithful in prayer (Romans 12:12).

Prayer covers all aspects of our lives; we daily make our needs known to God in prayer. When we feel insecure, we seek God's guidance in prayer. For people who acknowledge the total authority of a loving Father prayer is indispensable.

The greater your need, the more serious your prayer. Yet God knows about every need, even before you mention it to Him. Do not, however, think, "If God knows my needs, why do I need to bother Him with them?" A loving Father loves to hear the voice of His child in need, even if He knows what that need is. God will answer your prayer – not because of the urgency of your plea, but because of your faith and your willingness to obey Him.

When you pray you must always be sensitive to what God expects from you, as He often requires your co-operation in answering your prayer. If you are lonely and longing for friendship, ask God to give you a friendly disposition. You will suddenly discover how easy it is to make new friends.

If you are in need of money, God might make you aware of the difference between what you want and what you really need. Perhaps, in a practical way, He wants you to start living within your means. Through conversing with God, the Holy Spirit leads us to solutions.

There are, however, prayers that you can do nothing to help answer. These you must bring to God in childlike faith and leave them in His hands. Be alert, because the answer to your prayers might be presented in such a way that you do not recognize it as such if you don't have a sensitive spirit.

O Hearer of prayers, help me to be sensitive to Your voice so that I can contribute to the answers of my prayers. Amen.

SIMPLE BUT COMPREHENSIVE

"Teacher, which is the greatest commandment in the Law?" (Matthew 22:36).

JANUARY 22

Religion can become very complex and intricate when people try to regulate it. Within the Christian church there are so many diverse and even contradictory views that the average person can get totally confused.

When Jesus was asked what the greatest commandment was, He answered simply but clearly, "Love the Lord your God with all your heart and with all your soul and with all your mind." He then added the meaningful phrase, "Love your neighbor as you love yourself" (Matt. 22:37-39).

Self-love, which refers to the respect that I have for myself as God's unique creation, has got nothing in common with the monster called pride. In our day and age we find a serious lack of self-love – rather an indescribable feeling of uselessness. In Christ's eyes every person is precious. Reconsider your opinion of yourself and accept joyfully that you were created to be God's representative on earth.

Love your neighbor with the same love you have for yourself! Stop finding fault with others all the time; stop judging and condemning them. If people don't meet the standards you've set, be patient and understanding.

Nurture your love for God. The more you love God, the more this love will reflect in you. Everything the Father has is yours. Because you are His child, the wealth of His treasury is always available to you. Live a life of love, praise and gratitude towards Him.

If you do these things, then God's commandments will not burden you, but will give you wings to soar the heights in your flight of faith.

God of love and mercy, please help me to make love the central theme of my life. Amen.

LIVING FAITH IS PRACTICAL FAITH

So then, just as you received Christ Jesus as Lord, continue to live in Him ... overflowing with thankfulness (Colossians 2:6-7).

True Christian discipleship is an ongoing relationship with the living Christ. Perhaps you are one of those very fortunate people who had a profound and wonderful encounter with Jesus at a specific time in your life. You remember with excitement the exact day and date.

Or perhaps you are one of those people who cannot tell exactly when your relationship with Jesus started, but are fortunate enough to apply to yourself Paul's words about Timothy, "I have been reminded of your sincere faith, which first lived in your grandmother Lois and in your mother Eunice and, I am persuaded, now lives in you also" (2 Tim. 1:5).

It does not matter which of these two groups you belong to; what does matter is the quality of your relationship with your Savior. Although it is interesting to recall spiritual experiences of the past, the real test of faith is the state of your spiritual life at this moment. Do you share your joys and sorrow with your Lord? Are you guided by Him and do you obey His instructions? Do you spend time with Him?

The road leading into the new year may look difficult. You want to share your problems with Jesus, be guided by Him and wish to obey Him; yet obstacles in your way make you lose hope.

Perhaps it is time to stop concentrating on your problems and rather think about closeness with Christ. He wants to become part of your nature and personality. When this happens, your faith will become a practical reality.

Dear Lord and Savior, please take total control of my life so that my faith can be substantial and practical. Amen.

FEAR EXPOSED

Surely God is my salvation; I will trust and not be afraid (Isaiah 12:2).

God repeatedly tells His children not to be afraid. With Israel's crisis at the Red Sea, the Lord said to them, "Stand firm and you will see the deliverance the LORD will bring you today" (Exod. 14:13).

After Moses' death the Lord encouraged Joshua with these words, "Do not be terrified, do not be discouraged, for the LORD your God will be with you wherever you go" (Josh. 1:9).

God made similar appeals to Gideon, Isaiah, Jeremiah and Daniel. Through problem situations He calls on His people, Israel, to overcome their paralyzing fear in His holy name.

The implications for us at the beginning of a new year are crystal clear: as long as we take refuge in God and cling to Him, we can handle and overcome every fear in our lives.

At the birth of Christ, the message of the angels to the shepherds was, "Do not be afraid" (Luke 2:10). When Jesus walked on the water towards His panic-stricken disciples, He said, "Take courage! It is I. Don't be afraid" (Matt. 14:27). And in the last discussion with His disciples, Jesus talked to them about the future, comforting them with these words, "Do not let your hearts be troubled and do not be afraid" (John 14:27). Even today, in every situation where there is tension, anxiety, sadness or pain, the Lord lovingly says to us, "Do not be afraid!" You are His child and He loves you. Make the reality of this love the source of your life because "there is no fear in love. But perfect love drives out fear" (1 John 4:18).

Glorified Lord Jesus, please lead me out of the darkness of my fear. You know that I love You. Amen.

THERE IS NO EASY WAY

JANUARY 25

All hard work brings a profit, but mere talk leads only to poverty (Proverbs 14:23).

The elevator to success is out of order so you have to climb the flight of stairs laboriously, step by step. Today more and more people are looking for a shortcut to success.

Unfortunately these are mostly people who wish to get the most out of life without putting anything back into it. They are the "grabbers". An attitude like this always leads to a compromising lifestyle, a strong dislike of hard work, and sometimes even to dishonesty.

Nothing worthwhile comes easily. You must be committed and prepared to offer the best possible input. If you wish to attain really worthwhile goals, you must make sacrifices and show pride in what you do. Then you will also experience the joy of a job well done, although it might cost time and money, talent and dedication. If you want your achievements to be of any value, you must be willing to pay the price. It is an irrefutable fact that people don't appreciate the things that come effortlessly.

Jesus, our Perfect Example, worked hard and long hours in order to realize God's highest and holy objective for this world. He did so with tenacious perseverance, in the face of bitter resentment and sly hypocrisy. There were times when even His friends let Him down. Yet He persevered because there was so much at stake and He believed in His cause. By His trustworthiness He scored a victory over the world.

Whatever you attempt and undertake this year do it to the best of your ability. Backed by the power of the Holy Spirit you will achieve the fullness of life. "Be faithful, even to the point of death, and I will give you the crown of life" (Rev. 2:10).

Lord, You who assigned me to this task, make me trustworthy and dutiful to the glory of Your name. Amen.

THROUGH HIM WHO STRENGTHENS ME

Blessed is the man who trusts in the LORD, whose confidence is in Him (Jeremiah 17:7).

Everybody is searching for peace of mind but we all have to face the stresses and worries of life. How we handle these stresses is important.

If we look at Christ's lifestyle and the way that He handled pressure and tension we know that there was always a quiet calmness in and around Him.

No matter how turbulent or confusing the circumstances, He always created an atmosphere of peace and quiet. Even in the midst of the milling, noisy, pushing masses that mocked and scorned Him at the crucifixion, His very presence and love created an atmosphere of tranquility – even after He was nailed to the cross!

The composure that Jesus showed under pressure was the outcome of His unique relationship with His Father. He regularly isolated Himself in prayer and bared His soul to His Father. Then He was able to return to a stormy life with the peace of heaven in His heart.

To survive the storms of life, you must allow the living Christ into your heart and life and give Him full control. Allow His Holy Spirit to influence you and to control every word and decision.

When you know that the Prince of Peace is your Guide and Teacher you will be able to cope with any situation. You will be victorious no matter what life has in store for you because, like Paul, you can say, "I can do everything through Him who gives me strength" (Phil. 4:13).

You are my Keeper, O Lord my God. I place myself under Your control and in Your care. That is why I am assured of Your peace. Amen.

What Do I Do with My Burdens?

JANUARY 27

"Come to Me, all you who are weary and burdened, and I will give you rest" (Matthew 11:28).

Dare we go into the future carrying our heavy burdens? Today's Scripture verse is one of the most comforting, but at the same time the most challenging in the New Testament. Through the years it has brought strength and comfort to many people. Many a pilgrim, weary of life and its struggles, managed to derive new hope and inspiration from it. Have you accepted this gracious invitation?

Even though this invitation is powerful in its simplicity and all-inclusive in its application, it does create problems for some who respond to it. However, to take your problems and burdens to Jesus and to find the peace that only He can give is one of the most enriching experiences anybody could hope for.

Unfortunately people resist when they have to let go of their burdens. They tell the Master what it is that worries them and when they get up from their knees, they pick up those very burdens and worries, shoulder them once again and struggle forth.

Some people hesitate to cast their burdens onto Jesus because then they will have nothing to complain about and receive sympathy for.

Perhaps you have been carrying your burdens for so long that they've become part and parcel of your life. They have to be phased out of your life until you are rid of them altogether.

Make sure that you fill the void left by the cast-off burdens with the indwelling Spirit of Christ. Only then will you experience the peace which only Jesus, the Prince of Peace, can give you.

Spirit of Christ, fill my life so completely that I can be set free from every earthly burden. Amen.

Even Though ... Yet!

*Though the fig tree does not bud ... yet I will rejoice in the LORD,
I will be joyful in God my Savior* (Habakkuk 3:17-18).

Many people have a problem linking Christianity and joy together because they think of religion as solemn, serious and rigid. The result is that they miss out on many dimensions of a balanced Christian life.

Some people think that Paul's call to the Philippians to rejoice in the Lord is slightly vain and misplaced and does not suit this worthy man of faith, and that it was also out of place in those times of bitter persecution.

However, Scripture teaches us that there is always joy in God's presence. To experience this joy, it is imperative to live in total harmony with Him. This is where many people fall short because this harmony springs from a daily walk with Christ and a steadfast love for Him: a love that becomes the motivating force of our lives. Then you can rejoice in times of prosperity and adversity.

How we express our Christian joy depends on each individual's temperament. In God's household there is room for all kinds of people. There are those who will express their joy in a spontaneous, jubilant manner, while others will experience it in a more subdued or reserved manner.

Yet it is not the expression itself that is important, but the actual experience. Never judge people's inner feelings by their outward expressions. Whether you are outwardly vocal about the wonder of being God's child or whether you experience quiet, unspoken joy – the main thing is to praise Him from a heart filled with gratitude.

Jesus, Source of all my joy, thank You that my joy is not dependent on my circumstances, but on my relationship with You. Amen.

DO YOU QUESTION YOUR ABILITIES?

JANUARY 29

For it is God who works in you to will and to act according to His good purpose (Philippians 2:13).

There are some people who can't handle seeing others achieve success. These people see others doing things that they would never dream of attempting. Other people's successes just seem to emphasize their own failures and inabilities. The result is that some of us feel completely inferior in the presence of successful people. We are convinced that we could never achieve anything and all our attempts will end in failure.

If you have decided that you are a failure, at least stop blaming your circumstances. Sit down and honestly assess your abilities and your attitude towards life. If you are absolutely honest with yourself you might find that you are hampered by self-pity because of opportunities that you never had or the fact that people were not prepared to give you a chance in life. The result is an aggressive and hostile attitude.

Ask God to assist you through His Holy Spirit in this analysis. He will not only reveal your weak points, but lead you to the discovery of your strong points and hidden potential as well. He will also show you what you can become if you allow God to work through you.

Committed and successful service is not the privilege of a chosen few who have received special gifts. The most brilliant student, most captivating speaker, most talented artist can be used by God; but then, He uses the most ordinary people with no outstanding qualities to do His work every day. Anybody who is willing and who wants to do the will of the Father is used by Him. God Himself qualifies those whom He chooses to use.

Holy Teacher, help me to live for Your approval and not for the praise of men. Amen.

FORGIVENESS CAN HEAL

I will heal their waywardness and love them freely, for My anger has turned away from them. I will be like the dew to Israel (Hosea 14:4-5).

In our day and age much is being said and written about forgiveness and reconciliation. It is essential that we forgive one another, as forgiveness is one of the basic requirements of the Christian faith.

It is equally important that, once you have granted forgiveness, you reveal the quality of Christ's love by helping the person to accept your forgiveness with grace and to free himself from the burden of self-reproach.

When Jesus forgave Peter for renouncing Him, He did not leave it at that, but went on to restore Peter's self-respect by entrusting him with a very important commission: "Feed My lambs! Take care of My sheep!" (see John 21:15-19).

It is equally important that your love should be lavished freely upon those who have hurt or insulted you. That will be the balm that heals their pain, blame, guilt and remorse. Only then can a new relationship be built on equal grounds.

When forgiveness is asked, it should be given freely and generously. It should be linked to the abundance of Christ's love that is revealed by your conduct in the life of the one who received forgiveness. Through the healing power of Christian love, broken relationships can be restored. This love should be the distinguishing mark of all Christians.

Because Christ loves us so much and forgives us so often, we dare not withhold forgiveness and love from any person.

Loving Master, fill my heart with Your love to such an extent that my forgiveness of others may be sincere and healing. Amen.

BAN MONOTONY

JANUARY 31

He who was seated on the throne said, "I am making everything new" (Revelation 21:5).

The only difference between a groove and a grave is the depth! Monotony is the biggest enemy of a happy and full life. It makes everything that was once holy and beautiful, mundane and ordinary – it destroys the appreciation and excitement that are so necessary for a meaningful life.

It may be possible that the black shroud of monotony has descended on your life. Perhaps it happened so gradually that you weren't aware of it until it became a serious frustration in your life. Perhaps your life has lost its glitter and sparkle and you have come to terms with being stuck in a groove of routine. You no longer know the joy of excitement and keen expectation!

When you realize that your life has become monotonous and uninspiring, you have the power to do something about it. It might not be possible to change your daily routine because of set working hours and a scheduled program, but the rest of your time belongs to you to manage and spend wisely! A fixed work program should never rob you of the adventure of making new friends, relieving the burden of others, reading stimulating spiritual literature, or of taking every opportunity to appreciate and marvel at the grandeur of God's Creation.

If you manage to rise above the demands of your daily routine and find something to praise God for, you will discover that many other blessings from His hand will come your way. You will even experience a fresh, new meaning in performing everyday chores – you will be filled with joy and creativity because you are a "new creation" who belongs to Christ.

Savior and Master, You have lifted me from the rut of my existence and given me a new life. I praise You for that. Amen.

FEBRUARY

THE POINT OF DEPARTURE

"I am with you and will watch over you wherever you go" (Genesis 28:15).

Today is a significant point of departure in your journey to tomorrow. It is only when you acknowledge the importance of each day that you can build the future constructively. It is imperative to set a goal for yourself and work towards that. However, to get there requires successful planning, otherwise you will waste your energy and enthusiasm and achieve nothing. If you fail to plan, you plan to fail.

If you want to live a meaningful life, your goal must present a challenge. It must inspire you to attempt something that might seem beyond your abilities. Never fear or hesitate to start on something new or difficult. Only through used opportunities will you experience joy and fulfillment, intellectual and spiritual growth.

You might wonder where such a glorious goal is to be found. Part of the answer can be found in your job or profession. If your life has purpose you will always try to find new and better methods to carry out routine tasks with excitement and enthusiasm. Your greatest responsibility, however, is to do the will of God in all the circumstances He chooses to put you in as His representative. Doing His will, affords you the greatest joy and satisfaction.

To the uninformed it might sound pious and utterly impractical. Nevertheless, it is the wisest and most constructive thing you can do with your life. The road ahead will unfold before you in a most surprising way.

Holy Spirit, grant me the will and the wisdom to do God's will so that I may experience His joy and peace. Amen.

PIETY AND PRACTICE

So whether you eat or drink or whatever you do, do it all for the glory of God (1 Corinthians 10:31).

These days piety is not a very popular term. Many people mistakenly confuse this word with hypocrisy. Others think that being pious refers to a total inability to understand the crucial issues of life and to live in an impractical fool's paradise. Unfortunately this is the misconception created by many so-called "saints".

Many people are convinced that it is totally impossible to be godly and practical at the same time. The reason for this is that many of God's children display a form of godliness that isolates them from the daily struggle, heartache and pain of those who experience life in a different way. Godliness that isolates you from pain and suffering is not how Jesus lived on earth. On the contrary, He mingled with all kinds of people and identified with their suffering and pain – that was why they were drawn to Him.

Godliness is a remarkable Christian virtue – but it must be based on the realities of life, on the belief that Christ can handle these realities through you.

When Christ deals with human problems, He needs agents of His love who wish only to do His will. This is where true godliness emerges as a dynamic force. The person, who wishes to be a follower of Christ in the situation where God has placed him cannot be a hypocrite.

If Christ lives in you (see John 15:1-8) and you long for your life to reflect Him, you will develop a practical godliness that will glorify God in the service of your fellow man. And you will not even be aware of it!

Holy Spirit sent by God, teach me every day that my godliness must find expression in practical service towards my fellow men. Amen.

LET CHRIST LIVE IN YOU

If anyone acknowledges that Jesus is the Son of God, God lives in him and he in God (1 John 4:15).

The position in your life that you allocate to Jesus will determine the influence He will have on your life. If you are only prepared to admit that He was a good man you will probably admire His goodness, but it won't have a lasting effect on your life. He will remain on the side-line of your life. You might even find His doctrines acceptable and endorse the principle of doing to others what you expect them to do to you, as an acclaimed conviction of your own heart. This, however, is hopelessly inadequate.

The Holy Scripture elevates Jesus high above human goodness. He is part of the Holy Trinity and it is as such that the tremendous power of Jesus is seen and experienced.

When God dwells in you through Jesus Christ and the Holy Spirit, new horizons will be revealed to you. Your ability to love and forgive, to rejoice and to praise, to accept God's abundance and share it with others – these and many gifts of grace will become part of your character and personality.

Make sure that God's presence can be seen in your life, for then His gifts will be bestowed upon you according to the measure in which you are willing to receive them.

You'll find that closed doors will open; embarrassments will suddenly become opportunities; question marks will be straightened into exclamation marks because you walk with God. Christ made very special promises to those who love Him. He is always true to His word and your life will become enriched beyond recognition by your daily walk in His presence.

Thank You, Holy God, that I may walk in Your presence every day because You live in me. Amen.

REMEMBER WHO YOU ARE

You are a chosen people, a royal priesthood, a holy nation, a people belonging to God, that you may declare the praises of Him who called you out of darkness into His wonderful light (1 Peter 2:9).

Are you one of those Christians who feel unsure of your faith and therefore go through intense times of doubt and depression? On such occasions you feel tempted to give up being a disciple or communing with His followers.

Please allow me to remind you today that there are two distinctly discernible sides to your Christian life: God's side and your side. At your conversion and rebirth it was God who called you to live in harmony with Him; you reacted and became His disciple. This alone is reason enough for you to stand strong in your faith and to live the spiritual life with confidence and courage.

You belong to the living Savior. He bought you with His blood and accepted you as His own. When you start doubting or become depressed, don't put the blame on God, rather think about the fact that your relationship with Him is not as close as it used to be.

Always remember your rich inheritance and the kind of life God has called you for. Nothing will ever be able to bring as much satisfaction into your life as the right relationship with your heavenly Father. This world might offer you seemingly attractive temptations, but remember who and what you are in Christ.

You have been "chosen"; you belong to a "royal priesthood" and you have been "set apart". Muster all your strength to be true to this high and lofty calling. Even if you sometimes find it difficult to faithfully hold on to God – rest assured that He will never let go of you!

Gracious Lord, thank You for my high calling. Grant me, through the Holy Spirit, inner strength to live accordingly. Amen.

THE CHRISTIAN'S HOPE

We do not want you to ... grieve like the rest of men, who have no hope (1 Thessalonians 4:13).

The word "hope" is used to describe various perceptions. We say, "I hope the price of gold will go up"; or "My husband is sick, I hope he will be better soon." In these cases hope expresses our everyday expectations.

However, it also has another meaning: in the Tate Art Gallery in London hangs a striking painting by Frederick Watts. The title of the painting is "Hope". A beautiful woman is sitting on the globe. She is blindfolded and in her hand she holds a lute. All but one of the strings is broken. The woman sits bent forward touching the one string with her finger, listening. She is filled with hope – believing the best in the worst possible circumstances.

As long as Christian hope is alive, life cannot break us; we will not go down under the weight of our problems and afflictions. We know that God is able to make the best of the worst.

To experience comfort in adverse circumstances, know this: where Christian hope exists, no night is too dark, loneliness is not as painful and fear is less terrifying. Christian hope is optimism based on God's omnipotence. It is having faith in the future that fills your heart with joy when it feels like breaking. Hope sings along with Shelley that at the height of winter – spring is around the corner!

It is hope that gives us an invincible spirit. It is not from ourselves. That is why Paul says, "Christ in you, the hope of glory" (Col. 1:27).

This sinful world only knows a hopeless end; the Christian knows an endless hope!

Word that became flesh, thank You that Your Holy Word always brings hope when hopelessness threatens. Amen.

A CONCRETE FAITH

What good is it, my brothers, if a man claims to have faith but has no deeds? Can such faith save him? (James 2:14).

Christianity requires a balanced lifestyle because the Holy Spirit of God dwells in you. This is an inexplicable joy and encouragement that protects you against all kinds of wild figments of the human mind without hampering your enthusiasm for spiritual experiences.

The Holy Spirit always channels this zeal and enthusiasm into a well-organized life; otherwise it would become ineffective, one-sided and powerless.

Man is mainly what his faith makes of him. It serves no purpose to lay claim to a special religiosity if the love of God is not evident in your life.

Exuberant expressions of joy could certainly be the sign of an inner religious experience. As long as it lasts it fills you with great satisfaction, but the important question is whether it contributes towards your spiritual growth.

The requirement is always that your faith should lead you to become more and more like Christ.

Philippians 2:5-7 states clearly, "Your attitude should be the same as that of Christ Jesus: Who, being in very nature God, did not consider equality with God something to be grasped, but made Himself nothing, taking the very nature of a servant, being made in human likeness."

This kind of spiritual life rises above fleeting emotions and is always involved with a practical application of the Christian message.

Yes, there is a place for emotions in the life of a Christian. However, faith cannot grow and survive on emotions alone. It is impossible to believe in God unconditionally without serving your fellow man with love.

God of love, make me sensitive to Your will as well as to the needs of my fellow man. Amen.

PERFECT PEACE

Jesus said, "Peace be with you! As the father has sent Me, I am sending you" (John 20:21).

Peace is a word regularly used in conversations today. People use this word in a variety of circumstances, with various meanings and with a selection of motives. Your world might get torn apart by bad news; tension might build up because of worries; broken relationships might place your life under tremendous stress.

When these and similar adversities occur some people fall apart. They cannot take control of or handle the situation and fall into depression that drains them emotionally.

A classic example is the anxious, worried group of disciples of the Master hiding behind locked doors because their Leader had been crucified. They feared for their personal safety; they were guilt-ridden because they let Him down; they were worried and anxious about the future. Suddenly glory surrounded them in the form of the risen Savior and with Him came comfort, peace and consolation.

No matter what problems you may be facing now or in the future – that same living Christ is there to calm the storms of your life. He is there to stand by you so that you will be able to face every crisis and solve any problem.

If you are searching for peace of mind for your heart and soul invite Jesus into your life. He did promise, "Peace I leave with you; My peace I give you. I do not give to you as the world gives. Do not let your hearts be troubled and do not be afraid" (John 14:27).

Savior and Friend, set me free from all my fears and replace them with Your perfect peace and love. Amen.

PERSIST IN PRAYER

We do not know what we ought to pray for, but the Spirit Himself intercedes for us with groans that words cannot express (Romans 8:26).

When people need the healing power of prayer the most, they are often not able to pray. People find it difficult to pray when they are overwhelmed by great sadness. Often the only prayer at such times is the cry, "I cannot pray!"

However, sincere prayer is rooted in a search for God's will, an acknowledgment of your own shortcomings, your distress and your willingness to change and be enriched by God's love – under any circumstances. God doesn't answer prayers because they are perfect, but because He reaches out to people in distress with love and compassion.

It is not important how much or how well we pray, but simply that we do pray – that we humbly direct our hearts, minds and emotions to God. In this way we confess that God, the great Shepherd, is with us, even in the depths of darkness. Jesus says, "Ask and it will be given to you" (Luke 11:9). In your confusion and pain, just whisper a prayer asking for comfort, strength, wisdom or peace, and you will immediately experience the comforting touch of the Master. This will see you through the dark valley ahead, even if you stumble through it. His almighty hand will not let go of you.

Also remember that you are not praying alone. The Holy Spirit intercedes for you with the insight you lack at that moment. In your confusion and uncertainty the Holy Spirit prays for you according to the will of God. All God requires from you is to focus your heart on Him unconditionally. As Psalm 102:17 states: "He will respond to the prayer of the destitute; He will not despise their plea."

O Answerer of prayers, teach me to pray in such a way that I will rise from the depths of darkness towards eternal daylight. Amen.

THE ALL-SUFFICIENCY OF CHRIST

My grace is sufficient for you, for My power is made perfect in weakness (2 Corinthians 12:9).

Down through the ages man has been searching for the highest form of security for his life. This security often involves finances, personal safety or future plans. Fact is, man wants to be certain of his safety.

This is a praiseworthy quality to have and nobody should be criticized for it. However, these safety measures are often taken to extremes and then they become a burden. Many people lead a precarious existence because saving for the future has become an obsession. Others are constantly stressed because they spend so much time and energy securing their safety.

Whatever you do to safeguard yourself, always bear in mind that Jesus Christ needs to be your focal point in life. Only He can be your infallible source of security against the onslaughts of this world. Therefore, make sure that whatever safety precautions you take are carried out according to His will because it is when we are weak that His power is made perfect.

This is not only relevant to the temporal; but we have to put our trust in Christ in all areas of our lives. We especially need to be safeguarded against the attacks of the Evil One. We have a Refuge in our times of need and if we turn to Him when we are weak, His grace is sufficient for us.

Allow Christ to accompany and guide you along life's way and rest assured that you will be safe and secure. He is your ultimate guarantee for a safe existence.

Thank You Lord, that the words of the psalmist "The LORD is my shepherd, I shall not be in want" are applicable to my life as well. Amen.

Carry on Working Peacefully

"But now be strong," declares the LORD ... "Be strong and work. For I am with you, declares the LORD Almighty" (Haggai 2:4).

People often feel like giving up on life. The pressure and worries of their daily tasks take their toll. Lack of recognition causes people to want to throw in the towel because they work so hard and it doesn't seem to be appreciated.

While it is good, right and courteous for people to appreciate your input, a lack of acknowledgment may never be used as an excuse for giving up. Your main purpose in life should always be to please God in your job and to seek His approval. If this is the attitude with which you complete your daily chores you will be a true servant of the Lord, receiving inspiration regularly.

No matter how despondent you may feel, never forget that Jesus is with you in everything. In the most depressing circumstances, remember the example that Jesus Christ set: He was victorious through all kinds of discouragement and oppression – even until death on the cross.

When you are tempted to give up, turn to your Savior with your needs. He saves us from disappointment and despair; He promised to be with us always; He knows exactly what we are going through because He was tempted likewise. He went through the same experiences as we do today and much worse! In His strength and power people can overcome their depression.

Stay close to the Lord and trust in Him. He will give you inspiration to carry on working peacefully even in the face of severe obstacles – and you will experience the joy of a job well done.

I put all my trust in You, my Lord and Master, so that I can overcome my feelings of discouragement and disappointment caused by people. Amen.

RESIST TEMPTATION

No temptation has seized you except what is common to man. And God is faithful; He will not let you be tempted beyond what you can bear (1 Corinthians 10:13).

It would be a carefree and uncomplicated world if we were free from temptation. However, we are all subjected to temptation that comes in various forms and degrees of intensity. The wise disciple will take precautionary measures and in times of temptation will call on God.

We need a lot of grace to be able to identify temptation's harmful venom when it is hidden behind a friendly mask. We dare not underestimate the power of temptation and naively play along with it. Satan creates wonderful mirages of what we could achieve; his prey lives in a fool's paradise, continually assuring himself that he is in total control of his actions and emotions.

However, in a weak moment, temptation turns into an awful reality and fantasy becomes fact – a nightmare. Before you know it you have become the slave of your own desires and find yourself imprisoned by your own deeds. Then you are left with tears of remorse and sorrow.

The committed Christian resists temptation before it is too late. He humbly asks the Lord for wisdom to recognize its true colors and for the power to overcome it. This must happen before temptation gets a hold on your life.

How wonderful is the assurance that Jesus will never allow us to be tempted beyond what we can bear!

We also have the shining example of our Lord being tempted by Satan again and again. Jesus received the strength to overcome the Evil One from His Father – He is our Perfect Example.

Redeemer, grant me the power through Your Spirit to remain standing in the hour of temptation and to be victorious in Your name. Amen.

A Dwelling Place for God

Don't you know that you yourselves are God's temple and that God's Spirit lives in you? (1 Corinthians 3:16).

At the heart of every act of creation, lies the glory of God. Man was created by God to add to this glory by allowing Himself to dwell in them; thus reflecting His greatness.

God's goal has seemingly been nullified by sin, but God never gives up on His handiwork. The earthly, man-made temple was but a poor replica of what God was planning to do in the lives of His children, "You are members of God's household, built on the foundation of the apostles and prophets, with Christ Jesus Himself as the Chief Cornerstone. In Him the whole building is joined together and rises to become a holy temple in the Lord. And in Him you too are being built together to become a dwelling in which God lives by His Spirit" (Eph. 2:20-22).

With the coming of the Holy Spirit God made the cleansed heart of every believer His dwelling place. That is why we should ask ourselves, "Don't you know that you are God's temple?" This has been made possible because the Holy Spirit moved into our lives and made it a fit place for the holy God of the Universe to live in. That is why Paul could testify " I no longer live, but Christ lives in me" (Gal. 2:20).

Thus, the promise of Jesus is fulfilled as He and the Father live in us. This is a gift of God's grace that brings us to our knees in total admiration. The Holy Spirit makes us God's temple through His purification, provided that we unconditionally hand over the keys to each room of our lives in total obedience. On God's side there is not the slightest hesitation: when I open the door He will enter (see Rev. 3:20).

I bow down in adoration before You, my Father, because You have come to make my unworthy life Your dwelling place. Amen.

A FAITH THAT BRINGS LIFE

"He is not the God of the dead, but of the living. You are badly mistaken!" (Mark 12:27).

Spiritually there is nothing sadder than having faith that is dead; faith that was once vibrant with energy and life. It was once filled with joy and gladness. Then, due to neglect, it waned unnoticed and eventually died, or it was smothered by circumstances and matters that received higher priority. A dead or dying faith is interspersed with lame excuses, procrastination and increasing bitterness.

Fortunately God never changes. He is still the Author and Perfecter of your faith. That is why you have to realize that any decline in your spiritual life is your own fault and can never be blamed on God. This realization and confession is a good starting point for spiritual revival.

If you have a sincere, burning desire to experience a pulsating, living faith, the responsibility to develop it rests squarely on your own shoulders. God longs for you to have a living faith with Him at the center, which will allow you to live and not merely exist.

He did not leave you, nor did He withdraw His Holy Spirit from you. He is always available to you. The main problem that arises is usually that God has to make way for other matters in your life, which you regard as more important than Him. He cannot give you His fullness if your "house" is overcrowded with cheap furniture that is taking His place.

If you want your faith to be powerful and alive, God must be central to your life. Only then will His love drive out hatred; replace bitterness with friendliness; weakness with power and doubt will flee before a constructive, living faith.

Heavenly Father, thank You that Your Holy Spirit allows my faith to live – and that I can live because of this! Amen.

The Name Above All Names

"And I will do whatever you ask in My name, so that the Son may bring glory to the Father" (John 14:13).

The name of Jesus Christ is omnipotent. Christians have the assurance that this name has the power to overcome every evil spirit and can strengthen those who reverently take it on their lips in moments of weakness.

The Lord Jesus invited all who love Him to call on His name when in need or distress. Unfortunately, for many people this loving invitation has become a magic wand or lucky charm. They believe the words "in the name of Jesus" to be a magic formula that can change straw into gold. When we regard His name as such, we are regressing in our faith.

The importance of any word is never in the word itself, but in the power that sustains it and the belief behind the word when it is used. To pray in the name of Jesus Christ should mean that we pray with a heart and mind that are in accordance with God's will. That is why Jesus taught us in His model prayer: "May Your will be done on earth" (Matt. 6:10).

Therefore, when we pray "in the name of Jesus," we are not trying to twist the will of God to suit our desires, but rather to submit our lives to meet His requirements. If this is not the case, it is dishonest and wrong to pray in His holy name.

It is possible for everybody to have a meaningful relationship with God. However, this requires your life to be totally committed to Christ and that above all you should seek to do His will and not to satisfy your own desires. This will then enable you to realize and accept that His will for your life is best.

Lord Jesus, Name above all names – sweetest Name in heaven and earth – Jesus, wonderful Jesus. Amen.

THE TRAGEDY OF BEING LUKEWARM

So, because you are lukewarm – neither hot nor cold – I am about to spit you out of My mouth (Revelation 3:16).

Christian testimony has lost much of its power over the years because some followers of Christ fail to get excited about the Good News that has been entrusted to them.

We are born into a rich Christian heritage and have begun to take it for granted instead of always being joyful and enthusiastic about it. The result is that we have an impoverished, weak testimony to offer the world. While the flame of righteousness should be burning brightly in us, only a few burning coals are found among the ashes. Not nearly enough to light up the darkness.

The church suffers when its members don't become excited and enthusiastic about spiritual truths. Many church members know very little about the love, power and joy of the living Christ that needs to be shared with the world. A church with such members is a total failure!

Even though the failure of the church is a great tragedy, it is in fact the individual who has failed. The church is made up of people – God's people! Yet we often find that these people accept the principles of the church without accepting and knowing the Christ of the church.

It is Christ who gives you the power to be a passionate Christian. When you experience Christ living in you in a new way, a new world will open up to you and you will become excited because the Holy Spirit is at work in you. He does not only renew your mind, but sets your heart ablaze with an unquenchable fire of love for Him. Now your life can reflect the light of His wonderful love as you become the light of the world. No longer cold or lukewarm ... but on fire for Christ and His Good News!

Lord, keep my heart on fire with love for You so that my testimony to the world may be alive and meaningful. Amen.

GIFTS AND RESPONSIBILITIES

For it is by grace you have been saved, through faith – and this is not from yourselves, it is the gift of God (Ephesians 2:8).

In Christ Jesus God gave Himself to you as a free gift. This gift cannot be earned or bought. You only have to accept Christ in order for Him to become your own. However, the moment you accept Him, there are some responsibilities – and only as you carry out your responsibilities to God to the best of your ability will you experience the full glory and power found in a living faith.

When you recognize Christ as Lord of your life, you will have a constant desire to know Him more intimately and to obey Him. You have to develop a meaningful and positive prayer life because without prayer you will lack purpose and it will become impossible to grow spiritually. To strengthen the bond between you and Christ it is also important to control your thoughts, spirit and body.

After you have accepted Christ into your life and spent time and energy developing a positive prayer life, you will have to submit to the discipline of Christ's love in your life. Your value system will change completely and you will no longer wish to satisfy your worldly desires at the expense of your spiritual growth.

Christianity doesn't require any painful sacrifices. You are offered the privilege of an ever-deepening relationship with the Lord. Of course, it requires the termination of any activities that can hamper or ruin your spiritual well-being.

Fulfilling your spiritual responsibilities will bring great joy and pleasure to your life that you cannot compare to the small sacrifices that you were willing to make.

Lord, I lay everything that is not pleasing in my life at Your feet and pray that Your Spirit will guide me into fulfilling my spiritual responsibilities. Amen.

CHAINED TO THE PAST

Be made new in the attitude of your minds; and put on the new self (Ephesians 4:23-24).

Don't blame yourself for things that happened in the past. The danger is that mistakes, failures and defeats in your past can hamper your spiritual growth and rob you of the joy that God intended for you.

Maybe you can recall the times when you allowed a worldly attitude or lack of enthusiasm to rob you of the highest calling of your life. Such memories can cast an unnecessary shadow over the present. If you keep on fretting about what might have been, you not only allow the excitement of the present to pass you by, but you also open the door for depression. Remember, the past is history, the future is a promise – the present is really all you have!

A living, practical faith in Jesus Christ requires continual adjustments in your life. Your attitude towards life should alter all the time. Instead of always expecting the worst to happen, you must learn to accept that God only wants what is best for you.

When you become spiritually sensitive, fear of the past and the future is replaced by faith and courage. Unwillingness to forgive is transformed into the will to forgive and forget. Your life undergoes a new, lively phase of growth and even your health improves.

Always remember Paul's sound advice in Philippians 3:13: "But one thing I do: Forgetting what is behind and straining toward what is ahead." Then your spirit will no longer be controlled by your failures from the past, but by the Holy Spirit. He will point out the wonderful opportunities around you. What a liberating experience!

Lord and loving God, I thank You for the past, I rejoice in the challenges of the present and trust in You for the unknown future. Amen.

THE SPIRIT THAT GIVES INSIGHT

But it is the Spirit in a man, the breath of the Almighty, that gives him understanding (Job 32:8).

There are many ways to obtain insight in life. You can read a book, listen to inspiring music, or notice something in God's Creation that leaves you speechless. You then find it difficult to describe your emotions, yet you feel inspired, fulfilled and uplifted. You need such a source of insight and inspiration to turn to regularly when the monotony of life threatens to get you down. A book, music, a breath-taking scene in nature is not only a refuge for your soul, but it also gives you insight and a deeper knowledge of your existence.

However, the greatest source of insight and inspiration is found when you allow Christ into your life. Contrary to general belief, the insight which Christ brings is not only restricted to spiritual life, but includes and enriches every aspect of your life.

When you accept the fact that Christ lives and works in you, that He reveals Himself in and through you, your business, social and cultural life will take on a new dimension and new ideas will be born in you. Your horizons will broaden and your insight will deepen.

To experience the indwelling Christ, you are required to live in His presence at all times and allow His Holy Spirit to lead you. This is not an unbearable burden, but a wonderful privilege. While you are developing this lifestyle, the heartbeat of your life will be increased by the insight and inspiration that the Spirit of God reveals to you. Is it at all possible to live a quality life without the Spirit?

Loving Lord, I give You complete freedom to work in me through Your Spirit so that I can live close to the Source of understanding. Amen.

Shalom! Peace Be with You

The Lord turn His face towards you and give you peace (Numbers 6:26).

Shalom" is the Hebrew word for the most ideal situation in life. It includes fullness, wholeness and harmony in all areas of life.

It is a state of "being" rather than having; being what God intended you to be. It also depicts the type of relationship that should exist among people. Paul referred to this kind of peace when he urged the Christians in Rome to "make every effort to do what leads to peace and mutual edification" (Rom. 14:19).

This is the peace and harmony that should be present in families. Family life should never become a battlefield. It is only when families start living in peace that the world will experience peace.

However, without love there cannot be peace. A famous pediatrician once examined a feverish, very restless baby and remarked, "What this baby needs is love." He had not received any because love and peace were not present in that family. This is also the great tragedy of our feverish, unwell and restless world.

Shalom peace is a gift from God that He expects His children to minister to a world starving for peace. The world desperately needs people with the peace of God as a living reality in their lives. We have a duty to spread His peace not only because we are Christians, but also because we are bound by the command of our King who said, "As the Father has sent Me, I am sending you!" (John 20:21).

God is commissioning us to go out into the world and create relationships of peace so that God can rule in this world through His peace and be glorified.

O Prince of Peace, strengthen my will to share Your peace freely with everyone You allow into my life. Amen.

A Confession of Faith

"But what about you?" He asked. "Who do you say I am?" Peter answered, "You are the Christ" (Mark 8:29).

Sadly, many Christians have lost the joy of discipleship because they deny the sovereignty of the risen Christ in their lives. With some it is due to a feeling of self-reproach, while others honestly feel very inferior. However, the great majority are just plain unwilling to make a total commitment – a commitment which Christ requires from us if we really want to bear His name in the true sense of the word – Christian. Many rumors were spread as to the true identity of Christ, but when Peter was confronted with the question, he fearlessly replied that Jesus is the Christ, the Son of the living God!

This was Peter's simple, yet earth-shaking confession. It meant the transformation of his whole life. It was so radical and far-reaching that, in spite of the fact that he had denied Jesus earlier, the establishment of the Christian church is based on this confession. This proves the responsibility as well as the reward for His confession.

Every Christian will admit that being a true Christian requires total commitment to Christ. These same people will also speak about the ecstatic joy found in intimately knowing Christ as your personal Savior and Redeemer. And the world needs to see the practical, concrete proof of this confession in our lives.

Ask the Holy Spirit to enable you to confess your faith in the Lord Jesus Christ fearlessly and to live accordingly. You will then bow before Him in wonder at the joy and fulfillment it brings to your life.

Savior and Lord, I confess with joy: You are the Christ, the Son of the living God. Amen.

SPIRITUAL BACKSLIDING

I always thank God for you because of His grace given you in Christ Jesus. For in Him you have been enriched in every way (1 Corinthians 1:4-5).

Some people are utterly disappointed and disillusioned by the Christian faith. At one time they ventured onto this road with great enthusiasm, but their zeal faded. They are no longer part of the community of believers and they have lost all interest in Christian fellowship.

It is only fair to ask, "But what went wrong? Did Christ disappoint them?" Just the idea of Christ disappointing anybody is unthinkable, especially because of the vast number that can testify of His faithfulness.

The reasons why people backslide in their faith are many. Yet there are some common traits in this phenomenon. In these cases it is noticed that their relationship with Jesus has weakened and they neglect to pray. It is impossible to maintain a vibrant prayer life and at the same time be cold and indifferent. Gradually their involvement in Christian fellowship also waned and their criticism increased.

Clashes of will and interests also play an important role in spiritual backsliding and failure. When the Father reveals His will, it is sometimes rejected in favor of self-interest. In such cases conceit gains victory over obedience to the will of God.

If you realize that your faith is beginning to lose its luster, power and meaning, there is only one way: repent! Go back to the Father and ask the Holy Spirit to assist you in self-examination. Obey Him and experience the joy of a living faith again.

God of grace and forgiveness, grant me wisdom through Your Holy Spirit and help me to obey You. Amen.

LOVE: ABSOLUTELY ESSENTIAL!

... but have not love, I gain nothing (1 Corinthians 13:3).

There is no substitute for love – nothing can take its place. That is why the question that Jesus asked Peter in John 21 verse 16 is so meaningful, "Do you truly love Me?" This question reaches down to the roots of our relationship with Christ and touches on the quality of our fellowship.

Jesus doesn't ask, "Do you believe in Me?"; "Do you understand My teaching?"; "Do you confess My name?"; "Are you obedient in your service to Me?" or "Do you love My Word?" Although these are all important matters, they are secondary. The primary question is, "Do you truly love Me?" Only if your reply is positive can you approach the future fearlessly and with spiritual security.

Jesus repeated this question to Peter three times – almost as if He wanted to offer him the opportunity to make up for denying Him three times. Jesus doesn't reprimand him for his weakness; he doesn't require a guarantee that he will not do it again. All He asks is if Peter truly loves Him.

It is fair to ask this because Jesus had invested a lot in Peter. For three years Peter had the wonderful privilege of attending the "School of Christ". Even when Peter did not live up to the expectations that Jesus had for him, He did not leave him to himself. Jesus also prayed for Peter (see Luke 22:30) and – like for all of us – Jesus died for Peter. "Greater love has no one than this, that he lay down his life for his friends" (John 15:13).

Considering the trouble Jesus takes with us in all areas of our lives, it is only fair for Him to ask about our love for Him. It is also fair then that He should receive the reply, "Lord, You know all things; You know that I love You."

I dearly love You, Lord. Thank You for Your loving involvement in my life. Please help me to reveal this love through my life to others. Amen.

THE GREAT SEARCH

If only I knew where to find Him; if only I could go into His dwelling! I would state my case before Him and fill my mouth with arguments (Job 23:3-4).

You and I live in a computerized society where numbers have become almost more important than names. A new world order is rapidly rising where everyone will be equal. It wishes to melt humanity into a faceless mass where the fine nuances of the individual will be disregarded. People who enrich their generation through individuality are becoming very scarce.

One of the heart-warming truths of Christianity is that every person is important to God as a unique creation of His hand. Created in God's image, as His representative, man is filled with a nostalgic desire for the perfection he enjoyed before the Fall. Though sin has marred the image of God in man, and has created a barrier between God and man, man knows instinctively that he will not find rest until he comes to God.

In every human heart burns this desire that a state of joy, satisfaction, fulfillment, safety and peace will become a reality. This longing is expressed in various ways: some people become more restless, others hoard material possessions hoping to find fulfillment. Many wander through life aimlessly, hoping that their desire will be fulfilled in some or other miraculous way.

In reality, we are all searching for God and this search only comes to an end when you commit your life unconditionally to Jesus and become one with Him. Then you will find purpose and meaning in your existence here on earth.

Guide and Master, only in You do I find rest and my true purpose in life. Amen.

HARMONY AMONG DISCIPLES

But it is you, a man like myself, my companion, my close friend, with whom I once enjoyed sweet fellowship as we walked with the throng at the house of God (Psalm 55:13-14).

Christianity involves a brotherhood of believers. Nowhere in the New Testament do we find examples of Christian believers who lived in isolation. On the contrary, we read about their regular fellowship with each other.

One coal cannot make a fire burn. It takes many coals to light a fire, to keep it burning and provide heat. If a disciple of the Lord refuses fellowship, or ignores his fellow Christians, he will soon lose his glow and warmth of being a Christian and his spiritual life will wane!

It is difficult to determine the number of Christians who have lost their zeal for God because they refused to be part of a living Christian community. It is when we join forces with other believers, following the guidance and inspiration of the Holy Spirit, that we experience the power and warmth that make our faith a meaningful reality. To sing God's praises in union with fellow believers, to study His Word together and to share our experiences are inspiring and life-giving and should not be neglected.

Yet the greatest treasure of the fellowship of believers is the wonderful reality of Christ's presence among them. Didn't He promise to be in the midst of His children when they are gathered together? But for His presence to become a reality, mutual love and understanding must be prevalent amongst those who gather in His name. When Christians love and care for each other they give concrete expression to their love for Christ.

I really love You, Lord, and that is why I also love Your children and find it great to live in harmony with them. Amen.

PROCRASTINATION IS THE THIEF OF TIME!

And now, what are you waiting for? Get up, be baptized and wash your sins away, calling on His name (Acts 22:16).

Procrastination is a common human weakness. That is why there is so much unfinished business in our lives – things which we badly wanted to do, yet we just never got round to. Now we find it gnawing at our conscience in the form of regret and guilt. The tragedy is that an opportunity missed is not likely to come your way again.

It is our happy-go-lucky attitude that leads to procrastination. This attitude again originates from the misconception that there is a lot of time. Satan is also always there to convince us, "Why the haste? Do it tomorrow!" That was what inspired Agrippa's reaction to Paul's urgent call for repentance, "Do you think that you can quickly convert me into a Christian?" If only he had reacted quickly because for him it never happened.

What are you waiting for? You know that you have all the abilities and talents. You have every opportunity as well as all the help you need. Yet you are allowing your ideals and dreams to die. You never use your wings of faith to pursue those spiritual visions, but are satisfied with second best. You keep on plodding through the shallow, muddy waters of procrastination and neglect. Make a decision today that will put an end to this gnawing regret and do what must be done.

Do not put off until tomorrow because tomorrow may never come. You receive today from the hand of God and you will have to give account to God for what you did with today.

Gracious Lord, please keep me from putting off and neglecting issues that will influence my eternity. Amen.

THE MINISTRY OF INTERCESSION

You who call on the LORD, give yourselves no rest (Isaiah 62:6).

A self-centered prayer consisting of petitions is not what God meant prayer to be. We must realize that praying for others is a great privilege.

When interceding we become co-workers of our Great High Priest and Intercessor, Jesus Christ. Our prayers then become part of His perfect prayers and we serve in a world that is not even aware of it.

In the name of Jesus we pray for His body, the church; for our fellow men in need; for God's ministers in their service to Him; for the heathen and for the laborers in God's vineyard.

In all these activities we don't stand alone – we form part of the tight unity of millions of believers across the globe. To be involved in warfare until the victory is gained in His name is not only a privilege, but also a great responsibility.

That is why we may not give the leftovers of our time and strength to prayer. We should give our best and noblest to this lofty call and be faithful and devoted in our ministry of intercession. Rest assured that it will bear fruit in your own life as well as in the lives of those you pray for.

The ministry of intercession requires strict discipline. We must have a special time and place to fulfill this important duty. Our hearts must be tuned in to God so that His holy and perfect will can become a reality through our prayers. Thus, we become part of the throng of intercessors spanning the globe and causing miracles to happen.

O God who answers prayers, thank You that I can be a co-worker with Your Son in prayer. Please make me faithful and alert in this. Amen.

Is Your Workload Too Heavy?

"If a man remains in Me and I in him, he will bear much fruit; apart from Me you can do nothing" (John 15:5).

Perhaps the workload that you carry has become an unbearable burden. This can happen very easily and then your work loses its joy and inspiration.

The reasons for this can be many: you might be robbing yourself of rest and relaxation; you might have an over-developed sense of responsibility causing you to be a workaholic. You might be trying to carry an unbearable workload that no one expects from you except yourself. The result is that you are tense and nervous and dislike your job, the job that was once such a source of joy!

If this description fits you, it is obvious that you are trying to live and work without the supporting strength of Christ. You do not apply your Christian principles to your daily life. Your time and your work have hijacked your love for the Lord. Your values have become mixed up and your life is like a machine without a regulator to set the pace.

A tried and tested method to develop maximum productivity in your life is to make Jesus your active Partner; committing and submitting every aspect to His control. He has perfect insight into what life really entails as well as the demands it makes on you.

Therefore, start every day by communicating with God. You will receive the assurance of His continued presence with you. He will honor His promise to be with you wherever you may go. Then you will be full of confidence and experience the pride and joy of a job well done!

Eternal Father, You have given us the command to work. Please hold me so that I can feel Your eternal arms under me. Amen.

A Humble Spirit Enriches Your Life

Though the LORD is on high, He looks upon the lowly, but the proud He knows from afar (Psalm 138:6).

Humility is sometimes seen as a weakness, but nothing has ever been further from the truth. Humility is a true Christian virtue that improves our lives.

When our emotions are controlled by pride there is constant stress and strain. We are forever struggling with questions like, "Why is that person being favored above me?"; "I am better than anyone else." These and similar expressions are proof of a jealous and hurt spirit and destroys all the beauty in your life. A haughty spirit causes one to have an exaggerated opinion of your own importance.

Humility sets your character and personality free from the monster of pride. It creates a calm and collected disposition in your inner being. It makes you aware of the fact that you should not live in isolation and only for yourself, but that you are part of God's people.

A truly humble person is never lonely, because he realizes his need to be with others and enjoys spending time with them. The changing whims of society pass him by because he is able to forgive and forget. He does not need the facade that the proud person has to hide behind. That is why he is much more relaxed and approachable.

It is the humble person who is used without exception by God. This person realizes that he can do nothing without God and that is why he is deeply dependent on God.

The humble person readily accepts the guidance of the Holy Spirit and obedience comes naturally. He walks in humility with Christ and serves Him with joy and great satisfaction.

Lord Jesus, You who washed the feet of men, please keep me humble so that I can serve You effectively. Amen.

RETIRE WITH DIGNITY

The things you have heard me say in the presence of many witnesses entrust to reliable men who will also be qualified to teach others (2 Timothy 2:2).

Retirement can be a traumatic experience. Paul prepared Timothy to take over the torch that he carried with so much excellence so that he, in turn, could pass it on to someone else again. In humble honesty Paul could declare, "I have finished the race, I have kept the faith." Now he could graciously step down to make room for the next athlete to run the race.

One of the saddest things to see is a person who cannot let go when his time has come. This usually happens when a person has worthily served a cause for many years and has been thought of as indispensable.

As they grow older, the task becomes too taxing. Due to their unwillingness to let go of the reigns, the quality of their work suffers and the atmosphere at work becomes unpleasant. Much of what they have built up through the years is now broken down.

One should accept growing older philosophically. When your job has become a burden, you will earn the respect of your co-workers if you acknowledge the fact and step down in favor of someone younger. Of course it won't be easy! Seek support, guidance and strength from Jesus during this time.

He understands your changing emotions very well. He knew when it was time to hand over His ministry to the disciples! He will assist you to make this decision with grace and to the glory of His name if you ask Him in prayer.

Lord Jesus, please help me to know when it is time for me to make space for someone else so that Your Kingdom does not suffer because of my attitude. Amen.

MARCH

WISDOM IS TO PLAN

If the axe is dull and its edge unsharpened, more strength is needed but skill will bring success (Ecclesiastes 10:10).

Some people plod from one crisis to the next, without ever achieving anything worthwhile. They blame others or unfavorable circumstances for their misfortune while the core of their problem, is lack of proper planning. If you fail to plan, you certainly plan to fail! Without planning, your life will be chaotic.

Many dedicated Christians piously declare that they have entrusted their future to God and therefore leave the planning to Him. These people will always serve in the lowest ranks in God's army. Positions of spiritual responsibility will never be entrusted to them for the simple reason that they lack the discipline required for effective service.

If God wishes to use a medical doctor in His service, He will call someone who submits himself to the discipline of the medical profession. If He is looking for a trustworthy Bible translator, He will choose a master at Greek, Latin and Hebrew. Spiritual enthusiasm is commendable, but it should be combined with knowledge. Only then will you become a powerful and specific instrument in God's hand.

When planning for the future, take your strengths as well as the gifts that God has blessed you with and develop these to the best of your ability. Lay them at His feet as a sacrifice. You will realize that every gift that you received was for a very specific reason, and that God is waiting for you to return these gifts to Him so that He can use you more and more effectively in His service.

Holy Master, I thank You for every gift that You have given me. Help me to develop them all so that You can use them. Amen.

Don't Despair

"In this world you will have trouble. But take heart! I have overcome the world" (John 16:33).

A person's world can suddenly turn pitch-dark. So much so that many of God's children are inclined to despair. Has God withdrawn from our turbulent world? Certainly not! God will never forget His handiwork and He will not hand this world over to the powers of darkness.

Don't despair or become despondent. It is still His world and He is still in control despite evil powers and darkness. In God's own time the light will break through.

In Genesis 42 we read about Jacob's crises. His country was experiencing an excruciating drought and famine. He had lost his beloved wife Rachel. He believed that his son Joseph was dead. Simeon, his eldest son, was a prisoner in Egypt and to crown it all, his darling son Benjamin had been taken from him. It seemed as if his world had completely changed forever.

However, Jacob made the same error of judgment that many of us still make today. In his despair he started blaming others only to realize that God could change even the bad into something good. Because he expected the worst, he misjudged Benjamin's situation. It was necessary for him to relinquish Benjamin so that he could experience God's miracles. He mistakenly thought that Joseph was dead, while all the time God was using Joseph to feed his family as well as the whole world.

During times of darkness we need spiritual optimism. God is alive; He is in control; He cares for us in Christ Jesus. "We know that in all things God works for the good of those who love Him, who have been called according to His purpose" (Rom. 8:28).

Even when I go through dark valleys, I will not fear, because You are with me, in Your hands I am safe. Amen.

THE ROAD TO LOVE AND LIFE

Teach me Your way, O Lord, and I will walk in Your truth; give me an undivided heart (Psalm 86:11).

Most of us have the human tendency to want to lead our own lives, and then still expect God's blessing. When things go wrong, we are upset and wonder how God could have allowed it. The problem is that we did not seek God's approval or blessing on the plans that we made in the first place. We rushed along the paths that we have planned for ourselves with our own blind hearts and then wonder why things go so horribly wrong.

As God's child you must learn to accept His discipline, knowing that without it no spiritual growth or blessing is possible. God's discipline is never arbitrary and He does not punish some and excuse others – although it sometimes seems as if He does. The discipline that you experience is often self-inflicted reproof. When you disobey what you know is God's will for you, you eventually have to pay the price. When you purposely break His law and foolishly think you can sidestep the results, don't rebel when it seems as if things have turned against you. Whatever you sow, you will reap. If you sow the wind, you will reap a storm!

God is not calling us to a lifestyle beyond our reach, neither does He set goals that cannot be attained. Never be shortsighted and think that your own methods and ways are infallible.

God's way to true life and love requires us to sacrifice every impure desire. Because His way is always the right one, it is the only safe way for the follower of Christ.

Risen Lord, I worship You as the Way, the Truth and the Life. Help me to obediently walk on the path of life and love. Amen.

You Learn to Pray by Praying

Pray in the Spirit on all occasions with all kinds of prayers and requests (Ephesians 6:18).

Many Christians long for a deeper and more meaningful spiritual life. They instinctively feel there is more to prayer than what they are experiencing at the moment. Some plead incessantly with God to enrich their prayer life.

Many books have been written about prayer and although they have been studied carefully, no philosophy has ever taught the soul to pray. You can look for advice and guidance from those who are regarded as masters of prayer but this might create an overwhelming feeling of inferiority, insufficiency and even failure.

Your call might also be that of the disciples, "Lord, teach us to pray" (Luke 11:1). Perhaps you are expecting a miracle that will suddenly transform your ineffective prayer life into a source of strength and inspiration. If this does not happen, you become disappointed and disillusioned.

The only way to learn to pray effectively is through persevering prayer. Prayer journals can help you to organize and formulate your thoughts. But at their best, they remain a secondhand source of inspiration. When the Holy Spirit touches your spirit, you will experience such boldness in God's presence that your thoughts will be set free and you will be able to express your deepest emotions and desires to God.

Pray without ceasing, even when your prayer life seems fruitless. Persevere in prayer. You will in time experience a fresh awareness of God's love and presence when you pray. Remember, the Holy Spirit intercedes for you when you do not know what to say or how to pray.

Lord, You who listen to prayer, I reconfirm my faith in the power of prayer, and I resolve to dedicate myself to a life of prayer. Amen.

GOD KEEPS HIS PROMISES

The Lord is my helper; I will not be afraid. What can man do to me? (Hebrews 13:6).

We have assurance that God will never leave us nor forsake us. God never makes empty promises and in His omnipotence and grace He keeps His word. He is the God who makes His promises come true even when circumstances seem to prove the opposite. While Jacob was on the run, he received the following promise at Bethel one night: "I will watch over you, wherever you go" (Gen. 28:15). How wonderfully God kept that promise!

Joshua, Moses' successor, led Israel into Canaan, and received this encouraging promise from God: "As I was with Moses, so I will be with you; I will never leave you nor forsake you" (Josh. 1:5). Joshua experienced the wonderful presence of God every day.

Before David's death, he encouraged his son, Solomon, with these words, "Do not be afraid or discouraged, for the LORD God, my God, is with you. He will not fail you or forsake you" (1 Chron. 28:20). And God did just that!

In the epistle to the Hebrews we are assured that this promise is extended to include everyone who believes in Jesus Christ. When a loved one dies, it leaves a void that cannot be filled. It is then that you desperately need God's promises and they take on a new meaning. In your utter loneliness He assures you that you are never alone because He is with you.

God is righteous and holy and He will never deceive you. He is gracious and good and He will never forget you. Because He is eternal and true. He will never change. Nothing is impossible for Him for He is omnipotent. Whatever He promises, He can and will do!

Loving Father, thank You that I can depend on Your promises forever and into eternity. Amen.

AN EXPERIENCE WITH CHRIST

For to me, to live is Christ (Philippians 1:21).

Christian faith is a spiritual experience based on your relationship with the living Christ. Some people worship a historical Christ while for others He is veiled in mysticism. However you experience Jesus, He only becomes meaningful when you know Him as your personal Savior and Redeemer. This is an encounter in the first person singular with Christ who is alive. This alone makes your faith alive.

Unfortunately your faith might fluctuate according to your moods. One day you might be in the clouds, determined to live your spiritual life to the full. The next day you might be so downcast that you can hardly pray and you feel that the assurance of Christ's presence has sadly disappeared.

Whether the light of your faith is burning brightly or not, the glorious truth is that God's love for you is strong and powerful, unchanging like God Himself. It never fluctuates. God is close to you when you are close to Him, but also when you are drifting away from Him. His sustaining love is unfailing and eternal. This makes the reality of Christian love something which does not belong to yesterday or tomorrow, but it is here and now and has indescribable meaning.

Once you realize that the Christian experience does not only have meaning for the past or future, but for the present, it becomes relevant to modern life as well. Christ is with His disciples wherever they are. Remember it is He who said, "And surely I am with you always, to the very end of the age" (Matt. 28:20).

I praise You, heavenly Master, because You are Lord of the past, present and future. Amen.

CHRIST GIVES TOTAL SATISFACTION

"I have come that they may have life, and have it to the full" (John 10:10).

Everyone is searching for satisfaction and it is quite interesting to see how people strive to obtain this goal. Many are unhappy with their achievements and look back upon unfulfilled dreams and lost opportunities with a feeling of deep disappointment. The disintegration of the church of Jesus Christ into many groups, often in direct opposition to one another, is sufficient proof of this emptiness within man.

Regardless of what you have done with your life, whether you are satisfied or dissatisfied with it, you can testify right now that you are satisfied in your soul if you have met Jesus, have been born again through His Spirit and have surrendered yourself unconditionally to Him. That inner satisfaction is the fruit of a real experience with Jesus. Only that can give you permanent, joyous satisfaction. It is the point of departure into a new life of abundance in which your deepest desires will be satisfied.

To know Jesus Christ in His grace, His love and renewing strength, is to know peace that surpasses all understanding. You can obtain it from God alone through Christ Jesus. This is the result of the Christian lifestyle and cannot be experienced outside of Christ. He is the Source of this new, abundant life.

This satisfaction may never lead to dull self-contentment, but should rather spur you on to an ever-deepening experience with the Lord. The only form of discontent allowed in the Christian disciple is when he realizes that his knowledge of and love for his Savior has stagnated and no longer shows signs of growth and maturity.

Thank You, Lord, for the new life which You give me each day. Prepare me through the Holy Spirit to accept it readily. Amen.

CHRIST AND YOUR GOAL IN LIFE

Commit your way to the LORD, trust in Him and He will do this (Psalm 37:5).

A person who lives aimlessly can never know the joy of achievement or fulfillment. To live without a goal creates a happy-go-lucky attitude with the vague hope of something better to come. You then achieve what you have been striving for: nothing! Lack of purpose is the result of lack of motivation in your life.

Many people who are ambitious are willing to sacrifice everything to achieve their goals – their time, health, family life, social contacts and money. Because they channel all their energy into obtaining their goal, they are successful. The tragedy, however, is that once they have achieved their goal, they are left with the painful knowledge that in spite of all their efforts, they have missed out on something important.

If you deny the importance of your relationship with Christ, you have overlooked the most important aspect of your life. It is impossible to live a full, exciting life if you remain ignorant regarding the reality of your spiritual needs. You were created in God's image, and therefore you are a spiritual being.

Jesus Christ said in John 4:34 "My food is to do the will of Him who sent Me and to finish His work." If you wish to follow in the steps of the Master, you must say the same – regardless of what your job might involve. Whether you are a clerk or shop assistant, housewife or factory worker, teacher, doctor or pastor – your primary task as a disciple of Christ is to do the will of God. God has given you the gift of life so that you can serve Him with joy and purpose. Only then will your life have true meaning and direction.

I submit myself to Your will, O Father. Manage my life and sanctify my ambitions. Amen.

DEALING WITH PAIN

"Do not be afraid, O man highly esteemed," he said. "Peace! Be strong now; be strong" (Daniel 10:18).

There are many distressing things in life that cause us pain: an undeserved insult, the denial of your human dignity, being refused the acknowledgement that is due to you – these and many more can cause deep inner hurt.

The cure of this hurt is in your own hands because you only suffer as much pain as you allow yourself. Some people are very insensitive and cause pain on purpose, yet you dare not sink to their level by allowing their pettiness to destroy your life. When you allow people to hurt your feelings to the extent that you become depressed and revengeful, you reveal the exact same level of spiritual and intellectual pettiness as that of your tormentors.

Sometimes people do not mean to hurt you – your pain is self-inflicted because of self-centeredness and touchiness. It is a general weakness in many of us to overreact and take exception, even though no harm was meant. Control destructive emotions, otherwise you give others the power to destroy your joy and happiness.

When you are filled with the Holy Spirit and have committed yourself to the living Christ, you will experience and enjoy His protection against anything aimed at breaking you down. You will especially receive the ability to forgive those who hurt you. If you have His love in your heart and practice His forgiveness, nothing anybody says can wound you permanently. Love and forgiveness heal all wounds. All that is required of you is to be strong because of God's love for you.

Great Physician, thank You that You also heal my spiritual wounds. Please help me to be like You and to forgive and love to the very end. Amen.

CHRIST BRINGS THE WORD TO LIFE

Do your best to present yourself to God as one approved, a workman who does not need to be ashamed and who correctly handles the word of truth (2 Timothy 2:15).

The main source of information about Jesus is found in the New Testament. The prophets of the Old Testament prophesied His coming, but it is from the New Testament that we derive our image and experience of Jesus Christ.

The New Testament mentions that Jesus taught and preached, and we sometimes wonder if there are marvelous truths that He expressed that were not recorded.

How then is it possible that, even though such a relatively small part of the Lord's life and teachings was recorded in the Bible, He had such a tremendous influence on the whole history of mankind?

The Scriptures were inspired by God and the Holy Spirit enlightens the Christian believer to understand it. Through the Spirit of Christ the written Word becomes alive so that it can support you in moments of deep need. You have undoubtedly experienced moments when Scripture came to mind and you received a specific verse that was exactly what you needed in that specific situation.

Because you love God's Word you study it with zeal and enthusiasm. While the Bible contains all the knowledge that is required for your redemption and spiritual growth, your insight into biblical truths can increase through reading books about the historical and social background of biblical times and characters.

Let the Bible be central in your life. However, do not reject any book that can cast more light on what is written on those pages. You must especially not stop praying for the enlightenment of the Holy Spirit.

O Word who became flesh, thank You for Your immortal Word from which we can learn Your will. Amen.

FOLLOW CHRIST'S EXAMPLE

Trust in the LORD with all your heart and lean not on your own understanding (Proverbs 3:5).

You meet many people daily, either in your job situation or on a social level. Yet you hardly get to know any of them really well. You make small talk with them and you are often impressed by their cheerfulness without ever realizing what they are hiding behind their smiles.

Depression is awful and can be caused by various things. Lonely people easily feel rejected. To feel unloved and rejected can cast a permanent shadow of depression over one's spirit. To lose a spiritual battle can cause you to be very melancholic. To never achieve success can eventually break even the strongest spirit. These and similar factors all add to a feeling of dejection that settles on people's lives like a black shroud.

It is true that many people who suffer from depression do not hesitate to tell others about it. However, many hide behind a smile and only a very sensitive and observant person will make a true assessment of the situation.

It is not wise to judge someone at face value. How different life would be if we could try to understand and get to know people before we comment on their peculiarities!

One of the most important characteristics of the Christian disciple is an understanding, compassionate heart. To be able to see behind masks is one of the results of a true encounter with Jesus Christ.

God of love and understanding, thank You that I can learn how to love and serve others by following the example of Your Son, Jesus Christ. Amen.

PEOPLE'S NEEDS

Let us then approach the throne of grace with confidence, so that we may receive mercy and find grace to help us in our time of need (Hebrews 4:16).

The average Christian lives under very normal circumstances. He experiences joy, happiness, failure and success and also shares in the aspirations of the community he is part of. There are some followers of Christ, however, who stress the scriptural call for Christians to isolate themselves from this sinful world. They try to have as little contact as possible with non-Christians.

Such an attitude denies the very essence of Christ's incarnation, because He came to the world to save sinners. To do so He mixed with all, sinners – people who were considered unacceptable in His time. Scripture declares that Jesus died for sinners. How will they be able to know Him unless they see His beauty and power in your life?

If you know Christ as your Savior, you develop an understanding for others' needs. Because people don't talk about their needs, we should not take it for granted that they don't have any. Our deepest needs and desires often remain hidden. Through the guidance of the Holy Spirit Christians can become acutely aware of others' spiritual and everyday needs.

To listen sympathetically to a guilt-ridden person; to offer friendship and understanding to a lonely, sensitive person; to give of yourself rather than of your possessions: these are but a few of the many ways in which you can discover and ease another person's burden. Disciples who have had an encounter with Jesus and who live in continual harmony with the Holy Spirit will find this easy.

Please use me, Almighty Savior, to notice and alleviate the burdens of others by Your grace and under the guidance of the Holy Spirit. Amen.

MARCH 12

THE ALL-SUFFICIENCY OF THE CROSS

Who is he that condemns? Christ Jesus, who died – more than that, who was raised to life – is at the right hand of God and is also interceding for us (Romans 8:34).

We cannot subdivide Christ's redemptive work into separate compartments. To study His ministry apart from His death; to see His death apart from His resurrection is to do Him gross injustice. If we see the cross detached from the Resurrection, this cross becomes a symbol of the triumph over evil, and the sad ending of a failed ministry.

On Good Friday we readily identify with Golgotha. Yet we can never really share the deep sorrow and despair of those first disciples, because our knowledge of the empty grave illuminates the deep darkness of Golgotha.

Once the glorious reality of the risen Lord dawned on them, they saw Christ and the cross in a different light. Their very first message was "He has risen!" While we wish to identify with the cross of Christ, it is impossible for us to share in His physical suffering. But we have the glorious privilege of His invitation to accept His Holy Spirit and to experience the wonder of His resurrection.

In the cross we see what sin does when confronted with perfection – it uses every measure to destroy and to inflict pain. Then we not only see God's triumph in one mighty act of salvation and surrender, but we also learn that He is able to bring forth the very best from the darkest circumstances.

The purpose of His saving grace on the cross is completed in the Resurrection. Once we understand this we will be able to grasp the all-sufficiency of the cross.

Crucified Lord, we praise You that we can worship You as the One who triumphed over the grave, sin and Satan. Amen.

CHRIST ASSURES VICTORY

But thanks be to God! He gives us the victory through our Lord Jesus Christ (1 Corinthians 15:57).

Many Christians experience frustration that borders on despair when they suffer defeat. They try repeatedly to live victoriously, but from time to time they fall prey to some subtle, yet powerful temptations. Eventually they admit defeat and allow their faith to degenerate into a powerless philosophy without a trace of the reality of Christ in their existence.

Everybody who is a serious follower of the Master has experienced the severe pain of disappointing God. Not even the disciples were exempt from this.

No matter how many times you have failed in your walk with the Master, always keep your eyes on the Lord. Never allow His image to fade. You were destined for victory. Sincerely confess your failures as temporary defeats and view them as obstacles that must be overcome in the name of Jesus.

Never accept, believe or confess that you have been defeated by a momentary failure. Christ lived victoriously and He will give you victory over sin and failure if you faithfully trust in Him.

If you have been trapped or overcome by sin and feel unworthy to follow Jesus, rise above your failures and defeats and turn to Christ. Accept the power and strength that He offers – it is pure grace and love. This simple act of faith will result in the jubilant experience of success through Jesus Christ. Live victoriously from day to day!

Thank You, loving Master, for giving me victory in all circumstances through the Holy Spirit. Amen.

CHRIST AND OUR SUFFERING

Jesus commanded Peter, "Put your sword away! Shall I not drink the cup the Father has given Me?" (John 18:11).

Health, financial prosperity, social security and freedom from pain and suffering are all priorities for most of God's children. The desire to be happy is understandable, but it should never become the main purpose or top priority in the life of a true Christian.

The Christian is called to do the will of God through the power of the living Christ. Experience has taught that doing the will of God can bring about immeasurable joy, but also intense pain and torment. Jesus proved this through His life on earth. His torment in Gethsemane and suffering on Golgotha contradict the myth that the Christian way of life is an insurance policy against pain and suffering.

Christ has promised His living presence under all circumstances to everyone who loves Him, faithfully follows Him and who serves and glorifies Him. No Christian is ever left to suffer alone, because Christ promised to be with His children in every situation however dark it might seem.

To meet the challenges of life in partnership with Jesus Christ is the top priority of the Christian's life. The circumstances that you find yourself in might be beyond your control, or not what you would have liked, but His wisdom and support will enable you to accept the most bitter cup life can offer you. In His name and through His power you will be able to drain this bitter cup to the glory of His name.

Thank You, Father, that in my darkest moments of pain and suffering, You are with me and support me through Your Holy Spirit. Amen.

THE REALITY OF THE RESURRECTION

The angel said to the women, "Do not be afraid, for I know that you are looking for Jesus, who was crucified. He is not here; He has risen, just as He said" (Matthew 28:5-6).

Without the triumphant resurrection of Christ from the dead Christianity would have been a long forgotten and useless religion. Christ's teachings touch the heart of man, stimulate his thoughts and are the source of inspiration to many who strive to uplift mankind.

However, these things can be said about many other religions and their leaders as well. What makes Christ unique, is not only His doctrine and the inspiration derived from it, but His divine Person. He approached death fearlessly and overcame it gloriously. He triumphed over death and appeared to His disciples and others and promised to be with them always.

It is this living, risen Christ who rules in the hearts of people. We have all committed ourselves to Him because He is our personal Savior. He is not merely an organization, a teacher or a doctrine. We know from experience that He guides, comforts and strengthens His disciples at all times. We enjoy fellowship with Him on a daily basis and constantly experience the reality of His presence.

It is not always possible to explain our firm faith in Him. Often His followers have no theological background, but deep down in their hearts they just know that He is alive, that He loves them and that they are His children. Nothing can shake their faith in the resurrected, glorified Lord, because He lives in their hearts.

Jesus, I know for sure that You are alive and I want to praise You for this surety! Amen.

JESUS GIVES GOOD HEALTH

Dear friend, I pray that you may enjoy good health and that all may go well with you, even as your soul is getting along well (3 John 2).

It seems as if there are many people with split personalities. Sometimes we feel close to God and at other times we want to forget about Him. Our positive well-being and virtues are erased when evil is rampant in our lives. This conflict in our personalities causes friction in our minds and in our souls. In the long run inner turmoil can cause spiritual, mental and physical backsliding and sickness.

Jesus is the great unifying factor in the human personality. When He controls your life, you have a wholeness that results in a well-balanced spirit. This is revealed in your soul and ultimately also in physical health.

The inner healing that Jesus offers can be destroyed by sin and neglect. If you refuse to forgive others as you have been forgiven, your faith will lose its power and His Spirit will not flow and work through you any longer. When this happens, you fall prey to ailments like lovelessness, covetousness, pettiness, self-centeredness, bitterness, hatred, and many more. These things take control of your body and unavoidably cause physical illness.

The healing and unifying work of Christ can become a reality in your life if you open up your spirit to the Holy Spirit. To be inspired and controlled by the Holy Spirit is the secret of well-being in spirit, mind and body. Then you become a whole, mature and balanced person.

I worship You who grants good health so I can live life to the full and be fruitful and healthy through the indwelling Holy Spirit. Amen.

THE DEMANDS OF OUR TIMES

In all these things we are more than conquerors through Him who loved us (Romans 8:37).

We are constantly reminded that we are living in troubled and violent times. Society is radically changing: crime and broken marriages are the order of the day; international matters are in turmoil; evil and ominous powers cast their negative influences over the entire human race.

The average person does not remain unaffected by this troubling situation. There is fear of the future, the increase in the cost of living and a decrease in income, permissiveness and the ever-present threat of a nuclear bomb hang over us like the Sword of Damocles.

In the midst of this confusion and insecurity stands our eternal, unchanging Father. Only when you realize and believe that behind all this there is a God who cares and who is working out His plan of salvation, will your life be stabilized through unchanging spiritual values and truths.

If you put God in the center of your life, immortal qualities like stability, uplifting goals, inspired visions, love that rises above hatred, and a positive living faith will become the secure foundation of your daily existence.

It is possible, even in turbulent times, to live a balanced life free of fear, through the power of the indwelling Christ. To trust, as an act of faith that the Spirit of Christ is in control, will enable you to look at the chaotic circumstances of our day with trust and courage that only God can give.

Redeemer and Friend, thank You that I can live as a conqueror even in dark times because You have already overcome the world. Amen.

CHRIST GIVES SELF-CONFIDENCE

Dear friends, if our hearts do not condemn us, we have confidence before God (John 3:21).

So many people today lack self-confidence. They may appear confident and even overbearing, but behind their masks, they are actually insecure and unhappy.

There are many reasons why you may feel confident: when you have achieved success; when you are dressed tastefully; when you are financially independent; when you get along well with people – all these will give you some form of confidence.

Basically true confidence depends on more than outward appearance or human relations. It is born from the security of your close relationship with Christ. It creates order, harmony and stability in your spirit. When Christ is in control of your life, you know for sure that nothing can happen that you won't be able to handle with His help. This creates a confidence that enables you to lead a mature, balanced life even if you feel threatened by problems and insecurity.

To approach life in the Spirit and with a Christlike attitude has a practical implication. This implies that because you acknowledge His Lordship and have committed your life to Him unconditionally, you are no longer unimportant. You are no longer influenced negatively by every passing whim or threat.

Once you realize that you are Christ's companion and child of your heavenly Father, with strong convictions that you can maintain through His grace, you can approach life confidently through the Holy Spirit.

Thank You, Lord, that You bring out the best in me so that I can live life to the full every day with humble confidence. Amen.

CHRIST ENABLES ME TO SERVE

He poured water into a basin and began to wash His disciples' feet, drying them with a towel that was wrapped around Him (John 13:5).

Few Christians are called to high and prominent positions in God's Kingdom. Yet every task that He lays upon us, however insignificant it may seem, is of the utmost importance because it is part of God's master plan for the world.

Therefore, whatever your task may be in His Kingdom, do it to glorify God and never to glorify self or to boast about your achievements. The moment you take credit for any success, you will lose the purpose of your calling. Worse than that, you will lose the awareness of Christ's presence and guidance. It is only by remaining humble and close to Him that you will be able to do His will.

If you are living in harmony with Christ, no task will be beneath you. Do everything to the glory of God. You will forget about your own interests while seeking His glory. The most humble task will become a sacrament when dedicated to Him and performed with an attitude of praise and worship.

A true disciple of Christ serves the Lord to the best of his ability wherever he goes. Then the Master can lead him to new terrains and trust him with more responsible tasks in the kingdom of God. He can only achieve this when he has accepted the servitude of Christ and displayed this attitude in the world. Then we will not be getting into each other's hair, but start washing each other's feet. We won't be fighting for the crown, but for the towel!

Here I am Lord, use me to Your glory and honor and help me always to assume the attitude of a servant. Amen.

LET GOD'S LOVE GUIDE YOU

You have made known to me the path of life; You will fill me with joy in Your presence, with eternal pleasures at Your right hand (Psalm 16:11).

You can choose the attitude with which you start each day. You can press on confidently trusting in a loving Father, or you can walk reluctantly, paralyzed by fear and feelings of incompetence.

For many people life has lost its purpose. Day after day, month after month, year in and year out, they plod through a monotonous cycle. They don't really "live" – they just "exist". Nothing positive or exciting fills their empty hours. This is totally unnecessary. The future belongs to God ... and to you! In that order. When you put God first in your life, He becomes your inspiration and He will lead you every day as He promised.

To put God first in life will cost you. It requires discipline that is worth much more than a passing emotion. You will have to set aside time to be alone with Him; you will have to allow His Holy Spirit to imprint the character of Christ in you and you will have to obey Him unconditionally.

Be adamant about getting to know God better through regular Bible study and persevering prayer. Then you will discover that past failures really belong to the past while the future is bright and promising.

Christ has promised to be with you always. Live with Him every day and you will experience a new quality of life. You will receive only the best from Him if you allow Him to guide you in His love and to teach you how to live.

Dear Lord and Master, thank You that I can abide in You. Thank You for teaching me how to live and for giving me Your joy. Amen.

DISCOVER YOUR GIFTS

For this reason I remind you to fan into flame the gift of God, which is in you through the laying on of my hands (2 Timothy 1:6).

Many people allow their lives to become dull and boring because they do not appreciate God's gifts. They are overwhelmed by the achievements of others and are convinced that it is impossible for them to achieve anything worthwhile. Then they bluntly refuse to attempt anything new and become bleak spectators instead of living actively and creatively.

God has given each one of us at least one gift. It often happens that while we are developing this gift, many others are revealed as a result. Many people never discover their hidden talents. It might be due to ignorance, laziness or lack of understanding as to how they should go about discovering this hidden treasure.

Unfortunately little can be done to help those who firmly believe they have no talents. Because of their unbelief their talents remain buried forever. The lazy will always complain about lost opportunities and pretend not to be hurt by failure. Only the Holy Spirit can reveal their unbelieving, sluggish attitude and awaken their spirit to new life and creative activity.

To discover God's gifts requires a sensitive attunement to the guidance of God the Father as well as a willingness to dare to become active. It requires courage, and God never disappoints those who put their trust in Him. As you gradually follow His guidance He will enrich your life because you are obedient. Talents that you have been unaware of will then be revealed.

Father God, give me the courage and the will to obey You, to discover and develop every gift You have given me. Amen.

DO NOT JUDGE

"If any one of you is without sin, let him be the first to throw a stone at her" (John 8:7).

There is an awful human tendency to rejoice when someone else's weaknesses are revealed. This happens when a prominent public figure has made a mistake and the media starts to expose every sordid detail of this person's private life. Viewers and readers then piously judge the happenings. This reveals man's sinful nature: the more gruesome the story and the more gory the details, the higher the circulation of newspapers and magazines becomes.

This disgraceful condition is due to the fact that people feel relieved when they realize that there are other people who are equally wicked, or even more wicked than they are. They mercilessly transfer their own guilt onto the person who has been caught out.

If you have had a life-changing encounter with Christ and experienced the miracle of forgiveness only He can give; if He has set you free from the tension of hidden, unconfessed sin, then you will never rejoice in the fall or weakness of a fellow human being.

When someone has sinned and stands exposed before a cruel, imperfect society, you will be filled with compassion to pray for the guilty one. Often compassionate prayer is the only constructive thing to do in an atmosphere of doom and judgment.

It is very easy to judge another, but when you know and love Christ, you will avoid this destructive attitude and concentrate on love and forgiveness.

Gracious Redeemer, help me to practice the ministry of love and forgiveness. Guide and inspire me to do so through Your Holy Spirit. Amen.

A REFUGE IN TIMES OF DANGER

Every word of God is flawless; He is a shield to those who take refuge in Him (Proverbs 30:5).

A seasoned police officer who had never been shot at during his thirty years of service, still wore a bulletproof vest every day. One day he was shot from behind and the bulletproof vest saved his life. Fortunately, he realized that as long as he was wearing that uniform, he would be a target for criminals and therefore he was always prepared.

In much the same way God protects His children. Every Christian should know this. Because we belong to Christ, we are targets for Satan's attacks. He tries to destroy us with arrows of unbelief, superstition, temptation and despair. We always have to be alert.

When problems seem to overcome us, in times of sickness and sorrow, on days when we ask, "Why God?" – then we are most vulnerable to the attacks of the Evil One. Because we serve in God's army, we are Satan's targets.

That is why an intimate relationship with Christ is crucial. We must remain close to Christ because He is our refuge in our battle against evil.

When we are most vulnerable, let us hide in Him, our Rock. Without His protection we are exposed to the Evil One. Christ's protection not only brings us safety, but also great comfort. The Almighty God of heaven is willing to rescue those who seek His will and who obey Him unconditionally.

Almighty Protector, be my Shield and Rock in times of sorrow, weakness and doubt. Amen.

REVIVAL STARTS IN THE HEART

"Seek first His kingdom and His righteousness, and all these things will be given to you as well" (Matthew 6:33).

Some people tend to become disheartened because they badly want to rectify every wrong in the world. They believe that their convictions and doctrines will solve every problem of our time. In their zeal they forget that imperfection is part of humankind's sinful nature and that we are living in a world torn apart by sin.

It is impossible to create a new world without regenerated people. It is also useless to try and change if your relationship with God is not right. The best place to start reforming and healing this world, is with you. Draw a circle next to your bed, kneel in the circle and beg God to start revival within that circle.

It is not easy to accept the fact that unless you find yourself living in harmony with God, influencing others positively is impossible. Jesus said, "the kingdom of God is within you " (Luke 17:21).

We have to become aware of God's Kingdom first and allow it to take control of our lives before it will be revealed in our lives and characters. Only then can we start to influence those around us. We must constantly strive for perfection despite our shortcomings.

Jesus promised to be with us not only when we succeed but also when we fail. He will enable you to have a positive impact on the part of His Kingdom where He has placed you.

Faithful Lord, You are the center of my life and I praise You for Your victorious power that is at work in me. Amen.

LIGHT IN THE DARKNESS

The LORD is my light and my salvation – whom shall I fear? The LORD is the stronghold of my life – of whom shall I be afraid? (Psalm 27:1).

When thinking of God, we involuntarily think of a bright light that dispels all darkness. Christ declared that He is the Light of the world and His Word assures us that heaven is a place where God Himself is the light.

It is wrong to think that God is not present in the dark places of our lives. Psalm 23:4 assures us that, "Even though I walk through the valley of the shadow of death, I will fear no evil, for You are with me." In Exodus 20:21 we read that, "Moses approached the thick darkness where God was."

At all times and under all circumstances we can hold on to the comforting truth that God will meet us even in the darkest moments of our lives. No matter how dark your life might seem, God is there. In His own time He will miraculously transform the darkness into light.

Are you perhaps experiencing a dark moment of acute awareness of sin and remorse, confusion and indecision, insecurity, sickness or even the loss of a loved one? God is there for you! He is there to take your hand and to lead you out of the darkness into His marvelous light.

May you experience this abundantly in your life. Those who serve and love Him will not dwell in darkness forever. The light of His grace will always penetrate the gloom.

God of light and love, thank You that I may know that in my darkest hour Your light can and will brighten even the most intense moment of sorrow. Amen.

Unfair Criticism

Do not repay anyone evil for evil (Romans 12:17).

Unfair criticism is painful and causes deep wounds. It can influence your whole life negatively. Nobody likes to be criticized, especially falsely or unfairly! The closer you are to the person who criticizes you, the more painful it becomes. Spouses are often unfairly critical about their partners. You probably cannot avoid being criticized unfairly, but you can choose how you are going to react.

We can learn from many characters in the Bible who had to bear the brunt of criticism. Moses was criticized by the people God appointed him to lead.

The biggest blow, however, was when his own family joined in. His own brother and sister criticized him for marrying a Cushite woman (Num. 12:1). Aaron and Miriam were jealous of Moses and wanted to know if God spoke through him only (Num. 12:2). They even criticized him in public.

Moses is a perfect example when it comes to handling criticism. Firstly, he did not even defend himself against the criticism of his family. He knew that truth would eventually triumph – and it did! Secondly, he didn't take revenge which is normally one's first reaction when being criticized unfairly. You don't solve the problem that way, but actually make it worse. Rather discuss the matter calmly and sensibly.

Also remember to keep on praying during such times and ask God for the strength to handle all types of criticism for He will never forsake you.

My Lord and Guide, help me to handle unfair criticism with the right attitude through the Holy Spirit. Amen.

FAILURE – THE DOOR TO SUCCESS

"I am making everything new!" (Revelation 21:5).

Nobody is ever a failure until he accepts himself as one. Maybe your business is gradually falling apart, or your marriage is under a lot of strain. Perhaps everything worthwhile in life seems out of reach. You may have reached a crossroad and are now wondering if it is worth keeping on or if it would not perhaps be better to throw in the towel.

In unpleasant situations like this there are certain dangers that you should try to avoid. Always be aware of bitterness that might take root in your spirit. Perhaps you have been wronged, but if you allow yourself to become bitter, you will not be able to think straight or act constructively. No matter what setbacks you have experienced, don't add bitterness, as it will only increase the damage.

Also avoid feeling sorry for yourself. It will rob you of your determination to start anew and achieve success. It will make your so-called failure a reality that will in turn become obvious to everybody.

Rather be honest with yourself: Examine yourself and evaluate your situation realistically. If you have acted unwisely, admit it openly. This is the point of departure into a new victorious life. Concentrate on your assets: your self-respect, your will to achieve success, your loved ones who still believe in you, and your ability to complete a task successfully. No matter how feeble these things might seem to you, they will direct you on the road to success.

The lessons that failure teaches you might be expensive, but if they draw you closer to God, they are worth it. In this way your failures become the doorway to success.

Holy Spirit, teach me through Your power to conquer my failures and to rise above them to a new life in Christ. Amen.

THE PRESENCE OF GOD

The angel of the LORD encamps around those who fear Him, and He delivers them (Psalm 34:7).

If your faith is based on Scripture, it is founded on faith and not on emotion. Never fall into Satan's trap thinking that because you don't "feel" religious, you have lost your faith. If your spiritual life consists of emotion only, you will easily fall prey to every spiritual whim.

In times of disappointment and defeat you really need a steadfast faith. Then you also realize the insufficiency of purely emotional experiences. Faith in the abiding presence of God is strengthened when you allow Christ to take full control of your life – a requirement of the Christian faith that cannot be sidestepped. To ensure that this truth becomes an inextricable part of you, it must become an integral part of your life and mind.

If you constantly reaffirm this truth, not only on bright sunny days but also on dark days, it will become part of your nature. You will just know that God is surrounding and enfolding you with His holy presence. In spite of emotional fluctuations you will realize that you are being upheld by His omnipotence and love ... even in moments of depression, stress and tension.

If you turn to Him purposefully in every dark moment, He can and will become a constant reality. If it feels as if He is distant and isolated at this moment, it is your fault, not His. Then you need to do something about your relationship with Him. Reaffirm His living presence in your life by surrendering and committing yourself to Him anew.

Thank You, my Savior and Friend, that I am not controlled by my emotions but that I can hold on to You. Amen.

FORGIVENESS AND RECONCILIATION

"Forgive us our debts, as we also have forgiven our debtors" (Matthew 6:12).

We are living in an era where these words are relevant and meaningful. As Christians we belong to a religion where this concept plays an important role. All of us have to say this prayer and truly understand what we are praying. Literally it means: "Forgive us our trespasses in direct relation to our ability and willingness to forgive others." In order to able to do this, the following are required:

- We need to learn to understand: There is always a reason for a person's actions. Perhaps a secret worry; certain environmental or hereditary factors; misunderstanding or temperament. To know everything will enable you to understand everything which will in turn enable you to forgive. The love of Christ is our motivating factor.

- We need to learn to forget. As long as we are brooding on hurts and insults, there is no hope of being able to forgive. It's very dangerous to say, "I will forgive, but I will never forget." This makes it impossible for you to forgive and it actually means that you don't want to forgive. Only the purifying power of God's Holy Spirit can cleanse our heart from bitterness, otherwise it will consume us.

- We need to learn to love: This is only possible if Christ, the Source of love, abides in our hearts. He not only taught us to love and forgive one another, but demonstrated it with His life and especially when He prayed on the cross for those who crucified Him, "Father, forgive them, for they know not what they are doing" (Luke 23:34).

This is the language of love that we have to learn to speak. Only then will forgiveness and reconciliation become a reality.

God of love, teach me the art of forgiveness and reconciliation today. Make me an instrument of Your peace. Amen.

FAITH, LOVE AND DEEDS

"The King will reply, 'I tell you the truth, whatever you did for one of the least of these brothers of Mine, you did for Me'" (Matthew 25:40).

There is a kind of faith that is nothing but theological wishful thinking and speculation and is not practical at all. It does not result in deeds of faith and is unproductive and futile in God's Kingdom. Paul says in Galatians 5:6, "The only thing that counts is faith expressing itself through love."

If my faith doesn't lead me to a deeper experience with God, it is mere pretence and has no lasting value in my life. God is the Source of all true love and in order to have faith that is expressed in deeds, I need to live in unbroken fellowship with Him.

Loving Jesus Christ to the extent that His presence becomes a living reality in my life, will inspire my faith and His love will urge me to do His will. Firm belief and faith in the living glorified Lord, is the foundation of all Christian doctrines.

Faith can only be vibrant and meaningful when it is supported by love. Without love my faith will be warped and will never reach its full potential. Faith that pleases God and obtains real purpose, must be inspired by love.

When your faith finds expression in love, your religion becomes a practical reality in your everyday life. Then you start looking away from your own problems and start seeing a world that is calling out for help. Your faith is no longer mere speculation and pious words, but becomes love in action.

Holy Lord Jesus, our love for You has taught us to love and serve our fellow man. Make us faithful in this ministry. Amen.

APRIL

ON THE ROAD WITH CHRIST

Jesus Christ is the same yesterday and today and forever (Hebrews 13:8).

When looking back on the road you have traveled so far this year, you will most likely be able to recall times of joy and times of sorrow. You probably shared these experiences with certain people. If you have discovered new life in Christ, you undoubtedly shared some intimate moments with Him as well.

He has become a wonderful reality in your life. The moments spent with Him might have been brief and fleeting, but the memory of those times light up the present. You realize that He is your faithful companion in this confusing and stressful life.

When you start obsessing about problems and burdens, the reality of God's loving presence fades. The present troubles overwhelm you to such an extent that you forget the times when you experienced His presence and saving grace as a reality. Pressure caused by problems eradicate the memory of the blessings that you received from the Lord in the past. That is why a certain hymn writer implores us, "My soul never forgets the Lord, because the Lord forgets me not."

No matter how busy or how burdened you might be with worries and cares right now, become quiet for a moment and thank the Lord for the way in which He has guided you up to this point. Praise Him for His faithful love and patience; for His grace when He led you away from temptations. Thank Him for the power of His Holy Spirit that enables you to come out victorious.

Faithful Shepherd and Lord, I will follow You wherever You might lead because You have always been faithful. Amen.

WHAT ABOUT THE FUTURE?

God is able to make all grace abound to you, so that in all things at all times, having all that you need, you will abound in every good work (2 Corinthians 9:8).

Worrying about your future financial prosperity can have a very negative effect on your physical and spiritual well-being. This is especially true of people drawing near to retirement or those who have already retired. They fear the rising cost of living, unexpected expenses, serious illness and many other possible negative situations. The joy of looking forward to a peaceful lifestyle is clouded by worry.

It would be unwise and even foolish to consider retirement without having planned and prepared for it. Your future well-being and financial security are certainly high priorities. The fact of the matter is, however, that if you have planned your life in accordance with God's will, then He will take care of your daily needs. That is the point of departure for your faith.

Jesus Christ made a huge effort in teaching His followers the futility of unnecessary worry. He wanted them to trust God under all circumstances. These were not words spoken in vain, but the assurance that a loving heavenly Father will always provide if you live according to His will. Millions of God's children can testify to the truth of this fact.

If you are worried about your future, come and lay your worries at Christ's feet in prayer. Trust Him with your future and follow His guidance obediently and in faith. He will show you the way and will care for you in His Divine Providence. Not only is He the Almighty Creator, but also the loving Supporter of His Creation.

Lord, my God, I put all my trust in You because I know from experience that You will take care of me in the future. Amen.

THE MINISTRY OF ENCOURAGEMENT

Each helps the other and says to his brother, "Be strong!" (Isaiah 41:6).

For the average person today life is not so easy. The increasing cost of living; tense human relations; unemployment; poor health; droughts: all these and many more factors work together to make our lives difficult and complicated. Unfortunately many people accept it as the norm. They believe that discouragement and misery cannot be avoided.

As a follower of Christ you are not exempted from affliction and trials. Your attitude towards stumbling blocks is what makes the difference. When you experience problems and you complain about your lot in life or feel that God has disappointed you, you become part of the universal choir of people lamenting the cruelty and relentlessness of life. Then you merely succeed in increasing your misery and despair. You become part of the problem instead of part of the solution.

When the Holy Spirit abides in you and is in control of your spirit, He will prevent you from becoming entangled in depressing thoughts and negative attitudes. Instead of trying to find solutions that constantly evade you, rather leave your problems with Christ who already knows everything. Keep trusting in God. This trust will free you to continue your life without a thousand fears filling you with despair and hampering your progress every day.

Because you have the certainty that you can triumph over any negative circumstance through the power of the Holy Spirit, you will be able to encourage others in similar situations.

Loving Master, please help me to look away from my problems and myself and see the needs of others. Enable me to encourage others. Amen.

RESPONSIBILITY TOWARDS CREATION

The earth is the LORD's, and everything in it, the world, and all who live in it (Psalm 24:1).

When God created man He commanded him to, "Be fruitful and increase in number; fill the earth and subdue it. Rule over the fish of the sea and the birds of the air and over every living creature that moves on the ground" (Gen. 1:28).

Pollution has become a household term in modern society. Media coverage of scenarios where man is causing irreparable damage to our environment are regularly viewed. We hear about the destruction of marine life due to the pollution along our coastline. Once pure, fresh air has become so polluted that it is threatening people's health when inhaled. Green fields and crystal clear rivers have become dumping sites. The tragic results are predictable.

Pollution is not restricted to the tangible and visible. The standards of living have also been affected. Progress has become a slogan and excuse for people to pollute our moral and spiritual values. Foul language is heard every day; permissiveness and decline of Christian standards and norms are visible all around us.

God created the earth and everything in it – and it was good! He created man as His representative and entrusted the whole of Creation to him. In spite of all man's many failures, God saved mankind through the death and resurrection of Jesus Christ.

It is our duty as Christians to protect and preserve the beauty of God's handiwork. Pray fervently that God will give us the ability and the desire to do this, otherwise we are headed for self-destruction.

Thank You, Creator God, for the beautiful world You have given us as our heritage. Inspire us to protect and preserve it. Amen.

An Effective Prayer Life

Do not be anxious about anything, but in everything, by prayer and petition, with thanksgiving, present your requests to God (Philippians 4:6).

Of all Christian disciplines, prayer is by far the one practiced the most. It is also probably the one most misunderstood. So many people regard prayer as an emergency button to press only when they have their backs to the wall or as a lifeboat in emergencies. Others treat prayer as an opportunity to bring their wish-list to God, or they use it to get God's seal of approval after they have already made their own decisions. With these attitudes, it is no wonder that many people complain about unanswered prayers.

As with all other blessings, you must first establish a prayer relationship with God if you expect your prayer life to be effective and meaningful. Only then does it become a meaningful spiritual experience. You must admit to and acknowledge God's presence every moment of every day. Keep growing closer to Him while you study His Word and meditate on His character.

Always remember to thank and praise God for the wonderful privilege of prayer – the right to speak freely to the holy, almighty God. Then lay your fears and petitions before Him, asking Him to grant you only the things that fall in His perfect will for your life. Ask for grace to wisely handle every situation that might come your way. Wait on the Lord and be sensitive to the moving of His Spirit leading you along a path of peace and boldness. Obey His voice when His will for you becomes clear. Then you will experience a new dimension of effectiveness in your prayer life.

O Hearer of prayer, You have always been faithful to me. Make me faithful in my prayer life through Your Spirit. Amen.

LOVE UNITES PEOPLE!

Keep on loving each other as brothers (Hebrews 13:1).

In the midst of all the confusion and insecurity, hatred and disunity, murder and crime of our modern day, it is of vital importance to continually remind ourselves of our Master's command to love one another. While we are preoccupied with the demands of life, it is easy to conveniently forget this command. Whether we realize it or not, with such an attitude we can become indifferent to the pain and needs of others.

There are so many things today that lead to the devaluation of our Christian values. Therefore, it becomes more and more important for us to unite against the onslaughts of these undermining influences.

We must form a united front against the merciless attack against the body of Christ by the Evil One. The only effective way to do this is for God's children to be bound together by Christ's love. This love drives away all fear, "There is no fear in love. But perfect love drives out fear" (1 John 4:18). This love overcomes all evil including the power of Satan.

By reflecting the love of Jesus Christ in your life and loving others unconditionally as He loves you, you obtain the power to resist temptation ... also the temptation to cause discord among God's children. In this world filled with hatred and dividedness, showing Christ's love will be a forceful testimony of His power.

The more Christ becomes a reality in your life, the more sensitive you will be to the prompting of the Holy Spirit and the more able you will become to spread His love because it will flow through you to others around you.

Lord, teach me to love unconditionally like You love me. Amen.

TRUE PEACE

"Peace I leave with you; My peace I give you" (John 14:27).

All over the world people are desperately seeking peace and relief. Relief from tension and fear; from nervous tension and exhaustion.

What is the answer? What is your antidote against fear and tension? Where do you find the relief you need and long for to carry on in the rat race of the twenty-first century?

Some find relief in seclusion and meditation. Others turn to drugs and alcohol. Some find it only in the finality of death – often suicide when their burdens have become unbearable.

There is only one way to cope with life and find relief from everyday stress and tension. It is through unconditional surrender to the living Christ. He promised, "My peace I give you. I do not give to you as the world gives" (John 14:27).

Whatever problems you might be experiencing and despite the seriousness of any situation you may be facing, open your heart to the compassionate love of Jesus Christ. Allow Him to take complete control of your life. Make Him a part of your very existence and thoughts. Spend time meditating on His Word, sitting at His feet. Make Him your constant companion every second of the day and pray without ceasing.

Then when the storms in your life have subsided and your spirit becomes quiet, you will know that you have found the peace of God, "the peace of God, which transcends all understanding" (Phil. 4:7).

Prince of Peace, thank You for the peace that I experience in Your presence enabling me to weather every storm in life. Amen.

SURE OF FAITH

The Spirit Himself testifies with our spirit that we are God's children (Romans 8:16).

Some people experience their faith as real, dynamic and meaningful, while others find it dull, powerless and without any meaning whatsoever. It is one thing to accept the doctrines of the church intellectually, but something quite different to be able to say with conviction, "I know whom I have believed" (2 Tim. 1:12).

Of course doctrines, principles and confessions of faith are important, because they determine the basis of your Christian faith. However, more important are those moments when your heart rejoices in the presence of Christ and your spirit experiences the reality of the Holy Spirit.

Both the intellect and emotions have a place in our Christian experiences. The two should never contend to control our mind and soul. Rather, they have to complement each other meaningfully. Christ, our Redeemer, didn't come in the first place to advocate an ethical code; He came to invite everybody to enter into a special relationship with Him – a relationship that radically changes lives, making people aware of the reality of the living God. This certainty is greater than any emotion ever experienced.

You will have the assurance that God really exists, because you know that you belong to Him. You were there when it happened! When this blessed assurance descends on your spirit – the assurance that God is your eternal Father – your faith becomes intellectually acceptable and dynamically active. Then the sacrifice of His Son, Jesus Christ, takes on a precious new meaning. Then you shout triumphantly, "I know that my Redeemer lives!"

Holy Lord, I praise and worship Your name for the blessed assurance in my heart that You are my living Redeemer. Amen.

Do it Now!

Teach us to number our days aright, that we may gain a heart of wisdom (Psalm 90:12).

As you grow older, time becomes more precious to you. You become acutely aware of the years rushing by. Friends, family, colleagues pass away and you become aware of the brevity of life once again.

God determines the number of our days on earth and fortunately we don't know how long we will live. We cannot even predict the quality of our lives in days ahead. That is why today is of the utmost importance. Live life to the full and live wisely. As a believing child of the Lord, there is so much you can do today. Therefore, do not be caught in the quicksand of regrets about yesterday. Confess your mistakes before God and accept His forgiveness – then don't repeat the same mistakes. It makes a cheap mockery of God's grace.

You can start by spreading the good news of redemption through Jesus Christ by being a living example of His grace. Reveal the love and attitude of Jesus Christ through your words and actions today, and the world around you will become brand new. He will enable you to do this through the power of His Holy Spirit.

It is of the utmost importance that you realize now is the time to act. Don't suppress the urge to do a good deed; show your gratitude, the smile you have to share, the help you want to offer – do it now! Do not put off acting out of compassion and offering friendship. Tomorrow may be too late! Reach out to your fellow men and serve them in the name of Jesus Christ. If He then calls you home, the work that He gave you will have been completed. Do not waste your time – do it now!

Lord, my God, I am in Your service and long to fulfill my calling. May Your name alone be glorified. Amen.

YOUR PERSONAL WORSHIP

Come, let us bow down in worship, let us kneel before the LORD our Maker (Psalm 95:6).

Worship can entail the interaction of conflicting emotions. Sometimes you will be filled with a sense of awe that causes an irrepressible feeling of spontaneous praise. You then meditate on the greatness of God and feel like exclaiming with the psalmist, "When I consider Your heavens, the work of Your fingers, the moon and the stars, which You have set in place, what is man that You are mindful of him, the son of man that You care for him?" (Ps. 8:3-4). The greatness and omnipotence of God makes you aware of how fragile man really is.

At other times you lack the inspiration that sparks off worship and you wonder what you should do to create the atmosphere of prayer and adoration. While attempting to understand the eternal God through the life, words and works of Jesus Christ, your worship necessarily becomes more intimate. Jesus enables you to call the holy God your Father.

Through the teachings of Christ a bond of friendship develops between creature and Creator. Then worship becomes a personal and holy matter. How you worship God will necessarily be influenced by your personality and temperament. However, the Holy Spirit will lead you in your worship.

To see God through the eyes of Jesus Christ in your personal times of worship, will enable you to worship Him more intimately and affectionately. Wonder, awe, adoration, love and affection are experienced simultaneously when worship is offered in spirit and in truth.

Holy, Holy, Holy are You, Lord God of hosts. Draw me forever closer to You in worship. Amen.

A CHALLENGE TO DO SOUL-SEARCHING

O LORD, You have searched me and You know me. You know when I sit and when I rise; You perceive my thoughts from afar (Psalm 139:1-2).

Some people stubbornly refuse to do serious introspection. Some become angry because honest soul-searching can be painful and uncomfortable. It is then just easier to avoid doing it at all. The Holy Spirit reveals hidden weaknesses, twisted relationships, ingrained pettiness, and other sinful habits to you while you are introspective.

The quality of self-examination depends on your standards. If you have low standards, it will be revealed through your lifestyle. Only when you discover and accept the fact that God's standards are non-negotiable and not to be sidestepped, will you seriously strive to arrange your life according to His pattern.

This of course might pose a problem to you. To discover the difference between what you should be and what you know you really are, might seem like a gap that cannot be bridged. Can any man meet God's standards? In your own strength such a feat would be impossible, but God, in His grace, enables us. Paul says in Philippians 4:13, "I can do everything through Him who gives me strength."

If you rejoice in the forgiveness that He offers with childlike faith, if you allow His Holy Spirit in your life and stay constantly aware of Christ residing in you, then the value of honest soul-searching will become clear.

The Holy Spirit guides Christ's disciples in this soul-searching. He enables them to look at themselves in the light of God's holiness, and also in the forgiving grace of Christ Jesus our Savior.

"Search me, O God, and know my heart; test me and see if there is any offensive way in me, and lead me in the way everlasting" (Ps. 139:23-24). Amen.

REPLENISH YOUR SPIRITUAL RESERVES

I pray that out of His glorious riches He may strengthen you with power through His Spirit in your inner being (Ephesians 3:16).

If our lives are to have true meaning, they must have depth. To live a superficial life is to develop a poor, ineffective lifestyle. Then we will completely lack pure and holy objectives for our existence.

To live a profound life by no means implies that our lives must be somber and boring. On the contrary, the opposite is true because we discover dimensions of life that we were totally unaware of. A new quality is added to our spirits and immeasurable new horizons open up before us.

To live profoundly requires a certainty about the Holy Spirit's ability to work in and through you. Realizing that the Holy Spirit expresses Himself through people, you begin to fathom the immense potential in your life that is waiting to be revealed. The spiritual reserves that are available to a person are unlimited. They come from God and can never be exhausted. However, they can only be utilized when you accept and apply them in your personal life.

All the measures of God's grace are available to you and are ready to be used so that your life may be brought into greater harmony with God and can be used to the advantage of your fellow man. To be able to draw from these gifts of grace, it is imperative to spend much time and energy pursuing them.

Those who have the courage to live meaningful lives are rewarded beyond their wildest dreams. Test God – move out into the deep waters of His Spirit, "so that Christ may dwell in your hearts through faith ... rooted and established in love" (Eph. 3:17).

O Spirit of God, lead me into the depths of spiritual growth and strengthen my faith and love daily. Amen.

Self-imposed Restrictions

I can do everything through Him who gives me strength (Philippians 4:13).

Many people harbor thoughts of failure even before they have started a project. In a moment of inspiration they have a vision of what they can do and then start to realize their plans with zeal and enthusiasm. Suddenly insecurity starts gnawing – not concerning the project, but regarding their abilities. Thoughts like, "This is probably too big for me. I am not capable" or "I am not qualified for this and I have too little experience" control their minds and paralyze them with fear.

Never turn your back on a challenge because it seems too big. Accept it courageously. Always remember that you have resources hidden inside yourself that you have probably not even begun to draw from.

Your inability to accept the challenges might be caused by a lack of self-confidence. Perhaps someone called you a failure and you accepted their judgment without restraint. Perhaps you attempted a difficult task before and failed miserably and now you accept failure as inevitable. It is wise to remember that you are never a failure until you have accepted yourself as one.

As a Christian you will experience times of doubt and spiritual insecurity. You will wonder if you have the ability to be a disciple. Remember, it is then that the wisdom and power of the living Christ is at your disposal. Accept every challenge that comes your way in faith. Accept your own limitations, but accept the challenges in the name of the Almighty and He will let you triumph over your self-imposed restrictions.

Holy and faithful Master, in Your name I accept the challenges of life – also the challenge to overcome my shortcomings. Amen.

You Cannot Do it on Your Own

"Remain in Me, and I will remain in you. No branch can bear fruit by itself; it must remain in the vine. Neither can you bear fruit unless you remain in Me" (John 15:4).

It is a painful experience for you as a Christian to discover that all your efforts have been in vain. You have been working faithfully, yet the result is failure. If you have experienced this, you will know what a demoralizing effect it can have on your faith.

If you are experiencing such a time right now, you should become quiet and do some soul-searching. There are a few questions that you should ask yourself regarding the areas where you have failed: Did you follow your own selfish heart or did you honestly seek the will of God before you started? Did you make time for prayer, earnestly asking God if that was really what He expected of you – or did it merely fit in neatly with your own plans?

If you practice intimate fellowship with God on a daily basis, submitting all your plans and ideas to Him for approval and guidance, you will experience how the Holy Spirit takes over and guides you in the way that you should go. The more profoundly you are tuned in to God's will, the more certain you will be about God's will for your life. Then you will not foolishly rush into projects and ideas generated by your own shortsighted will.

Obedience is a sure sign of a committed life. Your greatest joy then will be to live in the center of God's will. If you obey God to His glory alone, every effort of yours will be crowned with success. If not, no matter how worthy your intentions, everything will fail. Always remember that He, the True Vine, warned us by saying, "Apart from Me, you can do nothing" (John 15:5).

Lord, I realize that I am weak. Draw me ever closer to You. Amen.

WHEN EVERYTHING SEEMS LOST

Do not grieve, for the joy of the LORD is your strength (Nehemiah 8:10).

There are times in life when dark clouds of sorrow and disappointment descend on us. The death of a loved one or breaking off a longstanding relationship – these experiences are traumatic. It feels as if a part of your life has died. When this happens, some people find it practically impossible to fill the void. The result is that they sink into inconsolable mourning. This can have devastating effects on their lives, and can be detrimental to their emotional, intellectual and spiritual well-being.

It would be foolish and insensitive to say that you should not mourn because you have been separated from someone or something precious to you. On the other hand, it is important to know that with Christ's loving support, you will be able to deal with your sorrow and loss.

It is unthinkable that God did not experience sorrow when His Son died on the cross, or that Jesus would not have mourned at the grave of His friend, Lazarus, and that He was not sad to part from His disciples. That is why we can draw strength from the glorious truth that the Father and Son understand our sorrow. Christ sent His Holy Spirit to be our Comforter in times of sorrow.

God's love, peace and joy carried Jesus through His most traumatic moments. By His grace we are able to work through our sorrows and come out victorious. Surrender yourself unconditionally to God, also in times of deepest sorrow and loss. Then you will bear your cross in a worthy manner, knowing that everything is not lost as long as God is there.

O Supporter in times of sorrow, thank You for being my power and strength in times of weakness! I praise You for Your precious comfort. Amen.

IF YOU ARE SORRY – SAY SO!

Against You, You only, have I sinned and done what is evil in Your sight (Psalm 51:4).

A great number of people find it very difficult to express remorse. They find it difficult to apologize. They might have said something that hurt someone else deeply; they might have done something that caused major pain and sorrow. When they think about it, they are very sorry about what they have said or done. Yet they fail to set matters straight. Or they offer feeble excuses that do not come from their hearts. Or, they try to ignore the damage that they have caused and try to justify their wrong words and actions.

This attitude is often caused by a false or exaggerated sense of self-importance. There are people who proudly boast about the fact that they will never admit that they are sorry. This only reveals their pettiness and immaturity.

The Bible, however, teaches us in Romans 3:10, "There is no one righteous, not even one." We have all sinned. A remorseful confession of our failures in our relationships with God and man is the first step to recovery for the one who has been hurt as well as for the one who caused the hurt.

It takes a mature person to confess his mistakes. It is also a generous, kind-hearted person who forgives those who genuinely confess their trespasses. This is how God demonstrated His love to us through the life and death of His dear Son, Jesus Christ.

It is not a shame, nor a sign of weakness to apologize. When someone has wronged you, you would certainly expect him to apologize. Dare a Christian do less than that?

Gracious Lord, help me to apologize or forgive when needed so that my life can be in harmony with You. Amen.

RESPONSIBLE FOR YOUR OWN DEEDS!

A man's own folly ruins his life, yet his heart rages against the Lord (Proverbs 19:3).

God is often blamed for bad things that He is not responsible for at all. It is His desire for all people to live in harmony with Him and to be happy and prosperous. Nevertheless He is blamed for people's failures and maladjustments in society. It never even occurs to these unhappy folk that if they had walked closely with the Lord, obeying Him in all things, their lives would have been completely different.

The undeniable truth, however, is that man must take full responsibility for his own actions. This should have a sobering effect on all of us. It is an unchangeable moral law that man reaps what he has sowed. In Galatians 6:7 Paul wrote about this to the Galatians, "Do not be deceived: God cannot be mocked. A man reaps what he sows." We can conveniently ignore or forget this law, but that will not change its validity.

If you are experiencing an unhappy or difficult time, and you feel a little aggressive towards God and life, be wise enough to return to God.

Don't fight life – try to co-operate for a change. You can only do this if you acknowledge the lordship of Christ in your life and express your total willingness to obey His will. He will lead you on a road of joy and success and you will enter a new dimension of life.

You will also be able to approach and handle your problems constructively. Essential values will receive their rightful place in your life and you will accept responsibility for your own actions.

Faithful Guide and Friend, please guide me through the confusing demands of life and hold my hand so that I will not stray from You. Amen.

How Do You Look At Life?

All the days of the oppressed are wretched, but the cheerful heart has a continual feast (Proverbs 15:15).

Because sin is such an awful reality in this world, there is the danger of it controlling our minds completely. There is also the very real danger of developing a "sin-syndrome" so that even the most innocent pastimes could appear sinful to us. Then we are forever compiling catalogs of possible sins. Unfortunately there are many disciples who are much more sin-conscious than Christ-conscious.

As a child of God you have been freed from sin and it should no longer rule your life. You must, however, always be alert. Even if you are standing, there is always the possibility that you might fall – especially if you rely too much on your own abilities. You can easily backslide when you disregard God's grace. Your redemption is no insurance policy against never sinning. That is why you have to be more tolerant and understanding towards the weaknesses of others. Always remember: "There but for the grace of God go I."

An unbeliever has reason to be depressed when he looks at the world around him. It seems as if everything is falling apart and a feeling of despair takes hold of his spirit. If, however, you have a living relationship with your eternal Father through faith in Christ Jesus, hope replaces despair; courage diminishes your fear and surprisingly, you discover a dimension in your life which fills you with hope even in the darkest moments of your life. Suddenly you are no longer preoccupied with sin.

You can look at life from God's perspective and put your faith and trust in Him. Then life is a feast!

Lord Jesus, I trust in You completely and strive to be what You want me to. Please assist me through Your Holy Spirit. Amen.

A
P
R
I
L

18

SORT OUT YOUR PRIORITIES

So that you may be able to discern what is best and may be pure and blameless until the day of Christ (Philippians 1:10).

A great weakness in many people is that they try to do too much. They have this misleading conviction that they have to agree to everything they are asked to do and that it is an unpardonable sin to say "no". Very soon they discover that due to the quantity of work, the quality is lacking.

Unfortunately this phenomenon can be observed especially within the church of Christ. A small group of willing people always have to do all the work. In many cases it is because nobody else is able or willing to do the job.

On the other hand it may also be because the volunteer enjoys being involved in as many aspects and projects of the church as possible. Often they cling to their many responsibilities to the disadvantage of the church and others who also wish to become involved. Inevitably too much pressure and responsibility take their toll. Projects are left incomplete and others are too scared to offer their help: with the result that the Lord's work suffers loss.

You must accept the fact that you cannot do everything simultaneously – it is not humanly possible. Often you block the way for many other children of God who also received talents to help with part of the work. They might be able to do the job equally well or even better.

It is, however, possible for you to undertake a job and devote all your attention to it. Your responsibility as a disciple of Jesus is to open up your mind and spirit before God and be sensitive to the guidance of the Holy Spirit. Then you will be able to distinguish what is really important to God.

Source of all wisdom, help me to know what is really important. May everything that I undertake bear Your seal of approval. Amen.

GOD HEARS!

The LORD will hear when I call to Him (Psalm 4:3).

Every person who longs to develop an earnest prayer life, has experienced moments of deep despair and loneliness at times. You expect prayer to satisfy the yearning of your heart and yet it often ends in disappointment and frustration. Such a person starts feeling that his spiritual efforts are futile.

During such times we tend to try and force God to listen to our requests. We keep on hammering at heaven's door in the vain hope that God will reveal Himself and grant us our petitions because Jacob contended with God all night at the ford of Jabbok and eventually met God face-to-face (see Gen. 32:22-31). The average person, however, only experiences sorrow and disappointment when his prayers remain unanswered.

What we too often forget is that when we desire to meet God in prayer, He is already there waiting for us!

Put God first in your thoughts. Then any tension built up in your spirit will be averted and you will become aware of God's wonderful, calming presence. Stop forcing yourself to pray and allow the Holy Spirit to pray in you. The Lord whom you have been seeking and who seems to be so far from you is already waiting to meet you in the quietness of your own heart.

The mistake you probably made was to allow your selfish desires to form a wall between you and God. Only when your desire to meet Him overrides your personal interests, will you truly become aware of His presence. When He occupies the prime position in your prayer life, He becomes a living reality. Then you discover with great joy that He is a God who hears ... and answers prayer!

Thank You, Lord my God, that You are always there when I draw near to You in prayer. Amen.

Obedience Has Great Rewards

Do what is right and good in the Lord's sight, so that it may go well with you (Deuteronomy 6:18).

Obedience to God is a key factor in being a Christian. In our day and age many people are disillusioned and complain that their prayers are not answered. Then they hold God accountable, even though He is not responsible for their petitions not being granted and their dreams not being realized.

If, however, we manage to get to the root of the problem, we would probably find that God was never included in their planning until they found themselves with their backs to the wall. Then they blame God for their failures. Somewhere along the line they strayed from God's way and started following their own hearts.

There is no doubt about the fact that God loves you. He confirmed His love for all people on Golgotha. Because of His boundless love, you should never doubt that God wants what is best for you. However, it is only when you live the way that He wants you to, that you can hope to obtain the maximum blessings upon your life.

God did not leave us in the dark regarding His will. His eternal Word reveals His complete will for our lives. In Christ Jesus, God demonstrated that it is possible for us to live righteously. It requires sacrifices, but if we are willing to be obedient to Him, we can rely on Him to reward us.

With the Scriptures as guide for your life as a Christian and through experiencing the love of Christ and the power of the Holy Spirit, you will receive the wisdom and strength to live according to God's will. Do this and you will receive abundant life from Christ's hand.

It is my delight to do Your will, O God. Thank You, Jesus, that You are my Perfect Example and that Your Spirit guides me. Amen.

BE SPARING WITH ADVICE

We hear that some among you are idle. They are not busy; they are busybodies (2 Thessalonians 3:11).

Some people thrive on controlling and manipulating other people's lives while their own lives are a mess. Their involvement in others' lives is often a smokescreen behind which they hide their inability to manage their own lives successfully. Many ineffectual lives are hidden behind a stream of advice to others. This only reveals their immaturity and lack of practical experience.

Self-control is a prerequisite for serving others with constructive advice. If you cannot make a success of your own life, how can you advise others on how to conduct theirs? Advice without understanding and the foundation of experience has little value at all. If you have walked a difficult path yourself, you will be able to give advice and tell about its joys and dangers.

It is only when you have struggled through life's problems yourself that you become aware of the intricacies of human life on earth. Then advice becomes a scarce commodity. It is born out of experience and is not dished out randomly when not requested; and even when it is requested, it should only be given if that person truly asks for it. Therefore, be careful when giving advice – there are far too many people who do not really want advice; they only want their own ideas confirmed.

Never give advice to someone else unless you have prayed about it first. After serious prayer you might discover that God has changed your mind radically about the advice you had planned to give. After praying, you will be able to advise more humbly and with much more wisdom.

Holy Spirit of God, please keep me from being a busybody. Give me a sensitive ear and a praying heart for those in need. Amen.

LIFE IN THE SPIRIT

If the Spirit of Him who raised Jesus from the dead is living in you, He who raised Christ from the dead will also give life to your mortal bodies through His Spirit, who lives in you (Romans 8:11).

Christ can live in you! The wonder of God's grace! In the crossfire of theological arguments and sectarian disputes, this glorious truth is often forgotten. Scripture clearly declares, "This is how you can recognize the Spirit of God: Every spirit that acknowledges that Jesus Christ has come in the flesh is from God, but every spirit that does not acknowledge Jesus is not from God" (1 John 4:2-3).

To belong to Christ unconditionally is a basic prerequisite for a true Christian lifestyle. Without His indwelling Spirit life becomes a burden that nobody can bear successfully. However, when His Spirit takes possession of our spirit and fills it, we find new meaning in life. And this brings immeasurable joy and peace to the heart.

When you allow God's Spirit in your life, a miracle takes place. You have taken the first step to Christian discipleship. You dare not, however, remain stagnant at the miracle of your conversion and rebirth. There must be continual and consistent growth in a Christian's life. You have to develop a deeper understanding of God so that you can faithfully obey His will. That requires a daily surrendering to Him.

When you allow the Spirit of God into your life, the miracle of transformation occurs. You no longer live to fulfill your own desires, but to do the will of God whom you love. Christ will be revealed through your life as a blessing to others.

Don't hesitate to walk in the Spirit. It is the only way to find fulfillment, joy and peace!

My Lord and Master, fill me with Your Spirit so that I can reflect Your love in this world. Amen.

God Is Always There!

My God, my God, why have You forsaken me? Why are You so far from saving me? (Psalm 22:1).

Few things can be as devastating as the intense feeling of being deserted. Yet many people live through this destructive experience every day. Perhaps they have purposely cut themselves off from society; perhaps they really don't have any friends, or perhaps as is often the case, they have been cut off from society by other people.

Should you find yourself in such a situation, you must do something about it immediately. Do some self-examination. Haven't you perhaps consciously erected a wall between yourself and others? Have you been so preoccupied with yourself and your own affairs that you have become indifferent towards your fellow man? Have you withdrawn from society into your own cozy kingdom? Are people not perhaps shying away from you for fear of being hurt by your indifferent attitude and behavior?

You do have a firm anchor on days like these – God who has promised never to leave nor forsake you. Turn to Him for advice and love in times of loneliness. Invite the Holy Spirit to take control of your life. When you have the attitude of Jesus Christ, you become an instrument of His love and peace. He will enable you to take the first step in bridging the gap that has developed between you and others.

Express loving interest in your fellow man. By doing this you will be rewarded with love from those whom you have served in love. The loneliness will flee and new joy and freedom will become part of your life. All this because you know through faith that God is always there!

Father, thank You for Your promise never to leave nor forsake me. Thank You for Your Holy Spirit that makes me worthy of relationships with others. Amen.

Do the Right Thing

Speak up and judge fairly; defend the rights of the poor and needy
(Proverbs 31:9).

It is so easy to excuse yourself by saying, "I mind my own business!" It is normally an excuse to neglect your Christian duty and not to become involved. There is a vast number of people who are not able to fight for their rights: the uneducated; the oppressed; the fearful; those who feel inferior, and many others. They are cautious to make themselves heard, or express an opinion, or stand up for what they believe in. The result is that they are in danger of losing their value as human beings.

If someone bears the name of Christ, he should be alert and sensitive to such situations at all times. If you come across such a situation, it is your duty to make sure that justice is done.

Jesus, our Perfect Example, never put any value on popularity. In every situation He did what was right in the eyes of God. He was a friend of sinners; He mixed with the outcasts of society; He made time for lepers; He expressed love to those who hated Him.

It is your privilege and duty to follow Christ's example. Follow His guidance and serve Him by serving those He sends across your path. Don't be too sensitive about public opinion – that will curdle every worthy impulse of your heart. Also remember that in the end you are accountable to God and not to man. Do what the Master desires you to do and your life will have new dimension of fulfillment.

This kind of action requires courage. Our Leader never said that the road would be easy. What He did say was, "Whatever you did for one of the least of these brothers of Mine, you did for Me" (Matt. 25:40).

Blessed Lord and Redeemer, please enable me to do what You want me to do and not so much what I would like to do. Amen.

Do Not Take Love for Granted

If I speak in the tongues of men and of angels, but have not love ...
I gain nothing (1 Corinthians 13:1, 3).

We take so many of life's most precious things for granted. We are part of a happy family and have security and love, but we forget to thank God for it. If you manage to make ends meet, despite inflation and rising costs, you forget to express your gratitude towards your heavenly Father for His care. There are people who love, trust and support you and perhaps it never occurs to you to show them that you love and appreciate them.

Let us start with God's love for us: How often do we take His love for granted? We even confess, "God is love" without being filled with awe and adoration. The mere fact that the Almighty God loves you and me is breathtaking and incomprehensible. It should be the most sensational discovery of your life!

The realization of God's love for you and the awakening of your love for Him, should lead to true love and appreciation for the people around you – especially those you come in contact with on a daily basis. Perhaps you have been married for a number of years and have children you can be proud of, yet you seldom assure them of your sincere love for them.

Perhaps you try to justify yourself by saying they know that you love them. "I provide a home, food, clothing – how can I not love them?" Yet a single word or special act of love from time to time is worth far more than all the material things you can give them.

Never take the loved ones in your life for granted: it will definitely be the death-knell for all of them.

I truly love You, Lord! Your love for me and my love for You make
my love for those in my life abound. Amen.

PURE WORDS AND THOUGHTS

May the words of my mouth and the meditation of my heart be pleasing in Your sight, O LORD, my Rock and my Redeemer (Psalm 19:14).

It often happens that when a few men are together, the topics of discussion, the language used and the crudeness of jokes sink to a level that is not worthy of a Christian.

Apparently such behavior guarantees their manhood. It is highly unlikely that they would behave like that in the company of their own family. But because they are with the boys, they develop a kind of bravado. They have a misconception that manhood depends on foul language.

The real tragedy is when women try to outdo men in using "sewer language" and other foul expressions. It is a sad state of affairs that speaks volumes of our moral standards.

It requires an iron will and the courage of your convictions to stand up against this. However, we must remember that these bravados might be hidden from family members and loved ones, but God hears them and knows about them.

Wherever people gather Christ is there in His love. He cares for them, He loves them and He is certainly filled with sorrow because of their behavior.

Swearing is a bad habit which can be broken by being firm and disciplined. Persevering in prayer to be set free is of the utmost importance.

When the quality of a conversation drops to the level of the sewer, we must think of the pain it is causing Christ and the damage it causes to our spiritual lives. Refuse to be part of it because your refusal might cause the wavering child of God to reconsider.

Please put a watch before my lips, dear Lord. Help me to honor You in my thoughts and my words. Amen.

BE STILL BEFORE THE LORD

Be still before the LORD, all mankind, because He has roused Himself from His holy dwelling (Zechariah 2:13).

Life is filled with extremes. There are moments of exuberant joy and then there are times of devastating sorrow; there are times of victory and times of defeat; periods of deafening noise and of tangible silence. The most difficult of all is when your soul longs for silence in the presence of God like the parched earth longs for rain. For some or other reason we find it very difficult to reach this state of silence.

Life is also full of challenges. There is so much to be done and the clamor around us often silences the inner voice of wisdom and blunts our conscience. You stay busy, work hard and make a lot of noise, just in case it should become quiet and you perhaps hear something you don't like. To allow your spirit to dwell in God's silence can be a totally new experience. Yet spending time in seclusion with God is invaluable.

Try to break through this silence consciously. Your mind might try to convince you that you have too much to do and your blunted spirit might tell you that it is a waste of time – and time is money! If you persevere with the help of the Holy Spirit, you might feel a little uncomfortable at first leaving all the things that you have to do and the things that you did not complete.

If you confess your shortcomings courageously and with perseverance, you will reach your full spiritual potential. Then being still before the Lord becomes a creative reality.

I am still before You, O holy God, so that I am able to hear what Your will for my life is and to be strengthened so that I can do Your will. Amen.

WHEN YOUR WORLD FALLS APART

I despise my life; I would not live forever. Let me alone; my days have no meaning (Job 7:16).

When we have set high spiritual objectives for ourselves and have aspired to live according to honorable principles, yet experience nothing but adversity, we are left with intense feelings of sadness. Then we wonder: where is this road leading?

If life has knocked you to the ground, there is only one way that your life can go: upwards! It is at moments like these that you have to be very careful that self-pity doesn't control your thoughts and emotions. When dark storm clouds are gathering, or the storm has already broken, search for something constructive and permanent to hold onto. This will bring you to God – the Eternal, Unchanging One.

You may doubt if anything constructive will survive the devastating circumstances that you are in. But remember that not even the darkest moment of your life can prevent you from making a fresh start. A lot of drift-wood might need to be cleared up first and make no mistake, it could be a painful process. However, you can start a new life right now and you can do it in the love and strength of Jesus Christ. He is only a prayer away!

If you feel like throwing in the towel and are so tired of fighting that you only want to be left alone, then your life has lost purpose and meaning and only despair remains. Even from the ruins of your life, Christ can make a new day dawn. You might feel broken, but it is for this very reason that Christ came to this earth: to heal broken lives and create new beginnings. He *can* and wants to do it for you.

When my life has fallen apart, O Lord, please take it in Your hands and make it new and whole. Amen.

BE FIRM WHEN MAKING DECISIONS

It will be as though a man fled from a lion only to meet a bear
(Amos 5:19).

There are times in every person's life when you are forced to make decisions. You are battling with a problem; you are experiencing trouble; you are involved in a delicate situation – and each time you are called upon to make a decision and take a stand. It might concern your family, your business or your personal life. Your decision might have far-reaching effects.

When you are in such a situation, one thing is certain: you cannot turn your back on the problem or wish it would disappear. That will not bring you any peace of mind. Jonah tried to flee to Tarshish when God sent him to Nineveh. Tarshish became a mirage in the desert that he never reached. One cannot run away from the responsibility of making decisions without getting hurt.

Try to avoid making crucial decisions and you will suffer from guilt as you are constantly reminded of your failure to make a decision. You tried to take the easy way out and only managed to increase your problems. You fled from a lion but a bear attacked you instead.

There is nothing we cannot do through the power and grace of our Lord Jesus Christ: and that includes being firm when making a decision. What seems impossible to man is possible with God. No matter how insufficient and incompetent you might feel when you have to make a decision, never fail to ask Christ's help and guidance.

Bring your problems to Him in prayer and then faithfully follow the road the Holy Spirit indicates to you. In this way you will be able to handle any crisis. Only then can you be firm when making decisions.

Thank You, Lord Jesus, that there is no problem that You and I cannot handle together. Amen.

MAY

CHRIST + I = PEACE

When the disciples were together, with the doors locked ... Jesus came and stood among them and said, "Peace be with you!" (John 20:19).

Modern-day Christians don't have the privilege of knowing Jesus in the flesh. Fortunately, His influence on lives does not depend on His physical presence. It can be experienced any time when fellowship with Him is sought. Through the ministry of the Holy Spirit, Christ is not confined to time or space, but He inspires, guides and renews the lives of those who seek His presence.

Certain conditions have to be met before the presence of Christ can become a reality in our lives. There is no substitute for the discipline of waiting on Him in silence. We must desire nothing from Him but to have greater love for Him. This requires discipline that is not inspired by diligence, but by love. His perfect love reacts to your imperfect love, making His presence a glorious reality.

The danger is that it can become a purely emotional experience unless it is expressed in practical terms. While you practice the reality of His indwelling presence, you become increasingly aware of the needs and desires of your soul. Should you neglect to react, you might smother the divine initiative and lose the awareness of His presence.

The Master is always with you, but a lukewarm acknowledgment of His existence will never create the same awareness of His presence as a burning desire for Him and a willingness to obey Him. May He be a living reality in your life this month, affording you great joy and perfect peace.

I praise You, loving Lord, for the fact that through love and discipline, I can become increasingly aware of Your living, loving presence. Amen.

Triumphant in Christ

May all who seek You rejoice and be glad in You; may those who love Your salvation always say, "The LORD be exalted!" (Psalm 40:16).

We all come into contact with people who wallow in self-pity. They feel life has treated them unfairly; that they are not appreciated enough and that they don't deserve all the misfortunes that they encounter. Inevitably they withdraw into themselves and pamper their misery. They harbor feelings of bitterness against the world in general and specifically against those they blame for their misfortunes. The circumstances in which they find themselves are never their fault, but are always caused by someone else.

The cause of their situation might be beyond their control, but how they react to it is their own responsibility. You can either break down under the burden of your misfortunes or you can overcome it triumphantly. You may not be responsible for a physical defect or for your poor financial situation, but the responsibility for most other things in your life is undoubtedly yours. How you handle your circumstances depend on the strength of your faith.

Both in Scripture and in everyday life we find ample testimony of people who overcame their shortcomings through Christ and lived a life of triumphant victory.

This experience can be yours as well. Believe unconditionally in God's promise that He would never disappoint you or leave you in the lurch; that Jesus Christ will always be with you and that the Holy Spirit will lead and teach you. With Christ as your Lord, you are living on victorious ground.

When You are for me, O Lord, who or what can be against me? In You I have the final victory. Amen.

GRACIOUS GOD, GRANT ME PATIENCE

Be still before the LORD and wait patiently for Him (Psalm 37:7).

How often do we not rush into a situation only to be disappointed when things don't go according to plan? The only comfort we have is that we are not the only ones who are foolish. Many people pay a high price for being impetuous. As a result they become despondent and lose their self-confidence. Naturally their enthusiasm is dampened and the pendulum of their emotional life swings from one extreme to another.

The main reason for this is because you neglect to lay your plans or problems before God, and wait patiently for His guidance. It has been proved repeatedly in people's lives, both in the Scriptures and in secular history, that God's methods and timing are always perfect. His concept of life is total and eternal. We, on the other hand, can only handle what we perceive in the here and now. That is why we should learn to practice the Christian virtue of patience.

Before you make any important decision; before you move into any specific direction; before making a vital change in your life, bring the matter before the Lord in prayer and ask for the guidance of the Holy Spirit. Then wait patiently on the Lord and be willing to be led by Him.

Above all, be sensitive to the voice of the Holy Spirit because that is the way in which God will guide you. Then continue in faith, being certain of the fact that, "In all things God works for the good of those who love Him, who have been called according to His purpose" (Rom. 8:28).

Heavenly Father, You are my Guarantee and Security and that is why I can approach each day confidently. Amen.

GOD, OUR FORTRESS AND REFUGE

He who fears the LORD has a secure fortress, and for His children it will be a refuge (Proverbs 14:26).

One of the greatest joys in life is the feeling of safety and security. It removes the tension from everyday life and frees you from a gnawing fear that can become a destructive force in human lives. In order to obtain this security, people are willing to sacrifice almost everything and will fight with all their might to fulfill this need. Yet few people manage to reach their goals.

Security does not depend on the size of your bank balance or the strength of your material assets. In actual fact it is a spiritual state of mind that reflects the quality of your faith. If you worship God and enjoy regular and intimate fellowship with Him, you will become increasingly aware of a growing faith and strength. It is impossible to have a true encounter with the living God, an active faith in Jesus Christ our Savior, and still be troubled by a feeling of insecurity.

If God is a living reality to you, you will not feel insecure or unsafe. This blessed assurance of the safety and security that you have found in Christ, will flow through your life to those you meet.

Make time to get to know God more intimately and the assurance of safety found in the Eternal Rock will become one of your most precious assets. Isaiah knew this place of refuge and could testify with confidence about what we have in God under the inspiration of the Holy Spirit.

In Isaiah 41:10 we read, "So do not fear, for I am with you; do not be dismayed, for I am your God. I will strengthen you; I will uphold you with My righteous right hand."

I trust in You alone, my God and Father, and that is why I can start each day with confidence. Amen.

M
A
Y

4

OVERCOMING FEAR

Surely God is my salvation; I will trust and not be afraid. The LORD, the LORD, is my strength and my song (Isaiah 12:2).

Fear has a destructive influence on human lives. Its effects are widespread and far-reaching. Often the origin and nature of a disease cannot be determined until it culminates in fear with decaying influences. Even though fear is often linked with danger that threatens us physically, it goes far beyond that. Immeasurable damage can be done on your nervous system and emotional state through psychological tension and stress caused by fear.

There is however, no watertight human solution to the gripping fear that people experience when their security is threatened, or when lifestyle changes beyond their control are forced on them.

How does one handle the inconsolable loneliness that follows the death of a loved one, or the devastating news confirming a terminal illness? The examples are innumerable, but often the results are identical – the feeling of helplessness and despair as that icy finger of fear moves down your spine mercilessly.

The only way to get rid of fear and to solve this problem, is to find refuge in God and in His love. His promise, never to leave nor forsake you, remains steadfast. In Christ, God's love expelled all fear from our world. Christ overcame the anguish of death.

Allow Him to lead you out of the jungle of fear so that you will be able to handle anything that comes your way in His power and strength. Only He can give you the courage to live victoriously in any situation.

I cling to Your perfect love, O Lord, so that I can overcome my fear. Amen.

EXPECT GREAT THINGS FROM GOD

"Go home to your family and tell them how much the Lord has done for you, and how He has had mercy on you" (Mark 5:19).

You can never excel spiritually or intellectually if you underestimate life. If you expect little, or nothing from life, that is exactly what life will give you. Then you have not yet learned to realize your highest ambitions through hard work and dedication.

Perhaps you were too hasty or keen to say, "I can't" while you should have said, "I'll try!" If this happens, you will plod along through the shallow waters of mediocrity, refusing to believe that you have a higher calling.

If you have the courage to get the maximum out of life, expect great things from life and from God. It is the enthusiastic spirit of expectancy combined with a resolution to achieve that will eventually lead to true greatness.

True greatness should, however, never be confused with foolish haughtiness or pride. A proud person seldom reveals greatness. Spiritual and intellectual wisdom that bears testimony to a quiet but ever-increasing co-operation with your heavenly Father is of the utmost importance. Once you have decided to become an instrument in the hand of the Father and make that the main aim of your daily life, you will discover that spiritual depth, insight into life and a growing sensitivity towards spiritual things, become the characteristics of your life.

When God is first on the agenda of your life and your spirit is in harmony with the Holy Spirit, you will experience true spiritual greatness.

In fellowship with You, Father, true greatness thrives and I learn to expect great things from You, so I can do great things for You. Amen.

M
A
Y

6

SPIRITUAL BACKSLIDING

But he did not know that the LORD had left him (Judges 16:20).

Spiritual backsliding is often so treacherous that it enters your life unnoticed. In a crisis, the degeneration is then discovered with dismay.

There is always a prelude to spiritual and moral backsliding. It usually starts when you neglect prayer and your relationship with Christ. It happens so gradually that you are seldom aware of it. You might even still appear to be very "religious" and carry on profusely with good works. This, however, is only a smokescreen to cover up your spiritual decay that is eating into your life like cancer.

At times you will be sadly aware of your spiritual backsliding. To make up for these shortcomings, you become more enthusiastic about "religious activities", but eventually you will have to admit your spiritual bankruptcy.

Some people make the situation worse by declaring publicly that a spiritual life is not worth pursuing. Few of us will be courageous enough to confess that our spiritual lives have failed due to a lack of disciplined prayer, studying Scripture and spiritual growth.

To experience the presence of God in your life, you have to practice consistent fellowship with Him. Talk to Him always and wherever you are; share your joys as well as your sorrows with Him; acknowledge and confess continually that He is with you as Immanuel! Then your spiritual life will experience abundant growth and take you to mountain peaks with God and your faith will be strengthened every day.

Loving Father, guide me through Your Holy Spirit so that I will be kept from spiritual decay and backsliding. Amen.

M
A
Y

7

TRUST GOD IN THE STORM

But when he saw the wind, he was afraid and, beginning to sink,
cried out "Lord, save me!" (Matthew 14:30).

The tides constantly change on the ocean of life. At times
there is a windless calm and you cruise along peacefully
while everything is going in your favor. But then, suddenly, ominous storm clouds gather and everything starts
going wrong.

It is easy to trust God when the sun is shining and the
water is calm. It is a different story when the storm breaks
and it seems as if your faith is not strong enough to handle
the challenges and confusion in and around you.

Peter's effort to walk on water teaches us a simple, yet important lesson. Jesus was at the height of His ministry and
Peter was basking in the glory radiating from Jesus. It was
then that Peter and his fellow disciples found themselves,
in obedience to the Master's command, in a frail vessel in
the middle of a raging storm. In the storm they lost their
faith and only thought about survival.

Jesus came to them in the storm and restored their
confidence. Peter, more impetuous than the others, took a
courageous step of faith and started walking on the water
towards Jesus. While he kept his eyes on his Master, he
was safe. When the storm drew his attention away from
Jesus and fear filled his heart and mind, his faith failed
him and he started to sink.

It is vitally important to keep your eyes fixed on the
Lord and remember that He is greater and mightier than
any storm that might threaten you. The storms of life are
indeed under His almighty control and bow before His
authority.

Lord and Master, I will trust You when the storms of life are
raging as well as when the sun is shining brightly. Amen.

THE LORD FORGIVES AND FORGETS

Praise the LORD, who forgives all your sins and heals all your diseases (Psalm 103:2-3).

A great tragedy for Christians is the fact that many sinners whose sins have been forgiven, cannot or will not forget about those sins. God has forgiven them but they refuse to forgive themselves. Psalm 103:9 clearly states, "He will not always accuse, nor will He harbor His anger forever." Billy Graham said that God casts our sins into the depths of the ocean, but we take a boat and row to that spot to do some fishing!

It is true that all people have sinned and fall short of the glory of God, yet you may never allow sins that have been forgiven to rule your thoughts. Sins of the past may not rob you of the joy that God has in store for you. As a Christian you are filled with remorse about your sins, and you confess them to God. Therefore, never allow the memory of past sins to hamper your spiritual growth.

If you have accepted God's forgiveness and approach the future in His name without the handicap of sins from the past, your future will blossom. God is already in the future, and as you move into it, He will show you the way. The Word of God teaches us a specific truth in this regard, "But one thing I do: Forgetting what is behind and straining toward what is ahead" (Phil. 3:13-14).

Therefore, free yourself from the grip of past sins. Stop reminding yourself of them and don't recall them all the time. If you do, they have authority over your life. God forgives and forgets. You have to do the same and move towards a richer, fuller life in Christ.

I gratefully accept Your forgiveness, O Lord. I remind myself continually of this fact and cannot stop thanking You. Amen.

THE SECOND MILE COUNTS

"If someone forces you to go one mile, go with him two miles"
(Matthew 5:41).

Palestine was under Roman authority. The Jews had to pay grueling taxes and were humiliated in various ways.

One of the most degrading Roman laws was that any Roman soldier had the right to command a Jew to carry his rucksack for one mile. The proud Jews obeyed this resentfully. They carefully counted the exact number of steps and when the mile was completed, they would throw the bag down in disdain.

Now Jesus comes with a surprising and challenging claim of Christian love: carry the bag for another mile. He wants to teach us that one only really starts living once the mile of duty has been completed and we have started with the second mile of love. It is the second mile that cancels out the monotony of life. You are filled with joy when you willingly undertake a task of love – even for your enemies.

The compulsory mile never brings joy. It is that optional giving of yourself, your talents and your time that brings joy beyond description. Willingness to travel the second mile indicates spiritual growth, because it is done with enthusiasm born out of love.

The cross on Golgotha is sound proof of the benefits derived from the second mile. Jesus' enemies mocked Him; they flogged Him and nailed Him to the cross – yet He prayed for them! The second mile is difficult, but more worthwhile. Jesus teaches us that it is much more important to express love than to stand on our rights. The second mile is the biblical antidote for unfairness. What a challenge! Are you willing to accept it in the name of Jesus Christ?

Perfect Example, help me to spot every opportunity to walk the second mile in obedience to Your will. Amen.

Being Your Own Enemy

"Sirs, what must I do to be saved?" (Acts 16:30).

One can very easily become one's own greatest enemy. Consider this thought-provoking idea. Each of us has many enemies: it might be your neighbor who irritates you with his saxophone; or an employer who delights in humiliating you; or just someone whose personality clashes with yours. There are many people we can label as the "enemy".

Strange as it may sound though, many people are their own greatest enemy. You are a mixture of emotions that are in constant conflict with each other. Some people try to hide an inferiority complex by being aggressive. Yet others believe they are infallible and can never admit that they have made a mistake. They stubbornly refuse to beg forgiveness – even from God. They become fanatics who never see the truth about themselves.

There are other weaknesses like self-pity, lust, jealousy and self-centeredness that get a hold on our lives to a greater or lesser extent. These are the evil and negative influences from which our personalities have to be set free.

When you have rid your life from destructive powers through the healing power of the Holy Spirit, they must immediately be replaced by positive, constructive influences – otherwise other evils worse than the first, come into your life to fill the void.

Until you've experienced the redeeming power of Christ, you will never taste the joy of inner peace and victory. The Holy Spirit wants to set you free from bondage. If you refuse, you remain your own greatest enemy.

Redeemer and Friend, set me free from the power of sin and help me to overcome evil in the power of the Holy Spirit. Amen.

In Times of Despair

Hear my prayer, O LORD, listen to my cry for help (Psalm 39:12).

Many people experience life as a series of crises. Religious generalizations and words of comfort do nothing to make their lives a little easier. Everything they attempt fails. They start believing that they have nothing to live for any longer.

When circumstances become difficult, it is not easy to think clearly, logically and constructively. Neither do you always know where to find help. It is a great privilege to have someone that you can trust unconditionally in a time of crisis. Such a confidant understands the value of keeping quiet and just listening. Talking to this person will free you from inner tension and enable you to unburden your heart – a mechanism that God has provided in His great love.

In these times remember the peace and calm that can be experienced in the presence of your heavenly Father. Even though your life might be a whirlpool of confusion, it is His desire for you to share in His peace. He is waiting for you to turn to Him so that He can give you peace. You may not be experiencing this peace right now because you have been overwhelmed by your appalling circumstances, causing you to become deaf and blind to the guidance of the Holy Spirit.

Through earnest prayer and meditation on God's Word, you can revive the awareness of God's presence in your life and rediscover His omnipotence. Your circumstances will then improve radically.

Faithful God, draw me closer to Your love through my failures and problems so that I can live victoriously. Amen.

M
A
Y

12

INDESTRUCTIBLE JOY

Rejoice in the Lord always. I will say it again: Rejoice! Let your gentleness be evident to all. The Lord is near (Philippians 4:4-5).

Perhaps the time has come for Christians to take stock of their attitude towards life. Galatians 5:22 lists the fruit of the Spirit. First we find love: the great indispensable. Secondly Paul mentions joy: an equally indispensable sign of redemption.

However, we find very little of this Christian joy in everyday life. We tend to experience our Christianity as somber, reserved, depressing and morbid. This is a sad denial of the life of joy that should characterize the life of the Christian.

Many people think we simply have to endure this life so that we can go to heaven one day. If, however, we do not practice the art of cheerfulness now, we will not appreciate the joy in heaven.

What the prodigal son in Jesus' parable missed most in the joyless country of sin was the joyful feasting in his father's house. That is why we, the redeemed, should become part of God's feast here and now. We do accept that our sins are forgiven, but refuse to express our joy daily. We cautiously and longingly remain on the edge of receiving invincible Christian joy, thus robbing ourselves and others of one of God's greatest gifts of grace.

The Christian's joy is in Christ Jesus – founded on an encounter with the Savior. In Christ God came very near to us – no, God came into us. Christ met God's demands and filled our past, present and future with joy. Therefore, our joy should be unceasing and everlasting, because Christ is its Source.

Jesus, Joy of our lives, Source of all true goodness ... we want to rejoice in You here on earth already, in preparation for heaven. Amen.

TRUST INSTEAD OF FEAR

Surely God is my salvation; I will trust and not be afraid (Isaiah 12:2).

Fear stalks its prey in every area of life: through sickness and death; insecurity; family problems; financial worries; unemployment. Each one of these causes its own kind of fear that in turn generates worry that robs you of your peace of mind. Once fear has caught you in its grip it can have a devastating effect on your physical, intellectual and spiritual capabilities.

Despite the persuasive power of advertisements, no watertight formula has been developed against fear and worry yet. Not drugs or sedatives or any other commercial product can protect you. Nobody can guarantee that your life will not be touched by the destructive influence of fear and its consequences.

All human aids are fallible because they are created by man. Human weaknesses and imperfections have been the source of great sorrow through all the ages.

Unconditional trust in God's omnipotence through Jesus Christ is the only formula to protect you against evil. Only then will you be able to handle life with confidence. Only then will you be able to overcome every problem that occurs. Hold on to Christ through your faith and love for Him. Pray unceasingly. Develop a deep and constant awareness of Christ's presence in your life.

Then you will be assured of peace of mind and security that are the results of knowing that God is always with you. Also remember that love is the best antidote for fear. As 1 John 4:18 says, "There is no fear in love. But perfect love drives out fear."

Father God, You are with me always through Your Son, Jesus Christ. Because I love You dearly, I shall not fear. Amen.

PATIENCE BEARS FRUIT

But do not forget this one thing, dear friends: With the Lord a day is like a thousand years, and a thousand years are like a day (2 Peter 3:8).

Impatience is probably the one characteristic shared by most people. Impulsive decisions are made; plans are promptly set into motion; answers are required even before the question has been properly formulated. And as the pace of life increases, people become more and more impatient.

Man is paying a high price for this hurried lifestyle: in our marriages; our family lives; our economy; our politics and, yes, also in our spiritual lives.

However, it should never be forgotten that God is supreme. He is in control and has a perfect schedule and agenda. Therefore, patiently wait on God. In His own good time He will reveal His perfect will to you.

If you are striving towards the best in life, looking for peace and fulfillment, you should submit yourself to the authority of God. Christ's whole life was a living example of this. He submitted to and obeyed God, even unto death on the cross on Golgotha. This brought Him glorious victory – and that is how it should be in your life as well.

Nothing that you do can change the great plan and will of God. The life He has planned for you is the very best. In order to establish a sense of stability and fulfillment, you should place yourself willingly in God's hands. Then wait on Him in faith and only act on His command. Therefore, be extremely sensitive to the guidance of the Holy Spirit. You will be enriched immeasurably by knowing that your life is consistently in line with His holy will.

My times are in Your hands, heavenly Father. Keep me patient in the knowledge that Your perfect timing will enrich my life. Amen.

OUR WONDERFUL GOD

To our God and Father be glory for ever and ever (Philippians 4:20).

The words "Praise the Lord" are repeated often in the Psalms – also in other parts of God's Holy Scriptures. Therefore, we should pay close attention to it. There are many Christians who praise and thank Him daily. Unfortunately there are also many who take His goodness for granted.

Some people urgently and impatiently seek God's help when they experience a crisis and take it for granted when God answers them. They carry on with their lives exactly as before and never give a second thought to the fact that God created the universe for His glory – and that their gratitude adds to that glory.

It will be worthwhile to become quiet for a while in this rat race and consider what your life would have been like without God's love and faithful care. How would you have coped with insecurities and disappointments? What would have happened if you had lost your job and were left without an income? How would you have felt if nobody loved or cared for you? What would the quality of your life have been if you constantly feared suffering from a terminal disease or death or uncertainty about the hereafter?

As a Christian, you know that you don't have to worry about any of these things because your heavenly Father knows exactly what you need. You have been redeemed through the blood of Jesus and can echo the words of Psalm 106:1, "Praise the LORD. Give thanks to the LORD, for He is good; His love endures forever."

Praise the LORD, O my soul; all my inmost being, praise His holy name. Praise the LORD, O my soul, and forget not all His benefits (Ps. 103:1-2). Amen.

M
A
Y

16

LOVE IS THE BRIDGE

We know that we have passed from death to life, because we love our brothers (1 John 3:14).

The tension and pressure brought about by human relations can often cause great unhappiness. People upset one another and disputes occur where peace and harmony should have reigned.

You tend to join the ranks of people who think, feel and act like you do. There you find unquestioning support for your views and opinions. As a result, you seldom bother about people who differ from you, and develop tunnel vision because you never care to reason with others. You refuse the stimulating exchange of new ideas and ideologies.

When you restrict your spiritual beliefs, convictions, confessions, testimonies and experiences to your own small inner circle, and exclude everybody else as misled beings, you are in danger of shutting the Holy Spirit out of your life by silencing His voice. The ways in which the Holy Spirit works rise far beyond personal religious vision and cannot be restricted by intellectual limitations.

In order to broaden your spiritual perceptions, yet stick to your convictions, it is vitally important to open up your mind to God's love. Then, where differences of faith separate you from other Christians, the love of God will bridge the gap.

To be able to love like that is only possible through the grace of God. If you find it difficult to love, allow God to love through you. Willfully break free from the isolation that causes spiritual apathy that denies the Father's love. Then you will undergo a life-changing experience that is only possible when you share your love.

Let Your love flow through me, O Source of love, so that I can build bridges of love to reach the hearts of others. Amen.

THE WORDS WE SPEAK

I always thank my God for you ... for in Him you have been enriched in every way – in all your speaking and in all your knowledge (1 Corinthians 1:4-5).

We often find ourselves in situations where we are compelled to say something. It might be words of comfort or encouragement; of sympathy or reassurance; it might be to congratulate or reprimand; we might even be expected to criticize. Everything we say can have far-reaching results on human relations or emotions. We have a great responsibility when deciding when or where to speak. Most important, however, are the words we speak and the attitude we reveal towards others.

Whatever we say should bear the sign of Christian honesty. It must also be said with the attitude of Jesus Christ. Somebody once said that love without honesty is nothing but sentimentality, while honesty without love is brutality.

Unless the situation requires that we express our views in public, we should always do it in private, especially if it is negative criticism or scolding. The timing must also be perfect, otherwise it would be better to keep quiet.

There is only one way in which we can be sure to abide by these rules. It is having a consistent, living relationship with the living Christ. Then we will be sensitive to the Holy Spirit and He will be our Advocate in our dealings with other people. Whatever we say will then be inspired by the love of Christ.

Lord, also of my senses, take control of my thoughts and my tongue so that I will not hurt anybody heartlessly or purposely. Amen.

M
A
Y

18

INSOMNIA

I lie down and sleep; I wake again, because the LORD sustains me (Psalm 3:5).

Blessed are those people who fall asleep the moment their head touches the pillow ... and then wake up refreshed. There are many, however, who fear going to sleep because it causes them anguish and mental confusion instead of refreshment.

If you lie awake at night, worrying about things that happened and that might still happen, it is important to remind yourself to control your thoughts and not allow them to torment you. If you can no longer control your thoughts, you will lose perspective during these sleepless hours.

The night then seems endless and the loneliness becomes unbearable. Fear takes control of your spirit and it feels as if you have no control over your life.

It is possible to overcome this situation and to sleep peacefully! Fear, doubt and worry can never hurt you unless you give them power over your thoughts and life. Remember that God is your loving heavenly Father and that He cares for you – whether you are asleep or awake.

Sleep refreshes not only the body, but also the mind and the spirit. Go to bed with your mind set on God and your heart full of praise. Cover yourself with the cloak of His love and experience His peace while you sleep. God bestows the crown of His blessings on His loved ones while they are sleeping. Claim that for yourself in faith.

Provider and Father, thank You that together with all the many other tokens of Your love, You also give me a good night's sleep. Amen.

WISDOM COMES WITH THE YEARS

It is good for a man to bear the yoke while he is young (Lamentations 3:27).

Some children today are easy-going and spoilt. They have bad manners, don't submit to authority, are rude towards adults and will much rather talk than work or participate in healthy exercise. They no longer get up when an older person enters a room. They talk back to their parents, have a lot to say when grown-ups talk, they have no table manners and intimidate their parents." Does this sound familiar? Well, Socrates noted that in 420 B.C.

Quite often the youth feel subjected to unfair and unreasonable criticism and restrictions; their opinions are never taken seriously; their ability to contribute to another's well-being is often ignored. This makes them rebellious.

While it is true that the youth have much to contribute towards society; that they are probably better equipped academically and intellectually than any other generation due to the development of modern education and technology, it is also true that nothing can substitute the positive experience that only comes with the years.

If you, as a young person, feel that you do not receive the recognition you deserve; if you are resentful because you are being restricted by older people, see it as an opportunity to be enriched by their experiences rather than regarding them with resentment or bitterness. The advantage of their practical experience plus your academic qualifications will benefit you greatly in years to come. Be patient and humble – just like our Master. May all young people's characters be pure and anchored in Jesus Christ!

Blessed Redeemer, make me willing to accept the wisdom which can only be gained through years of experience. Amen.

FREEDOM OR PERMISSIVENESS

Everything is permissible for me – but not everything is beneficial (1 Corinthians 6:12).

One of the problems today is people's desire to please themselves and do whatever they want. Fewer and fewer people consider the needs of others.

If your friends are people who wish to please only themselves, you will be caught up in a very subtle form of slavery. You will gradually become the prey of self-centeredness as our view on life becomes restricted and shrinks to selfishness and covetousness. You become blind and deaf to the interests of others and then suddenly one day you wonder why it seems as if the whole world has turned against you.

Self-interest, selfishness and self-centeredness are foreign elements in lives founded on God. A Christian is someone who has decided to serve the Lord irrespective of his own interests.

Those who wish to please themselves, continually cry, "I want!" and keep on demanding until they can say, "I've got!" This indicates their licentiousness. Their emotions dictate their desires without exception. Because they are unable to clearly see the outcome of their actions, they could pay a price that might be very high.

If you desire to please God, you will walk in faith and spend quality time with Him, meditating on His Word in prayer so that your life will be in accordance with His holy will. Serving God is not a form of slavery, but a meaningful and positive approach to discover the real values of life. The highest and truest form of freedom is to submit yourself completely to the will of God.

Lord and Master, I desire to please You in everything I do and to discover the real meaning and purpose of my life. Amen.

THE POWER OF THE CROSS

May I never boast except in the cross of our Lord Jesus Christ (Galatians 6:14).

It is impossible to think about the Resurrection without being confronted by the challenge of the cross. Remove the cross from Christianity and all that is left is a philosophy.

The cross was central in the mind of our Lord. Towards the end of His earthly ministry it controlled His thoughts and actions. Scripture teaches us that Jesus told His disciples in Matthew 20:18, "We are going up to Jerusalem, and the Son of Man will be betrayed to the chief priests and the teachers of the law. They will condemn Him to death." He knew that the cross was awaiting Him.

Christ was human enough to shy away from the death on the cross, but He accepted that by dying that way, He was doing the will of His Father. He could have summoned twelve legions of angels to save Him from the cross, but doing the will of the Father was His desire.

Jesus never tried to make the gospel attractive by promising payment for piety. He promised life, inner peace and joy, but they are all by-products of loving and serving Him unconditionally. He calls His followers to bear a cross to love sacrificially.

God's love urged Christ to accept the cross because He knew it was God's will for Him as well as for the entire human race. This kind of love Christ expects from all His followers. It can be very demanding, but it enables committed disciples to follow triumphantly in the steps of the Master. There is undoubtedly power in the cross!

Crucified Lord Jesus, I boast in the power of the cross and the knowledge that You endured it on my behalf. I praise You for it. Amen.

FAITHFUL TO LOVE

"If you love Me, you will obey what I command" (John 14:15).

Discipline is often rejected secretly with aversion. This creates an attitude that spoils the work you are doing. If you are forced into a strait jacket that is restrictive and frustrating, you cannot excel. The person that truly enjoys his work is the one who loves it and finds joy in doing it. Such a person is always on the lookout for new methods to become increasingly productive. He does not count the hours and neither is his salary of primary importance because joy is derived from completing a task successfully.

This is the attitude God requires from those who serve Him. Many people think that because they are serving the Lord, they are entitled to VIP treatment or special rewards. Others again hope that God is taking note of their excellence and is therefore reserving a special place in heaven for them. It is, however, true to God's character that He experiences great pleasure in those of His children who have discovered the art of serving with gladness and joy.

The Christian's faith and work must be founded on love and not on fear. It is impossible to enjoy either of the two if you are fearful of God. The driving force behind true Christian life and service to God is His love for you and your love for Him. When the quality of your service is determined by your love for Him, it becomes inspired and filled with gladness. Nothing you do is a burden and no sacrifice is too great if you possess His love and are possessed by it.

If your faith and service to God have become a burden and you regard everything you do as a sacrifice, it is time to flame God-given love into life again on the altar of your heart. Service is love in action.

Lord, nothing You want me to do can ever be a burden because I truly love You. Amen.

M
A
Y

23

CHRIST LIVES! HE IS ALIVE!

"Look at My hands and My feet. It is I Myself. Touch Me and see" (Luke 24:39).

In the very center of the Christian faith stands the triumphant living Christ. It is an undeniable fact by which the Christian faith either rises or falls. Remove Christ from Christianity and you might have a wonderful philosophy, but it will be stripped of the spiritual power that changes lives. It is Christ who gives power, purpose and meaning to generations of people.

Because Christ has triumphantly risen from the dead, His teachings are not theories but practical realities. It is not theological speculation, but a dynamic, practical experience. Millions of people experience the power of His living presence and trust in His eternal omnipotence to ensure that they are leading meaningful, purposeful lives.

To obtain such a positive experience requires a simple deed of childlike faith. Believe with your whole being that Christ lives – and that He lives in you – so that He can reveal Himself through you to the world in which you live. If you confirm this knowledge with your way of living, the truth of His resurrection will become a living reality.

Then you will discover that, while you are making a conscious effort to reveal Christ, He becomes a reality and His living presence is experienced increasingly in every area of your life. When you know that Christ is alive, and that He lives in you, you will move into a new spiritual dimension. It was Jesus Himself who declared after the Resurrection, "Blessed are those who have not seen and yet have believed" (John 20:29).

Risen Lord and Master, I know that You are alive and I pray that You will become a greater reality to me every day. Amen.

M
A
Y

24

INNER HEALING

"Forget the former things; do not dwell on the past. See, I am doing a new thing!" (Isaiah 43:18-19).

We cannot enter the future bearing wounds and hurts from the past. They need to be touched by Christ's tender, loving, healing hands.

We all had experiences we would rather forget. It might be a mistake that we made in the long-forgotten past, but the memory keeps appearing at the most inconvenient times. We fear that others might discover what we have done and that drives away any possibility of peace.

The memories of past sins can cause great disturbance in our lives. Do not suppress them or wish them away but bring them into the open through prayer so that God's forgiveness can erase them.

If you have hurt somebody and reconciliation is possible – do it now! Right all the wrongs in your life as far as possible. Then you can boldly claim the forgiveness that Christ has promised you. To experience His forgiveness is certainly one of the most enriching experiences in life.

Are you being tortured by memories of disappointments and failures from the past; unfriendly or nasty words you uttered; insults that you handed out? These sins can only rule your life if you allow them to. As long as you fret over them without doing anything about them, you are in their power.

The healing power of confession in remorseful prayer, can expel them completely from your thoughts and life. To experience this, you have to trust Christ unconditionally. It is He who grants you the final victory.

Gracious God and Father, thank You that You heal my painful memories and that You give me peace. Amen.

FAITH IN THE UNSEEN

"Because you have seen Me, you have believed; blessed are those who have not seen and yet have believed" (John 20:29).

The most important factor in the Christian faith, Jesus Christ, cannot be verified by mathematical calculations. When you try to understand who Jesus is and what He does, you realize that you are trying to explain the inexplicable.

Who can ever hope to solve the mystery of the incarnated Word? That is why Christ calls those who have not seen and yet believe, blessed. Life involves much more than the average seventy years we are given. Because we cannot fathom but only experience eternal values, like love, chastity and unselfishness, they reveal to us a minute particle of what eternity has in store for us, "However, as it is written: 'No eye has seen, no ear has heard, no mind has conceived what God has prepared for those who love Him'" (1 Cor. 2:9).

It is a most enriching experience to look beyond the temporal world through the eyes of faith. While you lose your existence in Christ, you become increasingly aware of your union with the eternal.

Many people see this as a mystical, emotional experience, but in actual fact it has a real and practical implication for your life here and now. Your view on the temporary is extended and all pettiness vanishes from your life.

When you start living with eternity in mind, you realize your oneness with the "crowd of witnesses" (see Heb. 12:1). Then the greatest treasure on earth is not the gifts of God, but God Himself – and your increasing knowledge of Him, and growth in grace through Christ.

Eternal God, give me a glimpse of how great You are so I can understand something of eternity. Help me to get to know You better. Amen.

M
A
Y

26

WANDERING THOUGHTS WHEN PRAYING

Three times a day he got down on his knees and prayed, giving thanks to his God, just as he had done before (Daniel 6:10).

Daniel practiced the discipline of prayer. This must have improved his concentration during prayer and curbed his wandering thoughts. He followed a strict prayer program. Though he knew that he could pray anywhere, the upper room of his house was his prayer sanctuary. It was his Bethel, the power station of his life.

He also had a fixed time for prayer. Everybody knew that Daniel had set aside three distinct timeslots for prayer in his busy day, in spite of the fact that he knew he could speak to God at any time. Time is a precious gift from God and should therefore be used wisely. Time spent in prayer is never wasted. On the contrary, it is the most productive and fruitful times of our lives.

Daniel purposely focused his thoughts on God. He opened his window facing Jerusalem, the earthly habitation of God for a pious Jew. Prayer concentration requires us to consciously set our minds on God. It is not difficult to concentrate on someone you love! Love allows you to identify with the one you are communicating with. Effective prayer is closely linked with your love for God. If you speak to God in faith and because you really love Him, your thoughts will not wander easily.

An English hymn writer once said, "Prayer is the simplest form of speech that infant lips can try." Because of a child's pure faith and simple love, he finds it easy to pray. And that must be the prayer language of every one of His children.

Thank You for Your Holy Spirit, O God of grace who directs my thoughts so I can derive the blessings from prayer that You intended. Amen.

In the Desert of Despair

God has given us the Spirit as a deposit, guaranteeing what is to come. Therefore we are always confident (2 Corinthians 5:5-6).

Our ability to remain hopeful and not lose courage is firmly linked to our obedience to God. Without it we lack the confidence to lead a meaningful and joyful life.

Obedience, however, is not the reluctant acceptance of something you cannot avoid, but a cheerful acceptance of His will for your life as the very best and the perfect wisdom.

All of us experience times of depression which often borders on despair. It is for those times that God gave us His Holy Spirit, to encourage us again. In obedience to the Holy Spirit it becomes your greatest desire to fulfill God's will in every situation that He might place you in – even in a Gethsemane of sweat and blood.

Initially you may find this very difficult, but when the Holy Spirit is working in your life, you will receive power to live a life that pleases God. It takes courage to not do what you want to do, but to do what God wants you to do.

A surprising by-product of obedience to the will of God is that you gain self-confidence and power in faith. Then you start living without fear and develop the courage to venture into new areas.

The key to this approach to life is love generated in you by the Holy Spirit. Love expels all fear. It is impossible to walk in God's love and in obedience to Him and be discouraged at the same time. This is a lesson that the Holy Spirit needs to teach us continually.

Come Lord, our Lord, and comfort our heavy, sinful hearts and heal our wounds and pain. Amen.

WHO AM I?

Therefore, if anyone is in Christ, he is a new creation; the old has gone, the new has come! (2 Corinthians 5:17).

To face an "identity crisis" is a common occurrence in people's lives today. Finding yourself is one of the most difficult, yet most rewarding searches that a person can undertake. Don't confuse this with another fashion-word, namely "image". Self-image is what you think people think of you, your reputation. Identity on the other hand is what God knows about you, your character. And the wonder of God's grace is that He makes people new! He knows us and with Him, we can take off our masks and allow the Master Potter to transform us.

Some people look at themselves in total awe and admiration. Self-admiration is the death-knell of all change. When one has no desire to change, one stagnates and eventually dies. That is why it is so important for us to open up our lives to the regenerating work of the Holy Spirit so that we can experience daily growth.

Some people look at themselves with great confusion. They live in constant insecurity. They might have a vast knowledge of science, technology and psychology, but their own person is one big question mark. They understand everything but themselves. For them there is only one way, Christ who changed a totally confused Saul into an inspired Paul.

Some people refuse to really look at themselves, because they are afraid of what they might see. This road leads to feelings of inferiority and can be just as destructive as to overestimate yourself.

Bring your life to Christ. He makes all things new – even people!

I praise You, my Redeemer, for making my life new so that I may belong to You completely and forever. Amen.

M
A
Y

29

CHRIST REQUIRES HUMILITY

There are different kinds of service, but the same Lord (1 Corinthians 12:5).

Overestimating yourself is a flaw in a person's character. Therefore it is very unfortunate that this shortcoming is common among people who work for the Lord. It makes what they do for Him most unattractive, and causes incalculable damage to the ministry.

Whatever you are called upon to do in service of the Master, always remember that you are called into service in order to glorify God's name alone. In His Kingdom there is no hierarchy or ranking. Jesus Himself is our example of absolute and total humility. During His life and ministry on earth, He was the perfect image of humility. He washed feet and taught that true greatness means to be the least in service.

We thank God for the scores of dedicated servants who are following in His footsteps today, humbly serving Him under difficult circumstances because their lives are totally and unconditionally submitted to Him. Just think of Mother Teresa who was called to serve in the slums of Calcutta in India. Every time we see someone like that, we hear the splashing of water in a basin and in our mind's eye we see our Lord with a towel, washing the feet of His disciples.

Never look down on the calling that someone has to fulfill in the kingdom of God, regardless of how insignificant it might seem. Always remember that you are part of the body of Christ in which each member has a role to play. The final result of all our labor is bringing more and more glory to God our Father.

Dear Lord, make my life a living example of Your humility and service through Your Holy Spirit. Amen.

GET TO KNOW GOD BETTER

My soul yearns, even faints, for the courts of the LORD; my heart and my flesh cry out for the living God (Psalm 84:2).

Most of us have a sincere desire to get to know God better. It should not, however, remain a religious sentiment but should become the language of your life, "As the deer pants for streams of water, so my soul pants for You, O God. My soul thirsts for God, for the living God" (Ps. 42:1-2). If you truly desire a deeper experience with God, no sacrifice will be too big.

One sacrifice God requires is your time. It is a precious asset and yet so many people waste it. If you use your time wisely, it will adapt to God's plan and purpose for your life. You will discover that while you are living according to God's time, you belong to eternity. When you realize this you will appreciate time much more.

The most time-consuming, yet the most beneficial exercise you can ever undertake, is to increase your knowledge of God through prayer and meditating on His Word. Nurture the personal relationship that God wishes to establish with you and which you cannot go without. The reason why your knowledge and experience of God's love is not more comprehensive could perhaps be because you did not spend enough time with Him during the past month.

Your yearning for God is one of His gifts of grace to you. As long as you experience a need to turn to Him and experience fellowship with Him, you will find Him waiting for you.

Lord, Source of my desire, only You can satisfy the deepest longing of my spirit. Enable me to get to know You better and better. Amen.

JUNE

YOU CANNOT GO ON WITHOUT GOD

JUNE 1

Where is the wise man? Where is the scholar? Where is the philosopher of this age? Has not God made foolish the wisdom of the world? (1 Corinthians 1:20).

At the beginning of this new month you need assurance about which way to go as well as which principles you should apply to get the most out of it. Through the ages man has been proud of his scientific, technological and educational achievements. It cannot be denied that remarkable progress has been made. Things that until recently lived only in people's dreams are now reality. However, it is significant to note that in spite of these very praiseworthy achievements, man still remains deeply dependent on the Almighty God.

Man has developed terrifying weapons and while these weapons are used for deadly and destructive work, mankind is asking God to end the wars and grant peace on earth. Giant progress has been made in aviation and space travel, yet when disasters strike, man turns to God in prayer.

Medical science has developed in leaps and bounds, but when medical treatment fails, loved ones are brought before the Great Physician in prayer. When death occurs, no form of medication can take the place of the peace and comfort God pours into the lives of those who mourn. Remember therefore, that in spite of man's achievements, God's love for His world remains constant and infallible.

Whatever sphere of life you might work or move in, it is important to remember to stay in close contact with Jesus Christ in everything you do or undertake. Without Him you cannot experience true fulfillment. Dare you venture into the new month without Him?

I put all my trust in You alone, Father, because You are almighty, omnipotent and omniscient. Amen.

LIVING TOGETHER IN HARMONY

Then make my joy complete by being like-minded, having the same love, being one in spirit and purpose (Philippians 2:2).

Over the length and breadth of the world people are living together – in families, in homes for the aged, in hospitals and in many other places. Wherever we are, the Lord brings people together in special relationships. It is no coincidence that we are grouped together the way we are. That is why our attitudes toward each other are crucial.

We are one in Christ and we "have encouragement from being united with Christ" (Phil. 2:1). As children of the Father we should live in harmony because our relationships with our fellow men are a clear image of our relationship with Christ (see 1 John 4:20-21).

Paul is pleading for harmony. Each one of us is a unique creation of God and we need to acknowledge and accept the fact that we are all different. But the binding factor is Christian love. When we are one in heart, it proves that we have gone to the trouble of getting to know one another. We share one another's joys and sorrows and have Christ as our goal.

Paul condemns selfish ambition and vain conceit. Unselfishness is an important Christian virtue: it means looking beyond my own interests. Paul advocates the kind of humility where the "one considers others better than himself". That is probably the most difficult requirement of all where people live together. But it has the greatest reward. If I sacrifice my desires for the sake of the welfare of another, then I'm following the Lord's example.

How can we do this? By adopting the correct attitude. We have the Perfect Example in Jesus Christ. May His attitude reign wherever His children are living together.

Dear Lord, help me to bring harmony to the society that I share with others, to Your glory alone. Amen.

MAKE JESUS THE CENTER OF YOUR LIFE

J U N E 3

When they looked up, they saw no one except Jesus (Matthew 17:8).

The true Christian life is rich in meaningful experiences. You may belong to a church where the fellowship you share with other Christians is inspiring. The service that you render to God may have developed your personality beyond recognition. Now you are enthusiastic because you are convinced that Christ is working in and through you. When you think back to the days before you knew Him, you are amazed at the change He has brought about in your life.

While you rejoice greatly in your spiritual experiences and are filled with awe at the wonderful things God has done for you, you should always be mindful that your joy and enthusiasm don't mar your submission and commitment to Christ Himself. He is the central Person in your spiritual life and growth.

Often when His followers testify to what Jesus has done in their lives they place the focus on themselves and their own achievements instead of on the living Christ. This egocentric attitude stealthily enters your life and then hampers the spiritual growth of other Christian disciples.

When Peter, John and James received a revelation about Christ on the Mount of Transfiguration and heard God speak to them, they were filled with awe and "saw no one except Jesus".

This should be the Christian's goal at all times and the summit of his spiritual experience. No matter how wonderful and praiseworthy your spiritual experiences might be, they are only valid if Christ is at the center.

Loving Master, through the power of Your Holy Spirit I want to keep Jesus at the center of my life. When I have You, I have it all. Amen.

TRUST GOD IN DARKNESS

Even though I walk through the valley of the shadow of death, I will fear no evil, for You are with me; Your rod and Your staff, they comfort me (Psalm 23:4).

JUNE

4

At one stage or another there are dark days of depression that border on despair in the lives of many Christians. For a time you might have experienced the living presence of the Lord, then suddenly doubt sneaks in unnoticed. Your enthusiasm is dampened by indifference and you become satisfied with a mediocre spiritual life.

If this is the case in your life, it is probably because your awareness of Christ's comforting presence has waned. You need a true, fresh experience with God to drive the darkness from your life. You need His Holy Spirit to keep you from becoming insensitive and careless. He is the only One who can restore the intimate fellowship that you experienced before.

In the darkness of doubt and depression, you should cling to your faith in an unchanging God. No matter how your moods or spiritual feelings might fluctuate, God's love for you remains steadfast, strong and secure. He loves you with an everlasting, unceasing love and even though you might be feeling far removed from Him at the moment, He is always close to you in His unchanging love.

One of the benefits of traveling through the dark places of life is the appreciation it brings when you see the light and sunshine of God's love again. You will also approach others' problems much more sympathetically. In this way God is able to use even the darkest experiences to the benefit and blessing of others.

Please hold my hand, Lord. I don't want to see far ahead – only one step at a time. Amen.

STUBBORN OBSTINACY

JUNE 5

Who can discern his errors? Forgive my hidden faults. Keep Your servant also from willful sins; may they not rule over me (Psalm 19:12-13).

Sometimes you decide to do something in your own way and according to your own will, regardless of how other people's lives or feelings are influenced by it. The stronger the opposition you experience, the more adamant you become to have it your way.

If you are certain that your way is without a doubt the right one, you will be influenced by the well-meant opinions of others. The person whose stubbornness is caused by a feeling of insecurity refuses to take advice from others or listen to their viewpoints.

One of the most difficult things to develop in life is the ability to not be prejudiced. Religious enthusiasm can blind you to a deeper understanding of spiritual truths. Your social background might cause you to be ignorant about the rights and desires of other groups of people. You are probably subject to so many influences that you have developed tunnel vision and refuse to consider – let alone accept – anything other than your own narrow-minded opinion.

The danger of this situation is that when God wants to lead you into a deeper understanding of Himself, you choose to follow your own way. This prevents you from growing spiritually. What you wish for yourself then becomes more important than what God wants for you.

It is impossible to lead a positive, meaningful Christian life if you always wish to choose and follow your own way and refuse to put God first in your life. Kneel before God and clear this matter today.

Guide and Lord, I do not always desire Your guidance. I want to control my life. Please lead me now. Amen.

CALL UPON GOD'S OMNIPOTENCE

"Not by might nor by power, but by My Spirit," says the LORD Almighty (Zechariah 4:6).

We are often required to do superhuman tasks and different people react differently to this. Some struggle along in their own power, frantically looking for help from others and fret about the results until the task is completed. In spite of the resulting satisfaction once a task is completed successfully, the price they paid in stress and nervous tension is often clearly visible. It is impossible to attempt great undertakings without suffering the consequences of worry about the final outcome of the operation. It can break you down physically and spiritually.

Have you ever considered sincerely laying your work before the Lord? Some people regard this as a ridiculous form of escapism and openly mock such a philosophy. However, God is just as important in your work environment as He is in your spiritual life.

Before you undertake an important task, take it to the Lord in prayer and seek the guidance of the Holy Spirit. If you live in constant fellowship with Christ, you develop a feeling of trust and security even though you are not exempt from hard work. You will experience an increasing realization that what you have undertaken is right because you did not attempt it in your own strength.

This is often what makes the difference between drudgery and job satisfaction. With Christ in your life, your heart will be in your work and you will do everything as if for Him. The Spirit of the living God is then at work in you and you will peacefully go about your work from day to day.

Gracious Father, I confess that without You I am unable to do anything. I rejoice in the fact that I can do all things through Christ Jesus. Amen.

WATCH OVER GOD'S TEMPLE

JUNE 7

Don't you know that you yourselves are God's temple and that God's Spirit lives in you? (1 Corinthians 3:16).

It is of the utmost importance that you take good care of your body without idolizing it. Whether you want to admit it or not, the Christian has a great responsibility to treat his own body with respect. You belong to God entirely: body, soul and spirit. If you have accepted Christ as your Savior; He dwells in you just as He promised to do (see John 15:1-8).

Of course there are numerous ways in which a person can abuse or scar his body and mind. An example would be using any substance excessively. It might be food - and few of us do not sin in this area at some time or another, it might be alcohol or drugs, or anything that could harm your physical well-being. What you read, your thoughts, the movies you watch and the language you use – all these can defile your mind and influence you negatively.

If you have been abusing your body or mind in any way, you can be sure that your spiritual life will suffer as a result. Unless you do something radical to counteract the damage, you will slowly but surely destroy yourself.

Whatever you might be doing, always bear in mind that Christ is not only aware of your actions, but is present while you are doing it. If you would feel guilty or ashamed if someone that you love saw what you were doing, then don't do it because Christ is living in you. Obviously you would not want to hurt or offend Him. What an indescribable privilege it is to be a temple of the living God!

Holy Spirit of God, take control of all my words, thoughts and deeds so that in all things I might be acceptable to God. Amen.

THINK BEFORE YOU SPEAK

The heart of the righteous weighs its answers, but the mouth of the wicked gushes evil (Proverbs 15:28).

JUNE

8

Impulsive comments are often not meant to be degrading and painful, yet they are. Most people have expressed an opinion or made a harmful comment without thinking and feel sorry about it immediately. A word spoken, however, cannot be recalled. A wise man once said that there are four things that cannot be recalled: the spoken word, an arrow that has been shot from the bow, a life that has passed and neglected opportunities.

On the other hand there is a category of tormentors who loudly and proudly declare, "I am a straightforward person, I say what I think." You may very well be frank when commenting on others, but isn't the love in your life perhaps a bit warped?

The apostle James admonished us to be "quick to listen and slow to speak" (see James 1:19). The art of listening is an integral and virtuous component of the controlled tongue. Attentive listening is the prelude to wise words.

The person whose spirit is in harmony with the Holy Spirit will resist the temptation to be witty at the expense of another person. To always be ready with a quick, cutting reply is a sign of intellectual and spiritual immaturity. It is a sign of a personality that is battling with insecurity.

Never make a hasty judgment or jump to conclusions. Take time to consider your views in prayer. If you are forced to act immediately, submit your thoughts to God. Then you will have insight into the problem. Your inner peace and calm will increase, thus enabling you to speak and act positively and constructively.

Help me to pray without ceasing, Lord, so that I will make wise and loving comments. Thank You for the help of Your Holy Spirit. Amen.

THE PRECIOUS GIFT OF FREEDOM

It is for freedom that Christ has set us free. Stand firm, then, and do not let yourselves be burdened again by a yoke of slavery (Galatians 5:1).

The people of Israel were very much aware of the meaning of the yoke of slavery. Throughout their long history they were often taken captive and carried away as slaves. In spite of the birth of Christ they were under the yoke of the mighty Roman Empire. Tragically they were also slaves in their spiritual lives: they were slaves of the very strict and loveless expressions of the Mosaic Laws as interpreted by the scribes. They were more interested in showing off their so-called piety and holiness than in applying the law in order to set people free.

The coming of Christ brought the love of God right into the homes and hearts of ordinary people. His death on the cross was their guarantee of forgiveness and deliverance. His resurrection sealed His promise that those who believe in Him will have everlasting life and be set free from the oppression of Satan. We dare not disregard such a magnificent heritage!

Accept with joy the sacrifice as well as the promise of our Lord Jesus Christ. Believe steadfastly in His great power. Resist Satan's consistent efforts to try and sow seeds of unbelief in your heart. Hold on to your personal relationship with the risen Lord at all times.

Experience the joyous liberation that only Jesus can give you. Then you will be freed from the fear of death. Christ has set you free once and for all; it is His precious gift to you. Treasure your freedom and refuse the yoke of slavery.

Holy God, thank You that through Jesus Christ I have been set free. Help me to appreciate my freedom through the Holy Spirit. Amen.

CHRIST OUR MEDIATOR

Therefore He is able to save completely those who come to God through Him, because He always lives to intercede for them (Hebrews 7:25).

The service performed by the Levitical priests was only temporary. It was passed on from one generation to the next.

With Christ it is totally different, "because Jesus lives forever, He has a permanent priesthood" (Heb. 7:24). Therefore, Jesus' priesthood is eternal. What a blessed assurance for the Christian disciple! This is something in our changing world that is unchanging and consistent. That is why Isaiah could already rejoice in Isaiah 59:20, "The Redeemer will come to Zion." That is also why Isaiah said in his description of the Man of Sorrows that "He poured out His life unto death" (Isa. 53:12).

Jesus acted as powerful Intercessor while on earth. In His High Priestly Prayer (see John 17), He prayed for His disciples and all those who would believe in Him because of the words of His disciples.

He assured Peter that He prayed for him not to grow weary in faith. On the cross He prayed that God should forgive those who nailed Him there. Now He is elevated to the highest glory and sits at the right hand of the Father, as King. There He fulfills His high priestly task of praying without ceasing for His children. And in His name we can also offer all our prayers and petitions to God.

Apart from all this, He gave us His Holy Spirit not only to teach us to pray, but also to purify and sanctify our prayers. We do not always know how we should pray, but His Spirit intercedes for us "with groans that words cannot express" (Rom. 8:26). He also wants us to follow His example and become intercessors.

Thank You, Jesus Christ, that You sanctify our prayers to the Father. I praise You for intercessory prayer. Amen.

THE HOLY SPIRIT AND SANCTIFICATION

JUNE

11

"Consecrate yourselves and be holy, because I am the LORD your God" (Leviticus 20:7). *"Be holy, because I am holy"* (1 Peter 1:15).

Holy is not a popular word in the modern man's vocabulary. For some people it describes sanctimonious people who look down on others. But in its purest and highest form, this word depicts a meaningful experience.

Holy means to be set aside and implies union and intimate fellowship with God. Every Christian should strive to achieve this goal. Many people avoid this to their own detriment as their spiritual lives lose depth.

Some people reject the very idea as impractical because of its high moral and ethical claims. It is impossible to live a holy life if your commitment to God is lukewarm. A truly holy person is totally and completely committed and his obedience to God is unimpeachable – and it includes every area of his life.

A sanctified lifestyle requires you to be aware of your attitudes and actions at all times. As a follower of the Master you have no excuse for harboring secret sins. You cannot hold on to the world with one hand while stretching the other half-heartedly towards God and expect to experience sanctification.

We find the guidelines for leading a holy life clearly set out in God's Word. Christ is our Perfect Example in leading a holy life. Therefore He also gave us His Holy Spirit and leads us into the truth of sanctification. The more sensitive we become to the voice of the Holy Spirit, the more progress we will make on the road to sanctification and the more joyfully and purposefully we will walk this road.

O Holy Spirit, sanctify me more every day and fill me with greater zeal for my Lord. Amen.

GRABBING OR GIVING?

"I am the Good Shepherd. The Good Shepherd lays down His life for the sheep" (John 10:11).

Helen Keller once said, "I find life a most exciting experience, and it becomes more so when I live for others." Not only was she deaf, but also blind!

A Christian dare not live only for himself. We come into contact with other people daily and as a result of this we influence the lives of others – even when we are totally unaware of it.

If you have made up your mind to live only for yourself and to never help anybody else unless you can gain something from it, you will soon find yourself in the company of such people. Your life then becomes a selfish drudgery without anything to make it worthwhile. You are then demoted to a "grabber."

The secret of a true, vibrant life is not to be found in what you can hoard, but in the love that you are willing to share. To be loved by others you first have to give freely and unconditionally of yourself and your love. To be a blessed person you first have to become a blessing. Then you are promoted to a "giver"! This is what Christ Himself came to teach us: He gave Himself – even in death.

Should you find this Christian claim too idealistic or too far removed from harsh reality, the only way to test it is on the anvil of personal experience.

Be willing to listen and not only to speak, to share friendliness without always expecting others to give it first. Allow the joy of the indwelling Holy Spirit of Christ to flow through you to others by expressing goodwill, sympathy and consideration. You will find this little stream of joy and kindness flowing back to you as a mighty river.

Heavenly Father, create in me the attitude of Jesus Christ, the Great Giver. Amen.

BEING ALONE

Jesus, knowing that they intended to come and make Him king by force, withdrew again to a mountain by Himself (John 6:15).

J U N E

13

A cry one often hears in our world today is, "I want to be alone for a change so that I can think things through and find myself again." This is an understandable desire in this hectic life we live.

At some stage every sensitive, thinking person has a need to be alone to re-evaluate and reconsider the standard of his values and priorities; to check the direction his life is taking and to adapt if necessary; to take his spiritual temperature and to make sure that he is spiritually fit and healthy.

Unfortunately being alone can often cause wandering thoughts, frustration and boredom. You start off with a desire to be alone with God, only to find other thoughts crowding your mind. Your quiet time then becomes a waste of time.

If conflicting thoughts force themselves into your mind when you desire to be alone with God, do not try too hard to drive them away as that would only make them more determined to stay. As the thoughts come to you, take each one and consciously lay it before the Lord.

Confess to Him that these thoughts are hindering you and preventing you from experiencing the intimacy with Him that you so deeply desire. Trivial thoughts will disappear in the presence of the Almighty God, or you will be reminded of someone or something that you need to intercede for.

However, never suppress your desire to spend time alone with God. Those are the moments that you come closer to Him and also understand the issues of life better.

My soul thirsts for You, O Lord, like the deer pants for streams of water. Amen.

An Unavoidable Decision

But if serving the LORD seems undesirable to you, then choose for yourselves this day whom you will serve (Joshua 24:15).

Many people find it very hard to turn their backs on worldly standards. They think it is praiseworthy to be regarded as one of the boys. To them it implies an invincibility that can meet every demand of life as well as an aggression that tolerates no resistance. Such a person may be regarded as wise when it comes to worldly things. The company he keeps determines his attitude toward success.

A man of the world always puts himself and his interests first. His social position, the extent of his financial assets, moving in the right circles – these things are of prime importance to him. Everything he does is aimed at either self-enrichment or self-assertion.

Superficially, not much seems wrong with such a philosophy in life. It is only when you have achieved all your goals, only to realize that you still have this haunting feeling of dissatisfaction, that it becomes clear that you must have overlooked a very important issue in life.

It is much more important to be a child of God than a man of the world. Trying to avoid this inescapable truth because you feel it might be a bit over-pious is utter folly. To be a person who recognizes God's authority in your life, means living close to the Center of love, joy and peace – thus experiencing true fulfillment and satisfaction in life. And this is where you have to make a very definite decision.

It is basically a choice between an artificial form of life that is too superficial to bring real fulfillment and the quality of life that only Christ can give you. The choice is yours – to not make a choice is to choose against God!

Lord, my heart chooses You as its eternal King. I praise You for the fullness and rich quality of life You give Your children. Amen.

WHEN CONTEMPORARIES BECOME FEWER

JUNE 15

Lord, You have been our dwelling place throughout all generations... from everlasting to everlasting You are God (Psalm 90:1-2).

This verse stresses a simple yet very important truth. For a while you enjoy the companionship of loved ones and true friends, but then the scene gradually changes. Those loved ones, friends and acquaintances are not around any longer. You realize that your circle of friends has shrunk. It happens to people leaving school, to persons moving or changing jobs and couples who lose a partner. This world can suddenly become a very lonely place unless you have a defense against such losses.

When this truth becomes a reality in your life, you have to guard against becoming depressed, morbid or to wallow in self-pity. In such situations it is quite possible to cry out in desperation with Elijah in 1 Kings 19:10, "I am the only one left."

To be able to adapt to a new lifestyle, you must be willing to start new friendships without feeling guilty or disloyal to the old ones. You must also be tolerant. You might find it very difficult to adapt to modern trends. However, you must give credit to the new generation for the sincerity of their efforts and their honesty. They are trying their best to make the world a better place.

Realize that the things that once were now belong to the past. Rejoice in sweet memories, but don't get caught up in them. Appreciate the knowledge that you gained from previous friendships and apply that knowledge to enrich new ones. Consciously search for opportunities to enrich the present, especially through friendships that God brings across your path.

I praise Your name, loving Lord, for all the beautiful things from my past and I trust You unconditionally for the unknown future. Amen.

RESIST TEMPTATION!

But each one is tempted when, by his own evil desire, he is dragged away and enticed (James 1:14).

JUNE 16

Temptation comes in various forms and at different times, but it always comes when your resistance is at its weakest. However, there are many ways to fight temptation. Some people try to ignore it, but this is seldom effective because eventually they give in to the destructive powers snugly blanketed in reasonable excuses.

Idleness loudly invites temptation into your life. When you have nothing to keep you occupied and no task to motivate you, your thoughts very easily get out of hand – with disastrous results. Therefore, be on the alert for destructive thoughts as they will fester inside you and contaminate your whole life. When temptation knocks for the first time, it always seems reasonable and acceptable. Don't be misled! The main objective of all temptation is to destroy your moral and ethical standards.

Prayer and reading the Bible have a unique role to play in building your resistance against temptation. Through prayer you enter into God's presence and draw from the well of His omnipotence. By reading your Bible you will begin to understand how ordinary people managed to triumph over temptations through the power of the Holy Spirit.

When you have brought these spiritual disciplines into effect, it is vitally important to start applying them in practice. Be constructive and ask for Christ's guidance and strength, keep your mind occupied with positive thoughts and you will not only be able to resist temptation, but will also destroy the enemy completely (read Luke 4:1-13).

Divine Lord, keep me alert for the subtle attacks of the enemy through the ministry of Your Holy Spirit. Amen.

FORGET YOUR FAILURES

We were born only yesterday and know nothing, and our days on earth are but a shadow (Job 8:9).

Because the past has such a tremendous impact on the present, some people feel inclined to hold on to the past and thereby miss many opportunities in the present. People love to linger on memories and past experiences. They remember past defeats, failures and foolish actions – unfortunately often at the cost of their victories, triumphs and successes.

If it is true that God has forgiven and forgotten your past sins because you asked Him to, then you must learn to forgive yourself as well. You have to forget those negative influences that prey on your thoughts and oppress your spirit. If you live in a state of continual regret, crying over what could have been, you rob yourself of the joy that can be yours today and of the inspiration waiting for you in the future. Then you are also denying your faith in God who said, "If we confess our sins, He is faithful and just and will forgive us our sins and purify us from all unrighteousness" (1 John 1:9).

If the path of your past lies scattered with the wrecks of noble expectations and lofty ambitions, give them to your heavenly Father – and forget about them! Confess your guilt before Him once again and make a conscious decision to forget the paralyzing past through the power of the Holy Spirit. Make it your intention to do better and to achieve success.

Working together with God in this way channels His power into your life. The iron grip that the past had on you will relax and you will be able to deal triumphantly with the present as well as the future.

Faithful Guide, I now make a decision to forget the failures of the past and, taking Your hand, I enter the future. Amen.

JOY IN PRAYER

You have made known to me the path of life, You will fill me with joy in Your presence, with eternal pleasures at Your right hand (Psalm 16:11).

For some people prayer is boring. This is especially true if the beauty of prescribed prayer has waned and it has become nothing but a habit. It smothers your longing for God. Prayer can also become an unbearable burden if it is only a meaningless repetition of words and phrases. Many people who discard orthodox prayers with disdain are painfully repetitive in their own prayers.

Prayer must be kept fresh and vibrant if you want it to achieve God's purpose. He never intended conversing with Him to be boring and dull. That is why the living presence of God and never our own needs and desires must always be at the center of our prayers.

You cannot be involved in praising and worshiping God without becoming intensely aware of the fact that you are in His holy presence. Praise is the doorway that leads you into the throne room of God. When you become conscious of being in His holy presence, you experience exceeding joy and glory like nowhere else on earth!

It is also praise that prevents our prayers from becoming meaningless. Praise uplifts you, despite your shortcomings, and creates a totally new relationship between you and God. While you praise and worship Him, you identify with Him through Jesus Christ. It strengthens your faith, joy, zeal and interest in life. Learn to praise God – and start living on victorious ground. "Praise the LORD. Give thanks to the LORD, for He is good; His love endures forever. Who can proclaim the mighty acts of the LORD or fully declare His praise?" (Ps. 106:1-2).

O God who answers prayers, teach me to appreciate the power and real value of praising and worshiping You. Amen.

GOD IS LOVE

All this is from God, who reconciled us to Himself through Christ and gave us the ministry of reconciliation (2 Corinthians 5:18).

The emphasis we place on sin has blinded us to the glorious truth that the living Christ looks beyond the sin of the individual. He sees what that person can be once he has been forgiven and cleansed.

It is possible to be ignorant about a sinner's potential. It is only through the insight granted by the Holy Spirit that you can see a potential disciple in every sinner. Only then do you begin to understand something of the mystery and depth of Christ's understanding and His redeeming love.

Sin is an awful reality and denying it won't make it disappear. On the other hand it should never become so overwhelmingly important that it overshadows God's love. The love of God revealed in and through Jesus Christ is the highest and most unconditional form of love.

Christ's love makes Him so unique. He is Love personified. In Scripture we find various expressions of Christ's love. This love reached its pinnacle when He prayed for those who had crucified Him.

Despite the opposite appearing to be true, His love is still a fundamental power in the world today. Even when rejected, this Love waits patiently to be used to create order out of chaos, to bring peace where there is hate, to heal broken lives. The creative omnipotence of God's love through Jesus Christ is unlimited. All we, His children, have to do is to claim it for ourselves and reveal it in our lives!

Lord, we praise You when we mediate on all that Your love can do. Thank You that I may say, "I truly love You." Amen.

What More Could You Wish For?

Not that we are competent in ourselves to claim anything for ourselves, but our competence comes from God (2 Corinthians 3:5).

J
U
N
E

20

If you are searching for the deeper meaning and purpose of your life, you are on an exciting and rewarding journey. Your search proves that you have the intellectual ability, spiritual vision and hunger of the soul to realize that you belong to a higher order. Therefore, you have to fix your eyes on what lies beyond the temporal and discover that you are an eternal being, created in God's image. Only when you become aware of this immortality, your life acquires positive meaning and God's plan for your life starts unfolding.

Without God life has no real purpose or meaning. It is He who gives life purpose and when His Holy Spirit takes control of your life, you become more and more aware of the magnificence of life. Yet most people search for happiness and satisfaction in things that lie beyond the boundaries of God's greatness and omnipotence.

A wise man once said, "He who does not find God all-sufficient is asking too much." It is tragic that many people are searching for meaning in their lives, but don't know what they want. They have rejected God because their concept of Him is too restricted to satisfy their needs and their dreams. If they would only broaden their concept of God and give Him free reign in their lives, if only they had the slightest idea of His omnipotence and glory, they would experience those deep, enriching facets of life that only God can give. With Him in our lives, what more can we wish for?

Great and mighty God, I honor and praise You for the vision You have given me of how great You are and for enriching my life. Amen.

PRIDE RUINS RELATIONSHIPS

JUNE
21

In his pride the wicked does not seek Him; in all his thoughts there is no room for God (Psalm 10:4).

Pride is a common and treacherous sin. Many so-called humble people become proud of their humility. Like the Pharisees, they thank God that they are just as good, if not better than other people.

Pride has a destructive influence on the human spirit. It not only creates false values by making an exaggerated evaluation of one's own importance, but also destroys the harmony that should exist among people. Being proud of one's nationality can be valuable when linked to a sense of responsibility, but when it regards others as inferior, it contaminates society and rejects Christian principles. False pride is a force that destroys human relations.

Scripture clearly teaches us that, "Pride goes before destruction, a haughty spirit before a fall" (Prov. 16:18). This happens because pride causes division between God and you. When your relationship with God is severed, no other meaningful relationship in your life remains intact.

The prophet Micah clearly indicated God's way to us when he said, "He has showed you, O man, what is good. And what does the LORD require of you? To act justly and to love mercy and to walk humbly with your God" (Mic. 6:8). The life of a true Christian is characterized by humility.

To walk in humility before God is to acknowledge His authority in your life and to realize that without Him you can do nothing. In such a relationship humility creates in you a justifiable pride in which you can rejoice because God is your Father. This pride keeps you on your knees and causes you to look at your fellow man with love.

Lord, I am grateful to be Your servant. Make me what You intended me to be through Your Holy Spirit. Amen.

COMPASSIONATE CARE

Then they sat on the ground with him for seven days and seven nights. No one said a word to him, because they saw how great his suffering was (Job 2:13).

Job's friends probably did not know why their friend had to suffer so terribly, there's no doubt about the sincerity of their sympathy. Without saying a word, they just sat with him for seven days and seven nights. Their wordless presence was a balm for Job's distressed spirit.

Even if many people today might have the time or patience to imitate Job's three faithful friends, the principle of compassionate assistance in suffering is a true Christian virtue. In your life you might be confronted with the suffering and sorrow of a dear friend. Circumstances might prevent you from doing anything to alleviate the pain.

This is a heart-rending experience, and can cause frustration as well as inner confusion. Do not allow these distressing circumstances to undermine your faith. Just trust in the omnipresence and omnipotence of God. You might even question the existence of God by asking, "Why do these things happen?" Keep God and His love in the foreground of your thoughts and confirm it in your heart with the words of Job, "Though He slay me, yet will I hope in Him; I will surely defend my ways to His face" (Job 13:15).

Hold on to your faith in the face of every kind of adversity. Your sympathy will increase and you will become a source of power and faith to the person who is suffering – even if you are unable to express yourself eloquently. Just knowing that you are compassionately and prayerfully present will be a great comfort to the suffering soul.

Strengthen me, dear Lord and Master, so that I may become a source of power and comfort to those who suffer. Amen.

UNITY IS STRENGTH

So we rebuilt the wall till all of it reached half its height, for the people worked with all their heart (Nehemiah 4:6).

There are various principles that can rule our lives. Some people advocate "Survival of the fittest" while others say, "The winner takes it all!" or "Each one for himself!"

These are the laws of the jungle. There are also people who believe that retaliation is the sustaining power in life. These and many similar principles influence the direction that the lives of well-meaning people take.

One very important principle that should never be overlooked is that of co-operation. Many people are so aggressive, that they achieve very little. Others again are so narrow-minded and cramped in their outlook that they make more enemies than friends because of their rigid dogmatic attitude. Lack of co-operation can ruin a case and cause much antagonism.

Co-operation involves working together. It is a constructive way of building bridges of friendship and understanding. Initially co-operation might be needed for the sake of survival, but it creates mutual respect and love when kept up persistently.

If co-operation has become a characteristic principle of your life, it should extend beyond human boundaries and include co-operation with God. Such co-operation with your heavenly Father has wonderful results. It involves doing what the writer of Proverbs said, "In all your ways acknowledge Him, and He will make your paths straight" (Prov. 3:6). Then His guidance becomes an inseparable part of your daily existence and your life will be a reflection of His will.

Redeemer and Friend, I am willing to co-operate with You so that my life can reach its highest potential. Amen.

SPIRITUAL BLINDNESS

"Lord, I want to see" he replied (Luke 18:41).

JUNE

24

It is inexplicable that so many religious people suffer from spiritual blindness. This was the case during Christ's life on earth and it still is today. People cling to a theological phrase or idea to such an extent that it dominates all original thinking and spiritual laws. The theological theme then often has a greater impact on the disciple than the Master Himself.

Religious doctrines should be stepping-stones leading to a deeper and more meaningful relationship with the living Christ. Such convictions are of cardinal importance as an expression of your faith, but the final test for any religious doctrine is whether it makes Jesus a greater reality for the one who believes it.

When the Holy Spirit takes control of a life, there is no room for doubt about Him who is the Truth. There are no petty or bitter arguments. A Christ-filled person views life compassionately and sensitively. He perceives the needs of mankind and tries to apply God's love practically and treats others respectfully as children of the same heavenly Father, even though they might deny His Fatherhood.

It is the duty of every Christian disciple to be spiritually alert and prepared at all times. To be spiritually blinded through dogmatic fanaticism, bitterness or an unwillingness to forgive, is to separate yourself from Christ, and to become totally powerless and blind. Allow Him to free you from everything that causes division between Him and you and that leads to spiritual blindness. His Spirit is able to open your spiritual eyes miraculously.

Lord Jesus, help me to see You as the way, the truth and the life. Enable my spiritual eyes to see You everywhere in my life. Amen.

SELF-DISCOVERY

For I know my transgressions, and my sin is always before me (Psalm 51:3).

It is very important to discover your strong points and gifts. It is, however, equally important to be aware of your weaknesses and shortcomings. A person who refuses to acknowledge any of his own weakness soon becomes intolerably proud. What is even worse is that when such a .person falls, he seldom receives any sympathy or understanding from society. On the contrary, it seems as if people rejoice when he received what they felt he deserved.

However, when you acknowledge your mistakes and are only too aware of your sins, it can also have a negative effect on your personality. If you continually refer to them, the burden will soon become too heavy. Your constant self-reproach and confession of guilt will make you just as boring and unpleasant as those who are proud and full of themselves and their own virtues.

If you are deeply aware of your weaknesses and sins, it should cause you to bow humbly before God. Then you will pray the sincere, heartfelt prayer of the tax collector, "God, have mercy on me, a sinner" (Luke 18:13). Having done this, you should accept the fact in faith that, through Jesus Christ's death on the cross, you are assured of God's gracious forgiveness and purification.

Do not carry the burden of past sins. Ask the Holy Spirit to guide you into the truth of redemption and forgiveness. Then approach the future with Christ's forgiving love. Set an example by living like a redeemed, committed Christian who has experienced the wonder of confession and forgiveness.

Lord Jesus, by gratefully accepting Your forgiveness, I learn from my mistakes and become equipped to live a life pleasing to You. Amen.

YOUR LIFE IS YOUR TESTIMONIAL

We know that we live in Him and He in us, because He has given us of His Spirit (1 John 4:13).

J U N E

26

In some Christian circles, testimonies play an important role. To tell about what God has done for you can then be a source of inspiration for the one who testifies as well as for the audience.

Testifying, however, involves dangers of its own because even here the Evil One actively tries to mislead God's children. Self-glorification is not the least of these dangers. Because Christ has saved us from sin, there is the tendency to overemphasize the vileness of our own sins to prove to others how deep the saving grace of God can reach. It is sad that many testimonies then become gross exaggerations. It is as if people want to boast about the extent of their sins and morbid self-examination then replaces the simple truth that will bring glory to Christ only.

Whatever testimony is given about Christ's redeeming, regenerating, healing love, it all still depends on the quality of the life behind it. Every Christian has heard a testimony from someone about God's regenerative love, expressed in glowing terms by a person who makes life utter hell for the ones he lives with! A businessman might testify about God's saving grace, while the methods employed in his business cannot bear the light of the Gospel. This type of testimony is futile – on the contrary, it badly damages the Lord's kingdom on earth.

A life that reflects the beauty of Jesus Christ is always a powerful testimony to the world. Perhaps it is never even necessary to say a word, but it always bears the trademark of true love.

Creator and Lord, help me to live a life that is a living testimony of Your love and guidance. Amen.

SLOW DOWN

JUNE

27

"Be still, and know that I am God; I will be exalted among the nations, I will be exalted in the earth" (Psalm 46:10).

To go on holiday is a privilege. It is good to escape from the grueling routine of life and to pause for a while. But it must not turn into a time of stagnation. It should rather be the constructive tranquility in which strength is renewed; a time for spiritual meditation.

Some people just have to be active. To them, working is the highest virtue and they regard with contempt those who slow down their pace and allow the world to rush by. To be busy all the time can have negative effects. It allows no time for meditation or constructive planning – let alone replenishing physical strength. If you are always on the run life inevitably becomes a blur.

The busier your life, the more important it is for you to make time to become quiet. Naturally one's brain is always active, but by ceasing your physical activities for a while to concentrate on positive and essential things, you have the opportunity to discover that times of inactivity can be beneficial too.

To become quiet in the presence of God can be the most constructive time of your life. You will discover the power of the Holy Spirit afresh. His wisdom and spiritual insight – and especially His love – then becomes a reality to you. To be too busy to spend time enjoying the presence of Christ is an indication that you are actually wasting your energy on unimportant matters.

After spending time in God's calming presence, you will once again feel inspired to be creative. You will discover that these quiet times in God's presence have become the most productive.

Faithful Master, teach me through Your Holy Spirit to slow down and to become quiet before You. Amen.

CERTAINTY OF FAITH

"However, when the Son of Man comes, will He find faith on the earth?" (Luke 18:8).

Much is said and written about the state of the world that we live in. While violence, permissiveness and anarchy are increasing , more and more people become convinced that we are living in the end times preceding Christ's second coming. It seems as if very little can be done to prevent society from falling apart and man from totally destroying the environment.

Whether there is any truth in these convictions or not, and in spite of the chaos that has a grip on our world, we should steadfastly hold on to Christ's standards. The fact that the world around us is in a critical state is no excuse for the Christian to stop battling the Evil One. We dare not sit back and wait for the Prince of Peace to come to bring man to his senses.

In spite of Satan's efforts to undermine the church of Christ, and notwithstanding the tremendous pressure that is building up against the Christian faith, it is your duty to honor and glorify the name of Jesus with your whole life.

This you do through His power that enables you to fight for His cause. The foundation of your conduct is your faith in Christ. At His return, whether He finds you working, or praying, you will hear from His holy lips, "Well done, good and faithful servant!" (Matt. 25:23).

To be able to do so persistently, you need to be certain that your faith is of a high standard and that can only be obtained through an intimate, personal relationship with your Savior and Redeemer.

Lord, my God, please strengthen my faith, so that when I am tested, I will not be found wanting. Amen.

A PRAYERFUL HEART

J U N E

29

In bitterness of soul Hannah wept much and prayed to the LORD (1 Samuel 1:10).

True prayer is more than just spoken words. It can be defined as an attitude of the heart. It is a conversation with God that determines your actions and brings about an awareness of God's presence in your life. This consciousness is not something that you only experience periodically, it is a constant feeling of being united with your heavenly Father. And this brings peace and purpose to your life.

The Master knew about the hypocritical Pharisees who voiced their long, boring prayers on street corners to be seen by the people. Christ warns such people when He says, "For they think they will be heard because of their many words" (Matt. 6:7). Prayer, however, is an emotional unburdening of the soul and at times there are outbursts of joy from a heart that stands in awe of God's love.

The joy of a prayerful heart is that it is with you wherever you go. In your quiet times you rejoice in the presence of the living God; distractions are restricted to the minimum and you receive His love and blessings in a very special way. When you step out into a very busy and demanding world after having prayed, you don't leave Him behind but you take Him with you because He is in the sanctuary of your heart.

The inexpressible mystery is that the risen Lord is always with you. That is why every job you do, every encounter you have, every discussion you take part in, can be a prayer to God. Then prayer is not a disciplinary burden in your spiritual life, but an exciting and practical experience with no boundaries or restrictions.

Create in me a prayerful heart, O Lord, so that I will be aware of Your presence at all times. Amen.

PRACTICAL CHRISTIANITY

"Now that you know these things, you will be blessed if you do them" (John 13:17).

JUNE 30

The communist Karl Marx professed that religion was the opium of the people; a candy-coated pill to make everyday life bearable; a pie in the sky when you die. What he actually meant was that people become so obsessed with religion that the things concerning their daily existence are of little value to them. Unfortunately it is often true that people become so heavenly-minded, that they are of no earthly use.

True religion acknowledges the authority of Christ in everyday life issues and applies His message practically. Praise to Christ must be visible in your relationships with other people. Without that your faith has no substance.

On the one hand we find those who are so enthusiastic about religion that they fail to apply the message of Jesus Christ practically. On the other hand there are those who want to force Christian standards on people without being inspired by the Holy Spirit, thus relegating the gospel of Christ to a "social gospel".

It is possible to become so enthusiastic about the content of the Gospel, that you forget the call of the Master to apply His message in practical, constructive service. It is also possible to sidestep Christ's challenge to live a holy and committed life by surrendering only to the social application of His message.

Between enthusiastic discipleship and Christian service, lies the road that the Master has sanctified: living in total harmony with God and your fellow man. When you have accepted this challenge in His strength, the world will know whom you belong to and in whose service you stand.

Perfect Example, thank You for enabling me through the Holy Spirit to accept the challenges of practical Christianity. Amen.

JULY

A GREAT EXPERIENCE

And to know this love that surpasses knowledge – that you may be filled to the measure of all the fullness of God (Ephesians 3:19).

Life is filled with many enriching experiences. Some happen so often that they are taken for granted – the love of family and friends; the miracle of a beautiful, sunny day; fellowship with trustworthy, understanding friends; to feel satisfied when everything is running smoothly; to have nothing to worry about – these are a few experiences that enrich us and add to our joy.

It won't be easy to establish what the greatest experience is. What is exceptional to one might be ordinary to the next. However, regardless of who you are, the one experience that exceeds all others by far is to be united with God through Jesus Christ. Nothing whatsoever can be a greater experience than getting to know God in Christ.

The level of this knowledge will depend on the quality of your commitment and surrender to Him. God gives Himself abundantly to all who accept Him in truth. His gift can only be restricted by your refusal to fully accept Him.

To be aware of God's indwelling presence is an experience that changes lives. You develop a fresh appreciation for the meaning and purpose of life. You start every day with a spirit of anticipation instead of getting caught up in the quicksand of self-pity and depression. This experience uplifts your spirit and gives you a fresh attitude and your daily existence is renewed because you are filled with the fullness of God.

Lord, because You live in me, I strive to honor and glorify You through my life. Let me grow in my knowledge and love for You. Amen.

AN AMAZING TRUTH

I pray that you … may have power, together with all the saints, to grasp how wide and long and high and deep is the love of Christ (Ephesians 3:17-18).

Annie Flint Johnson wrote a touching poem on the width, the length, the height and depth of God's love. She ends the poem, "The love of Christ" with the following stanza,

> How great is His love! It passes all knowledge,
> no man's comprehension its measures can be.
> It filleth the world, yet each heart can contain it:
> He 'so' loved the world – and He 'so' loved me!

Christianity can be described as a philosophy to a certain point. It can be explained logically and a devoted seeker can understand it intellectually. However, there is a point where it transcends reason and faith takes over.

When you become so conscious of the omnipresence of God's love that you no longer doubt His existence, your spirit experiences the liberating assurance that God really exists. The awesome wonder is that you not only love Him, but that He loves you, you belong to Him and He is in control of your life. Then your whole life is filled with the glory of God and praise and worship becomes a way of life.

Ordinary people like us may know God personally, and He knows us – this is the amazing truth and good news of Christianity. Christ taught us that as He is one with the Father, His disciples can live in unity with Him in the same way (see John 17:22-23.) Those who accept and love Christ, share in His unique relationship with God.

O Lord, let me live in close union with You, the True Vine. Amen.

On a New Road in Faith

Without faith it is impossible to please God, because anyone who comes to Him must believe that He exists and that He rewards those who earnestly seek Him (Hebrews 11:6).

Faith that is certain of what lies beyond the horizon is faith that overcomes the world.

When Columbus set sail in 1492 to discover new continents, he and his crew realized at some point that they could no longer turn around. They faced possible starvation; they could die of thirst and disease; some of the sailors considered mutiny. But Columbus persevered, "We are sailing on!" What faith in the unseen! How great their joy must have been when they first set eyes on the New World.

During the difficult times in our lives, we need this type of faith: a faith that says, "We are sailing into the second half of this year!" Such faith will enable us to handle immediate problems with maturity, and to trust in God for the future.

It is so comforting to know that God is aware of us and cares for us. He is able to support us in every situation. The only condition is that we must trust Him completely.

God is Spirit and cannot be perceived by the human eye. Faith, however, is the courage that urges us to continue beyond what the eye can see. Then God reveals the beauty of His love to us – what the eye has not seen, the ear has not heard and has not occurred to the heart of man, that is what God is preparing for His children who believe.

In faith we can meet our problems, our sorrows and ordeals with courage. We will safely sail unknown waters and reach God's "New World".

God of comfort, thank You that You richly reward those who steadfastly trust in You. Help me to trust You also in the dark. Amen.

WAIT FOR GOD'S ANSWER

Devote yourself to prayer, being watchful and thankful (Colossians 4:2).

Should you submit your desires to God and then wait for Him to answer in His own good time without having to remind Him? Or should you persevere and constantly remind Him of your needs and desires? This has been debated for ages by many followers of Jesus Christ. Everyone tried to prove their point through their own personal experiences.

The fact of the matter is that both sides can be right. True prayer is not governed by rigid rules and regulations. It is the expression of God's Holy Spirit at work in the hearts of His children.

It is surprising how the Holy Spirit adapts to the life, background and personality of a person, and how He longs to lead him into God's presence.

Under the guidance of the Holy Spirit, prayer does not always follow the obvious route, but often the ways that God has chosen to suit your personal needs. The result, however, is always surprising and encouraging.

Whatever road of prayer you are following, travel along it purposefully and faithfully, always conscious of His loving presence.

Then you will soon learn to recognize God's answers and will gratefully sing His praises for the way in which His Word is being carried out in your life.

I will wait on You, Lord, and when I impatiently want to take my own route, help me through Your Spirit to wait. Amen.

TAKE HEART!

Be strong and take heart, all you who hope in the LORD (Psalm 31:24).

Our courage will never be tested more severely than when a loved one dies. And that is exactly when we need it most – courage to move on while we would much rather look back; courage to reach out to others when we would prefer to withdraw; courage to make decisions that will affect tomorrow when we are still broken-hearted about yesterday. Don't allow death to rob you of your hope and courage.

Courage is built on two pillars: faith in your goals and trust in your abilities. God will supply the determination and the strength for both.

Fear and giving up without a fight cause despondency, but faith and perseverance always bring us victory. With the eyes of faith we look beyond the temporal to what is eternal. Death then becomes a milestone on the way to the Promised Land. While we are holding on to God's promises, our courage will grow and become strong. God didn't say that we would never be tempted or suffer trials, but He did promise that He will keep us safe.

The most enriching experience are not found in superficial pleasures, but in our most painful sorrow. If we hold on courageously in faith, sorrow serves a holy purpose in our lives. Romans 8:18 states, "I consider that our present sufferings are not worth comparing with the glory that will be revealed in us."

Therefore, take heart!

Loving Father, renew my courage and release me from my fears. Strengthen me to follow in the steps of Christ Jesus, my Savior. Amen.

THE HOLY SPIRIT CULTIVATES LOVE

God has poured out His love into our hearts by the Holy Spirit, whom He has given us (Romans 5:5).

The certain knowledge that Christ lives in you can bring about a mighty spiritual revival in your life. It inspires your thoughts, enriches you, generates new trust, creates enthusiasm and gives purpose and meaning to your everyday existence. It is the work of the Holy Spirit alone that assures you of your unity with the Source of perfect love.

No matter how powerful and inspiring you might find this mutual love between you and God, it must be firmly founded on the foundation of reality and practical faith. To declare that you love Christ, yet refuse to lighten the burden of another is a blatant denial of that love.

If you love Christ through the Holy Spirit, you become painfully aware of the needs of others and you will have an uncontrollable desire to do something about it.

If you proclaim that the love of God is in your heart, it will be revealed in your words, attitudes and willingness to serve others. God is expressed in your life through the love of His Holy Spirit and as a result you accept the full responsibility of your faith in love.

This love enables you to want only what is best for your fellow men, in spite of insults, pain or humiliation. This love includes your heart and mind, your will and emotions. It is a conscious effort to seek nothing but the best for others through the support of the Holy Spirit. The basis of this love is God Himself, and has been demonstrated to us through Jesus Christ and revealed in our hearts through the Holy Spirit.

O Holy Spirit, enlighten me and make Your love burn brightly in me. I pray this in the name of Jesus Christ, my Lord. Amen.

SUBMIT TO GOD

Today if you hear His voice, do not harden your hearts (Hebrews 3:15).

What a wonderful place this world would have been if every Christian did what God expected of him. He would have been as dedicated to Christ and his calling as humanly possible; his prayers would have linked with his daily actions; he would have become increasingly conscious of Christ's presence in his life at all times and in all circumstances.

God cannot give you more of Himself than what you are willing to accept. Your spiritual poverty is the result of your unwillingness to enter into a deeper relationship with God, or your hesitation to obey His revealed will. Only when you submit yourself to the will of God as revealed by His Holy Spirit, can you hope to experience spiritual growth.

Unfortunately there is a natural obstinacy in us that prevents us from doing what God expects us to do. God may expect you to do something specific, but you refuse to do it, and as a result you experience conflicting loyalties. Only when you have submitted unconditionally and with total dedication to God will you truly believe.

This call for total submission is not a form of spiritual oppression, but a glorious privilege from God's gracious hand. All His disciples are keen to share in it. If you experience the subtle guidance of the Holy Spirit today, obey Him keenly and unconditionally. Don't be stubborn and allow selfish interest to rob you of what God is planning for you.

Lord, my God, my life belongs to You and I joyfully and gladly accept Your perfect will for my life. Amen.

GOD IS INFALLIBLE

Where is the wise man? Where is the scholar? Where is the philosopher of this age? Has not God made foolish the wisdom of the world? (1 Corinthians 1:20).

Man has made tremendous progress through the ages and we are living in a very sophisticated era. Despite scientific, technological, medical, and educational progress, people all over the world are obviously living under considerably more pressure than at any other time in history.

Despite all man's achievements, young and old seem very restless. It is as if mankind is consumed by the uncertainties of the present and fear for the future.

It is only when you acknowledge the all-sufficiency of God, that you will be able to live life to the full. When you look at man's progress and its tragic results, you will soon realize that for many people life has become nothing but an uphill battle. Man is caught up in a modern version of slavery. He finds no peace or rest from man-made masters.

It is imperative that you accept and confess that true peace of mind and rest can only be found in Jesus Christ. He is the same for people of all ages. Unless you trust Him unconditionally, and allow Him to determine the pattern of your life, you will never be able to rid yourself of the destructive power of guilt and worry.

In Christ you will have the ability to achieve the goals that He has set for you and you will experience peace.

Lord Jesus, only in You do I find rest for my turbulent mind. Let me always live in the glorious knowledge that You, my Savior, are infallible. Amen.

JULY

8

WHEN YOU FEEL HELPLESS

In my distress I called to the LORD; I cried to my God for help
(Psalm 18:6).

There are times in life when circumstances threaten to overwhelm you. You feel incapable of handling the demands made on you. During such times you become acutely aware of your inability and weakness. Even your spiritual life seems unreal, almost non-existent.

Temptation is at its worst in times like these. They either attack you brutally or very subtly, but always when you are at your weakest. Even though you realize that your loyalty towards God and your self-respect is being threatened, it feels as if there is nothing you can do about it.

If your victory depended on your own strength, you would have had no hope at all. Numerous people, however, testify that when they called upon God in the name of Jesus when they were weak and incapable, a divine calmness came over their lives.

Their spirits were revitalized and they realized they were not fighting the battle alone. You only suffer defeat because you try to do things in your own power and don't trust in God Almighty.

God is not a figment of the imagination. He is an active Being who is ready to work with you in the harsh reality of your everyday existence. He is only waiting for your invitation to join you so that He can lead you to glorious victory.

Immanuel God, I thank You that You never forsake me but are always with me to lead me to victory. Amen.

A LOVING SHEPHERD

The LORD is my Shepherd, I shall not be in want (Psalm 23:1).

Palestinian shepherds treasured their flocks of sheep and goats. The community depended on them for their well-being. These animals provided them with meat, milk and cheese, while the wool and skins were used for clothing and building shelters. That is why the shepherds took very good care of their flocks.

They made sure that they had the best pastures and they protected them against any form of attack; they kept them safe by leading them along the right paths; they searched for those who had gone astray and brought them back to the safety of the fold.

Christians are precious in the eyes of Christ. Through His Word we know that He is the Good Shepherd. He is your personal Shepherd who takes care of your daily needs and protects you from all dangers. He leads you on the path of righteousness and when you go astray He compassionately goes looking for you and brings you back to the safety of His flock.

However, there is one very important difference between the Palestinian shepherd and his flock and Jesus, our Good Shepherd. The difference forms the essence of the Christian faith. To be able to enjoy the care and protection of the shepherd, the flock had to provide for the material needs of the community. Jesus on the other hand, offers you His care and protection because He loves you – and in return He only asks you to love Him.

Is the price for such divine, wonderful love too high for you?

I love You, O Lord. You lead me and know all the obstacles in my way and before I fall You have already taken my hand. Amen.

CONTROL YOUR TEMPER

A man finds joy in giving an apt reply – and how good is a timely word! (Proverbs 15:23).

There are many people who proudly declare that they are straightforward and therefore, they have the right to trample down others' feelings. When they disagree with something, they strongly express themselves and even become rude. Then they excuse themselves saying they were merely expressing their views. There is no way to justify the pain caused by such frankness.

Of course there are times when you have to take a stand for the sake of truth. The Christian, however, may never be sarcastic. Defending the truth must always express Christian love and understanding. Total honesty is much more effective when uttered in love than in anger.

Most people express themselves in the heat of the moment, when they are outraged and indignant – only to be sorry about what they have said afterwards. This is especially true when a latent fiery temper is just waiting to flare up at the slightest provocation.

A quick temper causes you to say things that you don't mean. Most of us have said things that we regretted later. A quick temper can be overcome by the assistance of the Holy Spirit. Submit your temper to God and ask Him to control it. You will experience wonderful results. As you grow in grace, God's control over your temper will increase. Your words will then be loving, tactful, constructive and healing.

Holy Spirit of God, guard my lips and keep me from losing my temper. Amen.

GOD WILL NEVER FORSAKE YOU

"I will never leave you nor forsake you" (Joshua 1:5).

To be left behind after the death of a loved one causes immeasurable loneliness and pain. Your spouse played a very important part in your life as friend, companion and confidant. Your loss is intensified when you are subtly excluded from the company of friends and even family.

The widow or the widower stands alone in the storms of life; alone when important decisions have to be taken, alone during festive occasions; alone in times of need and sickness; always alone in sorrow.

Who will listen to your complaints about trivial everyday problems; who will share your deep joy; with whom do you discuss the activities of the day? During the night you stretch out your arm to touch your loved one, but there is only emptiness in the dark night.

The only solution for this kind of loneliness lies in our relationship with God. Through faith and trust you can face life and make a fresh start again (see Phil. 4:13). Through the grace of God you still have something to contribute. Through your example and service you can help build God's Kingdom.

Trust God for the future – He will provide. Also trust Him with your sorrow and loneliness. There is such great need in the world around us: the sick, the old, and the lonely. There are many people who could benefit from your own experience and they need you because you understand. While helping others you will triumph in your hour of distress because you have accepted God's will for your life.

God of the lonely, our strength lies in being still and in trusting You. Give me that strength in my darkest hour! Amen.

PRAYER REQUESTS

Delight yourself in the LORD and He will give you the desires of your heart (Psalm 37:4).

For many of God's children prayer is one-sided. They probably have a list with requests that they wish to lay before God. Many of these requests are praiseworthy: they plead for a loved one to be relieved from pain or sickness; for revival; for safety and prosperity. There are also selfish prayers that express jealousy and envy. These prayers can never be brought to God in a spirit of love and will never reach the throne of grace.

The purpose of true prayer is fellowship with our heavenly Father. When this fellowship fails, it influences the effectiveness of our prayers negatively. Before asking Him for anything, you must first strive to experience the reality of His divine presence when you pray.

This is not always achieved. Some people become aware of God's presence almost immediately when they start praying. Others have to discipline their minds, capture wandering thoughts and consciously allow God to govern their prayers and their thoughts.

In the presence of God you discover that you are developing a sense of God's all-sufficiency. Then you realize that He already knows all your needs and desires. This does not make a prayer list unnecessary, but stresses the truth that God knows our every need and will provide. Prayer requests must always be secondary to your experience of the presence of God when you pray.

Motivate me, O Spirit of God, to get to know my Father better before I lay my prayers before Him. Amen.

DIVINE HEALING

Jesus rebuked the evil spirit, healed the boy and gave him back to his father (Luke 9:42).

Never doubt the fact that the risen Lord heals miraculously. Why some people are healed and others not, is a mystery that we cannot explain. To declare that those who are not healed do not have enough faith is not true, because many of them have great faith. Sometimes they have even more faith than the disciple who prayed, "I do believe; help me overcome my unbelief!" (Mark 9:24).

Healing of the body is of the utmost importance, but healing of the spirit is even more important. It is true that a bitter and unforgiving spirit can cause physical sickness.

Gossip not only influences others negatively, but also has a very negative effect on the character of the person spreading the stories. Slanderers are the source of destructive judgments and their venom often causes them to become sick.

When your spirit is well, you will have the right attitude towards life and the Holy Spirit's healing touch will flow freely through your body. This is a miracle from God that He performs through His Son, Jesus Christ.

You must get rid of everything that separates you from God. God has made forgiveness available through the sacrifice of Jesus Christ. He promised His recreating Holy Spirit to all who acknowledge His authority. When God's Spirit takes control of your spirit and body, you are renewed and healed by God.

Thank You for the healing power of Your Holy Spirit, O Lord. Work in me continually so that I will stay spiritually healthy. Amen.

SOMETIMES WE HAVE TO WAIT

A week later His disciples were in the house again, and Thomas was with them (John 20:26).

While the other disciples were jubilant because they knew that Jesus had risen, Thomas must have felt wretched in his confusion and unbelief. A week had to pass before he would be assured that his fellow disciples had not seen a ghost or image of the Lord, but a living, dynamic Personality.

In the Christian faith, waiting patiently plays a very important role. Many Christians have to wait long before they experience a true consciousness of the living Christ. Many prayed for long periods before their prayers were answered. The fact of the matter is that we cannot rush God. He has His own, perfect timing and it is only when you live in perfect harmony with Him that your waiting becomes meaningful and constructive.

If you are experiencing a period of waiting at the moment, and it feels as if everything has come to a standstill to the point that influences your relationship with God negatively, remember to wait patiently on the Lord. If you appreciate the divine influence of the Holy Spirit, He will reveal God's will to you in His own time.

Be patient and don't expect God to act immediately just because you are in a hurry. Learn to live according to God's schedule and open up your mind and spirit for His guidance. Then you will discover that waiting is often the beginning of new growth on your spiritual pilgrimage. It may be the most profitable time of your life.

Gracious Lord, my times are in Your hand, and I praise and thank You for it. Amen.

PUT CHRIST IN THE CENTER

He is the beginning and the firstborn from among the dead, so that in everything He might have the supremacy (Colossians 1:18).

When asked, the average Christian will immediately say that Christ is central in his life. Does he not pray in the name of Christ? Does he not honor and glorify the Lord? Does he not faithfully serve Him?

However, if we analyze our prayers, we will be surprised to discover how often "I" takes the place of Christ: "I want this", "Give me that, Lord" or "Bless me, Lord." Such requests do have their rightful place but if they dominate your prayers, you have put "I" on the throne.

To develop a Christ-centered prayer life, you must strive to think the way He wants you to and to act the way He expects you to. You should ask yourself daily, "What would the Lord have done in this situation?" or "How would Jesus have reacted?"

A Christ-centered prayer life is not restricted to times of prayer only. It must be practiced throughout your working day and every area of your life. Only then can He motivate you and be glorified by it.

The dedication that is required to develop such a powerful and practical prayer life is only possible when you have placed Jesus in the center of your life. The authority of Christ in your practical, everyday life is imperative if you want to live a victorious life. It is impossible to live effectively as a Christian if Christ does not occupy primary place in your life. Place Him in the center and live victoriously and joyfully.

Loving Holy Spirit, help me in my sincere effort to put Christ first in every area of my life. Amen.

CHRIST IS COMING AGAIN!

You ought to live holy and godly lives as you look forward to the day of God and speed its coming (2 Peter 3:11-12).

During His life on earth Jesus was often asked when exactly God's Kingdom would come? His reply was always the same, "No one knows about that day or hour, not even the angels in heaven, nor the Son, but only the Father" (Matt. 24:36). Christ, however, emphasized that His followers had to be prepared for it at all times.

Since Christ's ascension, many scholars, theologians, and Bible students have tried to calculate and prophesy exactly when Jesus would return. Nobody has been successful yet. The words that Jesus spoke to His disciples on the Mount of Olives are just as true today, "So you also must be ready, because the Son of Man will come at an hour when you do not expect Him" (Matt. 24:44).

Your only concern as a Christian should be to ensure that you live your daily life in accordance with the pattern that God has set before you. You must obey His commands in love; you must pray zealously; you must continually praise and worship Him and also study God's Word.

Be open to the revelation of His will for your life. Be ready and willing to serve Him among your fellow men. Then you will be fully equipped to eagerly await His return and, when He comes in glory, to receive Him with joy and gladness.

Lord, help me to be ready when You return. Let me work to the glory of Your name in the meantime. Amen.

ENTHUSIASM CAN FADE

"Because of the increase of wickedness, the love of most will grow cold" (Matthew 24:12).

The Lord's prophetic words are as true today as when He said them in biblical times. Since the birth of the Christian church there has always been some form of spiritual enthusiasm that has washed over exhausted men and women, encouraging them.

God renews His church through His Spirit from time to time. As soon as the enthusiasm created by the Holy Spirit starts to wear off, there is a decline in Christian testimony especially among those whose faith was burning very brightly during the time of revival. It is sad then when someone whose faith has cooled off pretends to look godly by doing all the right things.

Even though you might be a child of God, the experience of your rebirth could diminish if you do not grow spiritually. God, however, is always prepared to refresh you through His indwelling Spirit, so that you can have that divine zeal that makes you an effective disciple.

If you feel that your enthusiasm for the Truth and your fellowship with God are declining, be honest and confess this sad state of affairs. Be determined to find the cause of this in prayer before God. This will require confession of guilt and introspection under the guidance of the Holy Spirit.

It could be a traumatic experience, because no feeble excuses will last before the Father. He will reveal your weaknesses, but this revelation will lead to a renewed enthusiasm to live a life dedicated to Christ.

Search me, O God, and know my heart; test me and know my anxious thoughts (Ps. 139:23). Amen.

God's Abundant Comfort

"Blessed are those who mourn, for they will be comforted" (Matthew 5:4).

Just before our Lord's ascension He was deeply aware of His disciples' sadness at the prospect of His departure. They were stunned but Jesus understood man's need and He promised them a Helper, "I will ask the Father, and He will give you another Counselor to be with you forever – the Spirit of truth" (John 14:16-17).

Sadness and sorrow are concrete realities. How well do we not know that! That is why these words spoken by the Lord are such a glorious comfort. He was indeed the Man of Sorrows, who was well acquainted with grief.

Is there need or shortage in your home? Jesus didn't even have a place where He could lay His head (Luke 9:58).

Have friends disappointed you? His friends betrayed Him (Luke 22:48 and 58).

Do you battle with sorrow? In Gethsemane Jesus experienced such anguish that His sweat was like drops of blood falling to the ground (Luke 22:39-46).

Are you mourning the death of a loved one? Jesus cried at the grave of His friend Lazarus (John 11:35).

Do you feel forsaken, even by God? On the cross Jesus wept because God had forsaken Him (Matt. 27:46).

In the midst of our adversity, poverty, needs, cares and worries, Someone who understands and cares comes to us and says, "Blessed are those who mourn, because they will be comforted" (Matt. 5:4).

Not far from Marah with its bitter water lies Elim with its twelve fountains and palm trees. Trust God to lead you from Marah to Elim by His understanding, loving grace.

Thank You, Lord, for the Helper You sent. What really matters is not what I have lost, but that You comfort me. Amen.

WE WORSHIP A LIVING LORD

"I was dead, and behold I am alive for ever and ever!" (Revelation 1:18).

At the Lord's crucifixion, the disciples experienced severe emotional trauma. They knew that Jesus had died and they were not only filled with sorrow, but also with shame and remorse because of their actions. They had fled and left Him alone in His deepest need. Things could hardly have been worse for them. Then came the baffling news and discovery that their Master was alive. They rose from the depths of despair, insecurity and doubt to the mountaintops of inexplicable joy.

The Christian today may try as hard as he can to experience the excitement of that first Christmas, but will always have the disadvantage of not being there. The Christmas celebration that has become so familiar to us was still fresh and exciting to the shepherds and astrologers, to Mary and Joseph. Bearing this in mind it is also virtually impossible for us to relive the joy of the disciples when they discovered that Jesus had risen from the dead.

The fact that Jesus is triumphantly alive is true! It is also possible for His disciples today to experience His living presence if we allow the Holy Spirit into our hearts. He gave His Holy Spirit to all who accepted Him as Lord and King in their hearts. This dynamic presence makes the Christian faith a pulsating, exciting experience for everyone who has risen from the death of sin with Christ.

Without the Holy Spirit the Christian faith would probably have been a wonderful ethical code, but it is Christ who makes it a vibrant, practical and joyous reality. The Lord has truly risen!

Spirit of the living Christ, fill my life with Your presence so that my faith can be vibrant and enthusiastic. Amen.

THE POWER OF SILENCE

"In quietness and trust is your strength" (Isaiah 30:15).

There are many people who talk way too much and keep themselves busy with unimportant matters. They just cannot keep quiet or calm down. When they have nothing to keep them busy, they feel guilty and become irritated or find some insignificant task to occupy them with.

While constructive activity certainly has its place in life, there is a crucial place for withdrawing from the wild rush of life to meditate on the deeper aspects of life.

Most people find it much easier to concentrate on the problems of everyday life than on the reality that God is real and eternally good. Even a short period of time spent quietly in God's presence creates a new sense of balance and power that cannot be found anywhere else.

When you become quiet before God, you are inclined to take your tensions and confusions with you. The result then is that the time that should have led to inspiration and meditation becomes a time of greater confusion.

When you enter into God's presence, take off your worldly shoes of haste and noise, because you are standing on holy ground. Take your Bible or perhaps a spiritual book to help you achieve harmony with the Lord.

To reap the benefits and strength derived from being quiet before God requires dedication, perseverance and time. When these sacrifices are made the rewards are innumerable, because it is in silence that God's presence is best experienced.

I thank You, my Lord and Master, that I can meet You in the silence as a living reality! Amen.

AN ANCHOR FOR OUR JOURNEY

Your word, O Lord, is eternal; it stands firm in the heavens (Psalm 119:89).

How true the words of a certain hymn writer, "Around me is only change and decay!" The world we live in is constantly changing. New methods replace outdated ways; modern technology replaces old theories. It is virtually impossible to visualize the scientific achievements that have occurred during the past few decades.

It is amazing to think that these achievements will probably soon be outdated too. In spite of all the wonders of development, ordinary men and women feel scared and insecure because of the drastic changes that happen regularly. Man is looking for something more permanent to embrace to give him a feeling of security.

It is most comforting, in these times of breathtaking changes, to know that the Word of God is the one great, unchangeable Truth in our world. So it was in the past and so it will be in the future.

Despite anything that can happen; despite insecurity and instability – God reigns supreme and His Word remains the lamp which gives light as we struggle and stumble through the dark, winding passages of time.

You can be sure that change will continue to occur in your life and in the world around you, but as long as you hold on to Christ you will be able to deal with change, because you have a steadfast anchor in the great unchangeable One!

Thank You, O Incarnate Word, that even though mountains may fall into the sea, I have an eternal anchor in Your Word. Amen.

I Despair, Lord, of My Sin

"Go away from me, Lord; I am a sinful man!" (Luke 5:8).

On your way to spiritual maturity, you cannot avoid the dreadfulness of sin. This is the saddest truth about human life. However, the most glorious fact about God is that although He hates sin, He loves the sinner. In spite of our sin, we worship a God of abundant love and grace.

While following the Lord Jesus, Peter had to face the awful reality of his sin. He confessed, "I am a sinful man." It was a painful, but liberating confession. The Heidelberg Catechism states as a definite prerequisite for a happy life and peaceful death: "I have to know the extent of my sin and how utterly lost I really am."

It is not fashionable to even mention sin these days. Only old-fashioned spoilsports do that. Sin has become redundant: rather call it nervous tension; a psychological disturbance; mental illness or human weakness. If I replaced the label of a bottle of poison with one that says "Honey", the contents would still be poisonous.

Fortunately for Peter he discovered his sinfulness. His first reaction was, "Depart from me, Lord; for I am a sinful man!" How he despised himself; how much torture and struggle, failure and shame was not expressed in this cry. Where could he go with his sin?

There is but one place to go to with your sin – Christ. John 1:12 says, "Yet to all who received Him, to those who believed in His name, He gave the right to become children of God." Why must we go to Jesus? Because "He will forgive us our sins and purify us from all unrighteousness" (1 John 1:9).

O Lord, purify me with Your precious blood that was shed for me. Amen.

SELF-ACCEPTANCE

What a wretched man I am! Who will rescue me from this body of death? (Romans 7:24).

There are people who are so arrogant that they become totally unaware of the truth about themselves. What a person thinks he is and what he really is are often worlds apart.

In contrast to the person who thinks so much of himself, we find the person who despises himself and who cannot find anything good in himself. Humility is a Christian virtue but can turn into a stumbling block when taken too far. It can become a heavy burden that destroys all initiative and self-development.

If you are continually putting yourself down, you should not be surprised if people judge you at the face value you've given yourself. If you consistently run yourself down, insisting that you are very ordinary and incapable of achieving any success, you should not be surprised if people treat you as unimportant.

God has given every person a talent. However, it is up to you to discover and develop your gift. You will only be able to achieve this if you realize that you need not do everything in your own power. You are a child of the omnipotent, loving God. The whole purpose of your life is to glorify Him and to do His will. To make this possible, God has given you the Holy Spirit to live in you and work through you.

With such a wonderful Father and meaningful faith, you dare not put yourself down. The Holy Spirit in you makes your life significant and worthwhile.

Lord Jesus, because You live in me through Your Spirit, my life has purpose and meaning. I glorify Your name. Amen.

THE WONDER OF FORGIVENESS

Blessed is he whose transgressions are forgiven, whose sins are covered (Psalm 32:1).

Few things in life can be as destructive as a constant feeling of guilt and remorse. While you brood and fret, it grows bigger and bigger until it reaches overwhelming proportions. If you analyze these feelings rationally, you will find that they have been blown out of proportion. However, in your guilt-ridden condition you find it almost impossible to believe the liberating truth of forgiveness.

If you consider this seriously and prayerfully, you will realize that such an attitude is a gross denial of the sacrifice that Jesus Christ made on your behalf. The Son of God died on the cross for your sin. Through His death He took your sin upon Him. He guarantees you God's love and forgiveness. This is an irrefutable fact.

As a Christian you may never allow yourself to become depressed by the burden of your sin and guilt. It is important to confess your guilt when you realize that you have failed to do what He requires you to do. Praise and thanksgiving must form a part of your confession. Your loving heavenly Father has forgiven your numerous sins and He gives you a second chance to live the way He wants you to.

Live each day victoriously and freely share the forgiveness that He so freely and lovingly gives you. "Many are the woes of the wicked, but the LORD's unfailing love surrounds the man who trusts in Him" (Ps. 32:10). Write this promise on the tables of your heart and live accordingly.

Lord, I praise You because You have forgiven me. Amen.

BACK TO REALITY

"Men of Galilee, " they said, "why do you stand here looking into the sky?" (Acts 1:11).

When Christ prepared His disciples for His death, He told them that He would be going to His Father. He comforted and encouraged them by explaining to them that it was necessary for Him to go away so that the Holy Spirit could be sent to help them continue Christ's work on earth.

After this preparation, we find the disciples staring at the clouds, trying to see their Lord ascending to heaven. Then the angels called them back to the reality where their faith was challenged by the world.

Children of God are often tempted to become so absorbed in prayer, Scripture reading and meditation, that they lose touch with reality.

You should be on your guard during quiet times and time spent on other spiritual activities that help you to grow spiritually. It is equally important to practice your faith in everyday life. Just like the disciples had to witness the Holy Spirit at work in their everyday lives, we have to testify to the power that we receive from our fellowship with the Lord, by serving others in His name.

After having sought the will of God in your quiet times, you must move out into the world and do what He expects of you.

When He returns, it will not matter whether you are on your knees praying, or whether you are serving others and testifying in His name. The important question is, "Am I doing His will?"

Lord and Guide, through Your power and grace my life is fulfilled as I serve others in Your name. Amen.

DISCIPLESHIP REQUIRES OBEDIENCE

Do whatever He tells you (John 2:5).

Many people want to follow Christ on their own terms. They are willing to follow Him faithfully, provided they can do their own thing and as long as their faith does not cause them inconvenience. However, a disciple who wishes to please himself before obeying the Master has lost touch with reality and causes himself a lot of frustration and disappointment.

Effective discipleship requires unconditional obedience to Christ. Your life has to be in harmony with His will and you have to let go of everything that is contrary to that will. If this seems too restricting, it is because you don't fully understand the will of God yet. If you believe that God's will is restricted to a religious interpretation of life and think that you can exclude His authority from certain areas of your life, your lack of commitment will soon become obvious. The failure of your spiritual life is then a foregone conclusion.

Striving to obey God's will as revealed by the Holy Spirit, should be top priority in your life. To walk with God; to discern His will for you through prayer and meditation; to know the joy and peace derived from intimate fellowship with Him, is the reward of the dedicated, obedient disciple.

Obedience to the Master is not a responsibility that must be suffered, but an indescribable privilege that should be accepted and carried out with thanksgiving. Have you ever heard a bird complaining because it has to carry wings on its back – they are the instruments that make him fly high!

Lord Jesus, my Master, make me a true disciple who finds joy in serving You and doing Your will. Amen.

CHRISTIAN LOVE WILL TRIUMPH

"If you love Me, you will obey what I command. And I will ask the Father, and He will give you another Counselor to be with you forever" (John 14:15-16).

Christianity is being challenged by the world today. Numerous sects exist that claim to be founded on Scripture; Christian norms are replaced by worldly values in many areas of life; the Gospel is reduced to a mere social or political code; all these things make it exceedingly difficult to know what to believe or accept.

We praise God, however, that in the midst of this religious confusion, there is a powerful core of believers whose first, last and only love is the risen Christ. Their beliefs might vary widely, their traditions and spiritual heritage might seem irreconcilable; they might feel isolated because of racial and cultural differences, but in their hearts they have the same burning love for Jesus Christ. It is this true love that forms the center of the triumphant church of Christ on earth.

Christian love must be revealed practically. Mere social concern, however, is not Christian love – though Christians do care for the lonely and the poor. Christian love is inspired by the unselfish love of Christ and that is what distinguishes it from socio political service.

If you belong to a group that loves Christ, you will be able to rise above all differences and your view will be broadened so much that you are liberated from pettiness and narrow-mindedness. You will no longer judge fellow Christians by their doctrines, but by the depth and quality of their love for the Master.

God of love, may Your Holy Spirit and Your law of love govern my life. Amen.

ENCHANTING PEACE

Grace and peace to you from Him who is, and who was, and who is to come (Revelation 1:4).

Dante proclaims in *Paradise* as he worships God, that in God's will is his peace. This timeless and universal exclamation however did not originate with Dante, nor did the universal echo become still when he died.

The humble acknowledgment that all true peace flows from God is the highest form of human wisdom. The peace of God must captivate us before we can find true peace.

In every generation, poets, philosophers, prophets and teachers join in the choir as they confess with Augustine, "In the whole, wide world there is no peace to be found, unless we find it in You first, Lord!" Blessed is the man who has found his peace within God's love.

To know that we are His children, is more precious than jewels. Those who have found their shelter in God approach life with inner peace and calm. God's grace is so awesome that we can only bow down before Him in adoration.

Mordecai Kaplan, a Jewish theologian tried to describe this enchantment as follows:

God is the faith with which we overcome
the fear of loneliness, helplessness, failure and death.
God is the hope that like a flash of light
lightens up the darkest chasm of sin, suffering and despair.
God is the love that creates, protects and forgives.
He is the Spirit that hovers over the chaos man creates.
He transforms evil into a pure life through His omnipotence
and creates a new earth where peace reigns.

O Prince of Peace, thank You for the rest and peace that You have brought into my life. Amen.

CARPÉ DIEM – SEIZE THE DAY

Cast all your anxiety on Him because He cares for you (1 Peter 5:7).

The word "worry" literally means to "tear apart". And that is exactly what our cares and worries do to us. They break down our physical strength, cause painful ulcers, drain our energy and make us feel old. When we worry we are unable to handle life's problems or carry out our responsibilities.

We often worry about things that we can do absolutely nothing about. We are worried sick about what the future might hold, while we don't even know how long we will live. Because we cannot control the future, we are torn apart. All that we can do is to worry about our worries!

Worrying about the unknown and what cannot be controlled is Satan's subtle attempt to break us down and eventually destroy us. That is why Jesus forbids us to worry about tomorrow. If you continue to worry you are disobedient to God.

You should plan for the future, but not fret about it all the time. Otherwise you have no faith in God and His love or in His ability to provide and care for you.

Focus on today. Do whatever you have to do today. Pick all the flowers of joy and happiness that God wants to give you today. The future is in His hands, and He will provide.

Today is God's gift to us and Christ wants us to live one day at a time, trusting Him completely. Yesterday is a memory; tomorrow is a promise; all that you really have is today. Take hold of it and live life to the full!

All-sufficient Lord, thank You that I can leave all my worries with You, for You know what to do with them. I know that You will provide. Amen.

DON'T LOSE FAITH

"Be strong and courageous. Do not be terrified; do not be discouraged, for the LORD your God will be with you wherever you go" (Joshua 1:9).

The way we experience life emotionally varies and therefore we have to reassess our emotions regularly. At the end of July, the halfway mark through the year, is a good time to do so.

You might have experienced a period of great joy or achievement. Or perhaps you have gone through a dark time of sorrow and you feel spiritually depressed.

Depending on your personal experiences you will face the future with faith and enthusiasm or with fear and hesitation. In Joshua 1:9 we have God's everlasting promise that He is with us wherever we may find ourselves. What more can you wish for?

The way you feel about the future will be determined by your faith. You will either be inspired or feel hopeless. If you believe that nothing good will ever come your way, you make life difficult for yourself. Job quite rightly said, "What I feared has come upon me; what I dreaded has happened to me" (Job 3:25).

If you steadfastly believe in the eternal goodness of your heavenly Father, and are willing to allow Him to work in you through His Spirit, you are preparing yourself for a happy, prosperous future.

Wherever you might be, God is there to wrap you in His love and give you His grace. Such faith dispels all fear. All that God expects from you is steadfast faith in Him. Put Him first and approach the future with optimism.

Thank You, Father, that I don't have to fear the future because I trust You. You will hold my hand and lead me along the path that You have planned for me. Amen.

AUGUST

PLANNING FOR THE FUTURE

Unless the LORD builds the house, its builders labor in vain (Psalm 127:1).

We all make plans for the future: the school-leaver, the parent-to-be, the professional – yes, just about everyone does this at various stages in life. In some cases these plans never materialize and only stay dreams. Thorough planning often results in dreams and ambitions being realized. It was a wise man who said that, "He who fails to plan, plans to fail."

People who leave their future in the hand of either fate or Lady Luck find their future clouded by insecurity. In a Christian's life, however, fate does not play a part because God is always in control.

There is only one way that you can plan confidently for your future and that is by committing your life to God completely. Despite any plans that you might have made or feelings of insecurity or confusion that might fill your mind, you must share all your thoughts about the future with Christ. He wants you to share all your problems with Him too.

When you have done that you must trust God unconditionally and wait on Him. He will lead you into the future that He has planned for you according to His perfect will. He has a wonderful blueprint for your life!

Go into the future with your hand in His. You will undoubtedly become deeply conscious of His holy presence. You will be able to act confidently and experience peace of mind because you are acting in accordance with God's master plan for your life. This will give you total peace and satisfaction.

Lord, whether the future is bright or dark, I am safe because You are holding my hand. I confidently follow You because You know all things. Amen.

GO FOR GOLD

Do you not know that in a race all the runners run, but only one gets the prize? Run in such a way as to get the prize (1 Corinthians 9:24).

For the true Christian only very high standards should be good enough. Anything less is a poor substitute and has been rejected by Jesus Himself as inferior and unacceptable. As present-day disciples of the Lord it should be our goal and ambition to keep Jesus before us as our Perfect Example in everything.

It requires steadfast perseverance and strict self-discipline to achieve anything worthwhile in life. You will have to put aside your own desires and seek only God's divine purpose for your life.

The Master's call to serve Him in various spheres of life will become top priority and your own preferences will vanish. Much of what you will be required to do or undertake might appear to be most inconvenient as far as your lifestyle is concerned, but it needs to receive top priority in your life.

Without the support, power and grace of God you will never be able to resist the temptation to compromise or even give up. If, however, the Holy Spirit has full control of your whole life, you will receive the strength and ability to obtain the crown of life in the fullness of Jesus Christ.

He enables us to mine the gold of life that has little to do with earthly treasures and riches, but gives satisfaction, joy and peace. If we persevere to the end, He will reward us, "Be faithful, even to the point of death and I will give you the crown of life" (Rev. 2:10).

Jesus my Lord, Guide and Example, may my highest ambition be to honor You with my life and work. Amen.

READING THE BIBLE MEANINGFULLY

"Man does not live on bread alone, but on every word that comes from the mouth of God" (Matthew 4:4).

Far too often God's Word is read haphazardly, even by His committed children. It is almost as if the Bible has become a good luck charm or just a document.

Treating the Bible in this disrespectful and disconcerting way has not only impoverished the church, but has also resulted in spiritual shallowness in many believers. It is the direct result of disobedience and lack of discipline.

The Bible is not an anthology containing interesting proverbs and speculative theological suggestions. No, it is God's Word, conveying a true message and it should be read in a disciplined, logical manner. It comes directly from God and His power emanates from it when it is fully understood. Amos R. Wells expressed it as follows:

I supposed I knew my Bible, reading piecemeal, hit and miss,
Now a bit of John or Matthew, now a snatch of Genesis;
certain chapters of Isaiah, certain Psalms (the twenty-third);
First of Proverbs, Twelfth of Romans. Yes, I thought I knew the Word;
But I found that thorough reading was a different thing to do.
And the way was unfamiliar when I read my Bible through.
You who like to play at Bible, dip and dabble, here and there,
just before you kneel aweary, and yawn through a hurried prayer,
you who treat the Crown of Writings as you treat no other book;
just a paragraph disjointed, just a crude, impatient look.
Try a worthier procedure, try a broad and steady view:
You will kneel in awesome wonder
when you read the Bible through.

Lord of the Eternal Word, please open my eyes so that I can experience the powerful ministering of the Bible. Amen.

PIETY CAN BE OVERDONE!

Do not be overrighteous, neither be overwise (Ecclesiastes 7:16).

Having a "holier-than-thou" or an "I-know-everything" attitude is a sure way of driving people away.

Unfortunately there are many people who have fallen into this trap and this results in other people trying to avoid them. People who act sanctimoniously often scare others away from the church of Jesus Christ. It is also a most unfortunate fact that many people judge the church according to the shortcomings of a few so-called Christians.

Humility and meekness, understanding and patience are crucial characteristics of a true disciple of Christ. When you look at the life of our Lord as recorded in Scripture, you see that these traits formed an integral part of His character. If this is true, it is essential for those who bear His name to follow His example. There is no place whatsoever for spiritual pride in our lives.

Your prayer should at all times be that the Holy Spirit, in His grace, control your mind and lead you in the steps of the Master.

Submit yourself to His divine and perfect will and allow His Spirit to work through and in you – in your thoughts, words and actions.

Then you will be able to reflect something of the beauty of Christ and draw others to Him. His love and humility will be revealed through you.

Loving Father, please help me not to be spiritually proud or presumptuous. Make me, like You, a servant to my brother. Amen.

PEER PRESSURE

"But what about you? Who do you say I am?" (Matthew 16:15).

Man is born with a herd instinct. We all have a natural urge to belong to a group. When the crowd does something, it takes great courage to ignore public opinion and move in directly the opposite direction.

This starts in early childhood when a popular person with a strong personality leads the other children in the direction of his choice. Few children will dare to protest, even if they know it is wrong. During adolescence the desire to conform or agree becomes even stronger. Even among adults we find that the desire to be part of the group still remains prevalent.

Some people have become alcoholics or drug addicts because, at a specific time in their lives, they did not have the courage to follow the sober, healthy and safe road. They succumbed to the suggestion of "just try it once" because "everybody else is doing it". However, the experiment very quickly became a habit.

If you want to achieve a worthy goal in your life and develop a strong character, you must be willing to submit to God's guidance. Through His grace, you will be able to make the right decisions. Listen to Him first before listening to popular public opinion. Don't allow your life to be ruled and regulated by what people might think. It is not true that the majority is always right. If it were true, Jesus would not have been crucified by the loveless masses.

If you want to be true to God and yourself, you must live close to Him. It is only in intimate fellowship with Him that you can develop the individual personality that He has given you. Only then can you start reaching your full potential and live to the glory of God.

Lord, make me steadfast in following Jesus, so that I will not get carried away by the masses and public opinion. Amen.

GUARD AGAINST MAMMON

Keep your lives free from the love of money and be content with what you have (Hebrews 13:5).

The most common complaint today is about the rising cost of living, shrinking capital reserves and high interest rates. The result is that more and more people become obsessed about being rich. Society stresses the maintenance of a certain standard of living in order to keep up with the Joneses.

Few people consider economizing so that they can live within the limits of their income. Such an attitude necessarily causes stress and tension. The main objective in life then becomes the accumulation of riches.

There does however come a time when deep down you realize that money and possessions are not the only priorities in life. They might afford a comfortable lifestyle or a false feeling of security, but they can never bring total satisfaction. Earthly possessions can never be regarded as permanent. The presence of Jesus Christ as Savior and Redeemer in your life has eternal value and gives you an anchor which ensures your safety against the raging storms.

If you are searching for fulfillment and security in your life, turn to Jesus Christ. He is always with you and only in Him will you find perfect peace. Without Him life has no meaning and you are subjected to endless worries. With Him your life has true meaning and purpose – something that cannot be bought with all the riches and treasures of this world.

Lord, my God, in You only do I find fulfillment and true peace. Amen.

HOLY SPIRIT – SOURCE OF PEACE!

"Peace I leave with you; My peace I give you. I do not give to you as the world gives" (John 14:27).

In man's passionate quest for improvement and development adults and children all over the world are under a lot of pressure to achieve. The experts today call it stress. More demands are made on people and more and more is expected of the individual. At the same time people are trying everything to free themselves from the unbearable pressure under which they work and try to relax. Everyone is searching feverishly for peace of mind.

Of course there are man-made tranquilizers that are consumed in great quantities. We have to be grateful that these remedies do bring relief for numerous people. For many, however, it is the trapdoor to various addictions. There are many hidden dangers along the road in our search for peace of mind and rest.

Eventually there is only one way to ensure the peace that your spirit, soul and body are longing for, "My soul finds rest in God alone; my salvation comes from Him" (Ps. 62:1).

To know Him and to become quiet in His holy presence will bring real and permanent peace. In this the Holy Spirit is our Guide and Teacher. We have to rediscover this power station where we can recharge with help from above.

That is why Christ did not collapse under the stress and strain of the severest test of His life. He emerged triumphantly. Through the Holy Spirit we find rest and peace with God that surpasses all understanding.

O Holy Spirit, please give me the peace of God. Keep me from trying to find peace anywhere else. Amen.

WHEN PAST DESIRES REAPPEAR

They did not listen or pay attention; instead, they followed the stubborn inclinations of their evil hearts. They went backward and not forward (Jeremiah 7:24).

It is true that Christ can heal the deadly disease of sin. When truth becomes a personal, practical reality and it feels as if your whole life is filled with the glory of the Lord, thoughts of depression and failure don't enter your mind. For many people the period directly after their conversion is the most wonderful time of their Christian pilgrimage. Christ, and what He has done for them, is new and fresh in their hearts and minds while His grace is working powerfully in their spirits. They don't experience the slightest form of doubt or secret fear.

This state of bliss, however, cannot continue forever. Past sins start lurking threateningly and Satan uses all sorts of new temptations to lure new converts away from the Master. You start compromising with regards to certain social habits and before you realize it, you are back in your rut.

Eventually that which was new in your life disappears completely and that which seemed so promising is nowhere to be found.

The only safe defense mechanism against spiritual backsliding is to put Christ in the center of your life, to test all your standards against His, to turn to Him daily, to not compromise your Christian values and to be willing to lay down everything that does not meet with His approval.

Submission to Christ is not a static, emotional state of mind, but a dynamic influence that enables you to triumph over every demoralizing influence and to live victoriously to the glory of His name.

Please help me, my Lord and Savior, to live victoriously over all my sins and bad habits because You have set me free. Amen.

Decisions Must Be Made

Oh, the depth of the riches of the wisdom and knowledge of God!
(Romans 11:33).

Uncertainty can be very confusing and nerve-racking. Because many people are in a state of uncertainty they cannot make decisions. Depending on the nature of the decision, indecisiveness can have serious consequences, especially when it concerns business matters or the future or the lives of those who depend on you.

There are few things worse or more demoralizing than to stumble along in the gray area of indecision, especially when you need to make a decision quickly. You feel totally incompetent and hopeless, while your self-confidence is undermined to the extent that you are eventually unable to make even the most insignificant decision.

If you are living in an intimate relationship with Jesus Christ, you will find that you are in contact with Him on a day-to-day, even minute-to-minute basis concerning the different matters and problems of life.

If you remain sensitive to the inspiration of the Holy Spirit, you will find that you subconsciously lay all your problems before Him. Then suddenly you discover that you instinctively know what to decide and how to handle problems.

Share your problems with the Master in prayer and meditation and you will feel the weight of decision-making being lifted from your shoulders. Christ invited you to do just that in Matthew 11:28, "Come to Me, all you who are weary and burdened, and I will give you rest."

Lord, my God, I come to You with all my problems, knowing that You will help me to make the right decisions. Amen.

THE CHRISTIAN VIRTUE OF COMPASSION

Be kind and compassionate to one another, forgiving each other,
just as in Christ God forgave you (Ephesians 4:32).

Christianity has social responsibilities that cannot be side-stepped. It is so easy to become immune to the demands that you eventually become indifferent to the needs of others.

Perhaps there was a time when you were deeply moved by the poverty or deprivation of those who are less privileged in life but now it no longer bothers you. If you have allowed your conscience to be dulled because it has become so ordinary, an important part of your spiritual life has disintegrated. Without it you cannot be a fully committed child of God.

To go through life without becoming involved in others' needs, means that you make it impossible for the Holy Spirit to work through you. God fulfills His commission on earth through sensitive, obedient people.

It is not easy to have a sensitive conscience because then you identify intimately with the pain and need of others. It does however make you a more understanding person. A clear conscience is one of a Christian's greatest assets.

It is the channel through which God's grace flows in your life to reach others, it is the road along which He leads you to victory and keeps you in harmony with God and your fellow man. It constantly reminds you just how gracious and compassionately God treated you in your need.

When your conscience is clear, your attitude becomes more like Christ's and you are filled with compassion toward fellow pilgrims. Then you forgive as God has forgiven you, and you are kind and compassionate toward all who are involved in the battle of life with you.

Lord, please keep me sensitive and understanding. Make me
compassionate through Your Holy Spirit. Amen.

EMERGENCY PRAYERS IN A CRISIS

O God of heaven, the great and awesome God, who keeps His covenant of love … let Your ear be attentive to hear the prayer Your servant is praying before You day and night (Nehemiah 1:5-6).

Sometimes we find ourselves in a situation where we need an immediate answer. Let us then follow Nehemiah's example: let us take refuge in God through prayer. In this way we will be able to maintain our intellectual and spiritual equilibrium. We are then appealing to the highest wisdom and omnipotence that is available.

It is amazing how God answers the crisis prayers of those who fully trust Him. A quick prayer is an emergency line linked directly with God. He answers us even before we have expressed our prayers in words if we are willing to submit our will to Him. We then glorify Him through our faith and trust.

Emergency prayers can, however, never substitute regular times of drawing aside with God for intimate fellowship. It is only in a crisis that you can call on God this way because you know what it means to call on Him.

The emergency prayer is your protection in danger; the saving grace in temptation; your directive in confusing circumstances; your peace and calm when anger threatens to overpower you. God always listens to His children's anguished cries and is waiting to respond.

Often people are amazed and surprised by the prompt – and often simple – answers that God gives in response to emergency prayers. They even ascribe it to "chance" and then fail to bring honor and thanksgiving to the One who deserves it. In this way many of God's miracles go by unnoticed and we suffer irreparable damage.

Thank You, Father God, that my prayers in an emergency also reach Your throne of grace and that I am blessed by Your answer. Amen.

Don't Fear Criticism

Whatever happens, conduct yourselves in a manner worthy of the gospel of Christ (Philippians 1:27).

At some stage in your life you will be criticized. If you do something, you will be criticized for doing it the wrong way. If you do nothing, you will be criticized for being lazy and detached. Whether you are a success or a failure, somebody will judge you one way or another. Even our Lord and Master, the most perfect Person who ever walked the earth, could not escape tattlers and slanderers.

It is useless to try and please everybody. If you want to impress people hoping for temporary popularity, you will never achieve anything worthwhile, and eventually you will be rejected by the same people you wanted to please.

Criticism can cause a lot of pain if you allow it to. If you have done your best, the least you expect is appreciation. Instead of that you often receive unfriendly and unfair criticism. Such comments are often all the more painful because they come from people who have never attempted anything themselves or who have less knowledge or are less capable than the one being criticized.

The only person I know of who is not being criticized is a mummy in the British Museum who was embalmed two thousand years ago – but then, for the past two thousand years he has not lifted a finger!

The most important thing is to live with integrity and honesty before God, according to the principles laid down in His Word. Don't always ask, "What will people think?" Rather humbly ask, "Is what I am doing now the will of God for me?" Such an approach will counteract the venom and impact of negative criticism.

Lord and God, to live and work for You makes me immune to criticism. Amen.

GOD CANNOT BE RESTRICTED

As a prisoner for the Lord, then, I urge you to live a life worthy of the calling you have received (Ephesians 4:1).

It is amazing how many Christians have a poor opinion of themselves and their calling. They live under the false impression that excessive modesty is acceptable and pleasing to God. Even though these people may have special gifts and qualities, they never achieve what God intends them to.

If, in your quiet moments of prayer and meditation, you conclude that you will never be able to achieve anything worthwhile, you must ask yourself why you have come to that conclusion. Be absolutely honest with yourself and with God.

If you claim that you know your shortcomings and are living within those limits, it is possible that you are looking at your natural potential without considering what God can do through you. You might feel ineffective, but if you combine your resources with those God has put at your disposal, you could achieve great things!

Don't waste your time and spiritual resources lamenting the things that you cannot do. Hold on to the glorious truth that if you dedicate yourself to the Master to the best of your ability, He will use you beyond your wildest imagination.

Place yourself in His hands and let your prayer always be, "Use me, O Lord, use even me." Such a commitment to the will of God will reveal hidden talents that you never realized you possessed. You will experience the deep satisfaction that is the reward of those who strive to do the will of the Master.

I lay my weaknesses in Your hands, O my Savior, so that I can be strong in Your strength. Amen.

STILL AN APPRENTICE IN OLD AGE

They will still bear fruit in old age, they will stay fresh and green
(Psalm 92:14).

Our life on earth leads to eternity and every day we are preparing ourselves for it. That is why we should, within the confines of our unique personalities, use each day optimally, right up to the end of our lives. However, this can only happen if we are bound inextricably to Christ Jesus.

It is an impoverishing error of judgment to assume that you can be of no use any more because you have reached a certain age. In earlier days the following motto appeared on the Spanish coat of arms, *Ne Plus Ultra* (there is nothing more). This indicated that Spain had discovered all the existing world of that time.

When Columbus discovered a whole new world in 1492, the motto changed to, *Plus Ultra!* (There is much more). For man in his ripe old age, there is much more to discover and experience.

The influence of the ageing Christian is immeasurable and of a very unique quality. It bears the sign of rich, personal experience and spiritual depth of insight. The fruit of a righteous life is produced in silence, but with power and abundance.

Let us therefore, whether we are young or old, regard every day as a gift from God, as an apprenticeship or training school for eternity. Let us do this out of gratitude towards our Creator for the privilege of being alive.

O precious Life-giver, please help me not to waste my life, not even in old age. Amen.

Be Careful with Labels

What I mean is this: One of you says, "I follow Paul"; another, "I follow Apollos"; another, "I follow Cephas"; still another, "I follow Christ" (1 Corinthians 1:12).

It is so easy to be shunted onto a siding in your spiritual life. Perhaps your conversion was most dramatic, or perhaps you gradually moved into a deeper, more intimate experience with the living Christ. How you got to know Christ is not important. The actual reason for praise is that your heart is filled with the glory of Christ's divine presence and that you rejoice in the reality of your faith.

It is only natural to regard how you met Christ as important. You especially enjoy the fellowship of those who went through the same training school. By doing this, you automatically accept the name of a group that follows a specific aspect of Christ's teachings that you can identify with. This is quite understandable, but you should be careful that this does not prevent you from having fellowship with Christians from other denominations.

Should this happen your faith will be impoverished because you refuse to experience a wider and richer spectrum of Christianity.

Never allow a religious label, even if it has a rich tradition, to cut you off from other Christians who also truly love the Lord. The variety of Christian disciplines and doctrines can enrich your life. It should be viewed against the background of Christ's love and understanding for us.

Love is the most important test for any doctrine, teaching or religious discipline. It rises above all differences and binds God's children together.

God of love, please help me to rise above all the differences that cause division between other Christians and myself. Amen.

TREASURES IN FRAGILE CLAY POTS

We have this treasure in jars of clay to show that this all-surpassing power is from God and not from us (2 Corinthians 4:7).

Eastern kings of ancient times used to store all their treasures in earthen pots. A crude tin lamp can cast a bright light and a tattered book can contain lofty thoughts – in the same way these plain earthen pots became the bearers of precious treasures.

This is exactly what it is like in the kingdom of God: plain fishermen became disciples; the bearers of God's treasures. Paul compares our lives to these earthen vessels in which we carry the glorious message of the Gospel of Christ. Life surrounds us with problems and obstacles, while Christ surrounds us with His glory.

The earthen vessel is the image of human frailty and mortality, of fallibility, contamination and impurity, but it is also an image of the Potter's ability to recreate our lives with His hands, to the glory of God.

When God calls us as disciples, we shrink back because we are so intensely aware of our imperfection. But the King is sovereign and does with His clay pots as He wishes. God does not necessarily call the ones that are capable, but He empowers those He calls. We may never lose the sense of awe at the realization that God uses us – sinful as we are – to bear His treasures! We may never draw attention to ourselves instead of focusing on God. The glory of your life must always be God's. You must live to be His witness and let His glory shine through.

Gracious Master, please make me worthy of bearing Your treasures so that You will receive all the glory and honor. Amen.

PERFECT PROTECTION

For He will command His angels concerning you to guard you in all your ways (Psalm 91:11).

Loneliness is something that the Christian pilgrim is not spared during his journey on earth. In spite of the crowds of people around him, he can sometimes feel utterly alone. If this feeling becomes overpowering, people are inclined to start fretting about the deeper meaning of life. They then start getting involved in numerous activities, hoping to counteract their loneliness. Yet this does not seem to be the answer to their problems.

One obvious weakness of some believers is that they don't seem to grasp the magnitude and greatness of life, especially those things that lie beyond that which we can see. They believe what the Gospels say about Jesus, but they have a problem accepting the spiritual realm.

Then there are those who are absolutely sure about the existence of another world as described in Hebrews 11:16, "Instead, they were longing for a better country – a heavenly one. Therefore, God is not ashamed to be called their God, for He has prepared a city for them."

Nowadays, the church has to endure numerous attacks from outside, and, unfortunately also from within its ranks; from those who confess their beliefs but deny their faith by their actions. Remember that the triumphant church in heaven is much larger than the warring church on earth.

When you feel lonely and depressed by what is happening in the world, remind yourself of the true church of which you are a member through faith in Christ Jesus. Because you love God, the angels are on your side, and in obedience to God's command, they are protecting you.

God of heaven and earth, thank You for the invisible host that strengthens and protects me at all times. Amen.

THE CHRISTIAN'S DIVINE DESIRE

I want to know Christ and the power of His resurrection and the fellowship of sharing in His sufferings, becoming like Him in His death (Philippians 3:10).

The spiritual goal of every true Christian should be to become more like Christ every day. How you strive to obtain this goal will determine the nature of your Christian testimony.

If you regard Christ as a social or political reformer, your testimony will speak of it. If, on the other hand, you interpret the teachings of Christ as purely spiritual and exclude everything materialistic, you are in danger of alienating yourself from everyday life.

The danger exists that you can become so involved with the way Christianity functions, that you lose sight of the Great One who is leading the way. The moment you stop following Christ as your Guide and Leader, your spiritual life receives a tremendous blow. Your service will no longer be motivated by divine love. Immediately your life loses its unique character as a true Christian witness.

The center of a Christian's life is Christ! Your most divine longing should be to know Him and to put Him first in your life. You must be filled completely by His Holy Spirit.

Then you draw from the Source of true inspiration and your testimony becomes effective. Your sincere desire will be satisfied when you are truly conscious of His guidance and living presence. An ever-deepening fellowship with your Savior will be revealed and will be pleasing to God.

This divine longing will only be satisfied if Christ is given the prime position in every area of your life.

Lord Jesus, my Savior and Redeemer, I have no greater desire in my heart than to put You first in every aspect of my life. Amen.

DO NOT SUCCUMB TO TEMPTATION

When the devil had finished all this tempting, he left Him until an opportune time (Luke 4:13).

All people, but more specifically God's children, are continually subjected to temptations. This does not necessarily involve committing deadly sins. You can also be tempted to tell "white lies"; keep the extra change that you were given; eat and drink excessively; omit important information when filling out official forms. Many people find these examples so insignificant that they don't even regard them worthy of consideration. But they can become temptations that violate your Christian principles and integrity.

You will undoubtedly be aware of that feeling of inner satisfaction when you have managed to overcome temptation. You know that in resisting the desire to sin you have achieved victory for yourself and for Christ. This feeling of achievement creates peace of mind that only comes with the knowledge that you have done your Christian duty through His power and grace.

However, never become over-confident or blasé when you have managed to overcome temptation. This feeling of peace that you are experiencing could be the calm before a storm. You can be assured that Satan has not given up on you and he will mobilize his whole satanic force against you if need be. Then, when you least expect it, he will attack, trying to make you fall.

Persevere in your efforts to obey God in everything. He will not allow you to be tempted beyond what you can bear. Remain in close fellowship with Christ at all times and He will indicate the perfect way for you to follow.

When You are with me, Lord Jesus, I will receive grace to resist and overcome every temptation. Amen.

INTERACTION IN FRIENDSHIP

He who walks with the wise grows wise, but a companion of fools suffers harm (Proverbs 13:20).

There is a well-known proverb that says, "A man is known by the company he keeps." It is true that involuntarily the company we keep rubs off on us – especially in the spiritual domain.

After your conversion you started a new life and your interests changed radically. Because past, probably worldly, friends did not change their interests, a deep gulf developed between you. This is inevitable, yet so disconcerting to you that you try to compromise with them.

You might try to keep these old friends by urging them to experience something similar to what you did. Your motivations and desires are noble and worthy of the Christian disciple. It is, however, very dangerous to attempt because you are a newborn child in Christ.

The language and emotions of your former way of life are still very much a part of you. If you continue to visit the old meeting places, you might find yourself losing your grip on your new life. Eventually you might find yourself right back where you started before your conversion – also concerning your spiritual welfare. Old habits die hard, while new ones have to be established.

If God has burdened you with the spiritual welfare of your former friends, accept the responsibility, but first make sure that your spiritual reserves are strong enough to handle their opposition and probably their mockery as well. Don't hesitate to call on a mature Christian to help you and don't stop praying for those friends!

Please protect me, Lord, from friendships that could harm my relationship with You. Amen.

A DAILY BLESSING TO OTHERS

"A man can receive only what is given him from heaven" (John 3:27).

Perhaps you would have liked to believe John the Baptist's words quoted above, but your job might not be inspiring and you detest every moment of it. You might find it difficult to believe that God planned it that you should be doing the job that you are doing now.

It is possible that you accepted your present job because the salary was good; the hours suited you; it was not a very demanding position and you didn't have many responsibilities. Therefore, the idea that God put you in such position might sound totally ridiculous. If your job can have a positive impact on your society it can become a channel of constructive service to the world around you.

No matter how insignificant your job might seem you have the opportunity to express God's will for your life. When you have become a willing instrument in His hands, even the most menial task will radiate a heavenly glow that will drive out feelings of boredom and inferiority.

Your job could be God's calling for your life provided that it does not harm your fellow man. Therefore, whatever you do, do it to the best of your ability, as if you are doing it for Him. Then you will discover that God will lead you and strengthen you through the Holy Spirit.

You will find that your job can become exciting and challenging and you will experience job satisfaction like never before.

Gracious God of the workplace too, help me to make my daily job a channel of Your blessing for those who touch my life. Amen.

PEACE WITH GOD!

He came and preached peace to you who were far away and peace to those who were near (Ephesians 2:17).

Christ is our peace! He made peace with God on our behalf. He removed the sting from the law that brought an end to the enmity that existed between Creator and creature. He changes sinners into Christians; He makes the old nature new.

It is He who broke down the wall of separation and enmity between God and man, "Therefore, since we have been justified through faith, we have peace with God through our Lord Jesus Christ" (Rom. 5:1).

It is this same peace that also enables us to live peacefully with our fellow men. So we start involving ourselves in those activities that will advance mutual peace (see Rom. 14:19). We become messengers of peace.

This peace also permeates marriages in a wonderful, healing way (see 1 Cor. 7:15). It brings joy to a family as it influences the lives of each family member. This peace grows in us as the fruit of the Holy Spirit (Gal. 5:22-23). It creates spiritual unity and togetherness, which is made possible by God's guidance (Eph. 4:3). It is also forms an important part of the Christian's character (James 3:17-18) as a "peacemaker."

Eventually it also leads to peace of the soul, because man has inner peace. Everything that was wrong before has been removed and Christ is now the center of our lives.

We also have a foretaste of heavenly peace and joy. That is why, in the final analysis, our peace depends on our living relationship with God.

Lord Jesus, teach me every day that my peace is to be found only in You. Let that be the source of my joy, my hope and my salvation. Amen.

A Faithful Hero

"I have had enough, Lord," he said. "Take my life; I am no better than my ancestors" (1 Kings 19:4).

An emotional breaking point differs from one person to the next, but is determined to a great extent by our faith in God, Jesus Christ and His Holy Spirit.

Elijah reached his breaking point when he fearfully fled from Jezebel. There he sat under the broom tree, wishing that he were dead.

There are times when the pressures and demands of life become too much for us. Relationships turn sour; everything you attempt seems to fail and bad decisions start taking their toll. Suddenly your faith is in danger. You no longer experience prayer to be a motivating force in your life. You question the meaning of life and desperately look for a way to escape – even if it means death!

There is a deep-rooted cause for the specific frame of mind a person finds himself in. The summit of Elijah's triumph when he became a hero of faith was suddenly reduced to a broom tree – and despair.

Perhaps he should have shown more maturity in regaining emotional balance so that not only the mountain top experience, but also the valley experience could take its rightful place in his life. Physical stress requires a time of rest. Sometimes we try to do too many things at the same time and then fail to complete anything.

Examine your life in the light of the Holy Spirit (see Ps. 139:24). You will rediscover the miraculous grace of the living Christ in your life. Then you will be able to accept challenges in His name and in His power, without having threatening Jezebels haunting you.

Good Shepherd, thank You that I can cling to You in faith even when I despair. Amen.

KEEP YOUR WORSHIP FRESH AND NEW

Sing to the LORD a new song, His praise from the ends of the earth (Isaiah 42:10).

It is very easy to fall into a rut when worshiping. Worship in your church might be conducted rigidly without any variation whatsoever; your personal devotions may follow the same pattern day after day and even your prayers may seem the same. The result of all this will be a dull, monotonous relationship with God.

Your times of worship should be vibrant and exciting. If this is not the case, you should seriously examine your pattern of worship and prayer.

Do not hesitate to experiment with new approaches. Even if seasoned, tested methods of worship have stood the test of time, variation in worship will prevent it from becoming lifeless.

When doing Bible study, use different translations – even another language can be exciting. Try using a concordance to shed more light on the meaning of Scripture, thus revealing deeper truths to you. Make use of spiritual literature that will explain parts of Scripture to you or highlight new concepts. Read songs in different languages and from different denominations. Find out what the younger generations sing when they praise God – you may find a totally new approach there! Read your Bible aloud. If you are used to meeting with God in the privacy of your room, move out into nature and allow God to speak to you.

Never be hesitant to vary the form or type of your worship. Change will bring a deeper dimension to your praise and worship. Just make sure that Jesus Christ remains the center of your worship.

Glorified Lord, I want to sing You a new song! Lead me through the Holy Spirit to worship You in Spirit and in truth. Amen.

THE HIGHWAY TO TRUE PEACE

"I will strengthen you and help you; I will uphold you with My righteous right hand" (Isaiah 41:10).

There is but one way out of all negative, disconcerting and terrifying experiences of life – the highway to God! This is the road we have to take when we are burdened with frustration, disappointment and failure, sorrow and pain. Jesus extended a hearty welcome to all of us when He said, "Come to Me, all you who are weary and burdened, and I will give you rest" (Matt. 11:28).

There is no situation that God cannot handle. There is no problem that He cannot solve. Nothing is so tangled that He cannot unravel it; there is no heart that is so broken that He cannot heal it.

Our problem is that we feel we should first try to put things straight ourselves. When we fail, we call on psychologists and counselors to help us. When they can't help us, we become anxious and fearful, hopeless and inconsolable. And all the while God is waiting to help us if we would only turn to Him!

Let us alter our procedure: let us go to God the moment a problem or crisis occurs. Lay it before Him honestly and prayerfully. Above all the storms that are raging in us, we will hear the glorious promise, "So do not fear, for I am with you; do not be dismayed, for I am your God" (Isa. 41:10). Test the Lord in this also, and see if He will not be true to His Word! Don't waste time and energy taking the road that your blind heart lead you on. There is a highway for you to take to the throne of grace. Jesus Himself said, "I am the way the truth and the life" (John 14:6).

May you, in the midst of your tension, unrest and insecurity, experience God's incomparable deliverance.

Almighty God, please keep me from trying to solve my own problems, and then coming to You when I've failed. Amen.

ORGANIZATION VERSUS MESSAGE

I appeal to you, brothers, in the name of our Lord Jesus Christ, that all of you agree with one another so that … you may be perfectly united (1 Corinthians 1:10).

Nowadays there is the misconception that the more disorganized you are, the more spiritual you are. Through the ages people have tried to recapture the "simple gospel", to overthrow all rules and disciplines followed by the Orthodox Church in an attempt to enjoy the so-called freedom people believe the early church had.

From the moment Christ founded His church on earth it has been organized. Human error and shortcomings often had a detrimental effect, but from what we read in the book of Acts, it is clearly the history of a new community that co-operated in a disciplined way to establish a new church. For a modern-day Christian therefore to look and long for a church with little or no organization, is to search for something that never existed.

Organization in some form is imperative. It is only when the organization becomes more important than the message that the true meaning and importance of the message is lost. Christian organization must always be secondary to the message of Jesus Christ.

Even though Christianity is divided into numerous organizations that form various branches within the church, it serves one central purpose – an ever-growing, purer love for Jesus Christ, the King of the church. Therefore, Christians should be united and single-minded. Where this love is missing, the church is no longer worthy of the Christian name, because the Spirit of Christ won't be there, no matter how excellent the organization.

Great Example and Leader, I want love to be the top priority of my life. Help me to live in harmony with my fellow Christians. Amen.

GOD'S PERFECT TIMING

Who knows but that you have come to royal position for such a time as this? (Esther 4:14).

Have you ever considered the possibility that God has placed you in your current situation for a specific reason?

Perhaps, at the moment, you find matters very difficult and tense and would rather have been anywhere else than where you are right now. Because of numerous problems, you are perhaps praying earnestly to God to either change your situation or to solve your problems.

If your prayers are not answered in the way you want, you have to consider the possibility that perhaps God put you in that place and that situation on purpose so that you can influence or change it for the better through the Holy Spirit. Should you not maybe have a more positive attitude towards your circumstances? Escapism is never the solution to the problem.

When everything seems to be going wrong for you, don't harbor any thoughts of defeat or surrender; but earnestly ask God what He wants you to do. Then be sensitive to the guidance of the Holy Spirit in the situation you are in.

Many of God's children can testify that if you sincerely ask your Father for guidance, He uses various ways to reveal His will to you. Does He want you to bring peace where there is strife? Do you have to reveal His power to those who are weak? Do you have to show understanding where there is misunderstanding? Do you have to be faithful to Him when everybody else seems to be unfaithful?

Before asking God to move you, make sure that He has not chosen this particular place for you because He needs you right there.

Father, keep me from taking my own selfish way. Let me live so close to You that I will understand Your will for my life. Amen.

FALSE PIETY

So, because Jesus was doing these things on the Sabbath, the Jews persecuted Him (John 5:16).

False piety is most probably the most despicable form of Christian conduct. During Christ's ministry on earth, the elite of the temple made use of every opportunity to criticize and undermine His work by accusing Him of not keeping to the letter of the law. After all, Moses laid down the law at God's command, and they submitted to it relentlessly excluding everything else – especially love.

The more Jesus tried to prove to these people that God's love was greater than anything else, the more they mocked and persecuted Him. Their loveless and rigid approach to the law earned them the respect of the people, not because of love or a sense of righteousness, but for fear of the consequences of disobedience. They were able to hide their own shortcomings behind the dubious cloak of authority and respectability.

As a Christian you have to be continuously on the alert not to succumb to the temptation to judge and criticize others. Always remember that there is not one person on earth who is fully righteous. Self-righteousness and loveless pride harm Christianity tremendously because it lacks the most basic ingredients of your faith: love and compassion.

Therefore, make the love and compassion of Jesus Christ the main ingredients of your testimony so that you will never disappoint the Master. A world torn by sin will also benefit from it.

Loving Father, let me remember that Your love saved me and keep me from becoming legalistic and self-righteous. Amen.

Renewed Strength

But those who hope in the LORD will renew their strength. They will soar on wings like eagles; they will run and not grow weary, they will walk and not be faint (Isaiah 40:31).

We often use the excuse, "I am too busy! I don't have the time!" Busy with what? What is it that you don't have time for? When you sit down for a change to try and get your priorities right you will find that you are often kept busy by matters of minor importance. If you are too busy to spend time with the Lord, you are indeed too busy!

Greek mythology tells the story of Sisyphus, the proud and haughty king of Corinth. Because of his arrogance, Zeus decided to punish him severely. With his bare hands he had to roll a big marble rock to the top of a steep hill.

Every day at daybreak he started and towards sunset he had almost reached the summit – but in some mysterious way the rock always slipped from his hands and rolled back to the valley. The following day he would try again, but with the same disappointing result. In this way he aimlessly wasted his strength day after day.

The new, exciting and adventurous things in life had vanished. He became the slave of a monotonous routine. Every day he got out of bed with great effort and started the drudgery of his day before going to bed again filled with frustration. Day in and day out, year in and year out.

What is the solution to this get-up-go-to-work routine; this desire for renewal? There is only one answer: Christ!

Therefore, make time to get to this divine power station so that you can charge your life and ideals with enthusiasm and innovation every day. Wait on the Lord to give you wings like an eagle so that you can soar.

O Lord, please keep me from monotonous drudgery. Renew my strength through Your Holy Spirit and make my life a spiritual adventure. Amen.

Build Up Your Hidden Resources

The precepts of the Lord are right, giving joy to the heart (Psalm 19:8).

Superficial faith is exposed in times of crisis. When things go well your faith may prove to be exuberant and meaningful, but when things start going wrong, it crumbles. How is it possible to obtain faith that can survive disasters and adversities?

There is no instant formula for obtaining a dynamic, powerful, sustaining faith. It is the product of a life lived consistently close to the Lord; a life so submitted and dedicated to Him as the highest priority.

If we want our faith to grow to maturity we have to work at it. The Bible is an indispensable manual of instruction and inspiration for the Christian. Perhaps your circumstances prevent you from joining a Bible study group, but it should not keep you from learning verses from the Bible off by heart. If you allow them to accumulate in your heart and meditate on them, you will discover their true meaning in practice, in times of spiritual or temporary need and crisis.

Remember that the risen Christ is more than a theological statement: He is a living reality in your heart and life. Wherever you are, He is there – invisible, yet dynamically present. At times your daily tasks and duties will require your full attention – God is there too. Even when you disappoint Him, He remains your constant companion. Teach yourself to be consciously aware of the living presence of Christ and He will become a daily reality to you.

The Word of God, the Word that became flesh and the Holy Spirit build up your moral and spiritual strength and when you need it in difficult times, it will be available.

Good Shepherd, I use every opportunity to replenish my spiritual resources. Thank You for the assistance of Your Holy Spirit. Amen.

THE PEACE OF GOD

Every man will sit under his own vine and under his own fig tree, and no one will make them afraid, for the LORD Almighty has spoken (Micah 4:4).

People constantly complain that we are living in times of great insecurity and violence, and there is so much proof around us to validate this argument! All over the world there are unmistakable signs of violence, unrest and anarchy. Governments and leaders come and go; social unrest and poverty cause much worry and need. People ask, "What can we do about this? How will it all end?"

Two of God's greatest gifts to mankind are His love and peace. Jesus Christ came to live among us as the Prince of Peace. He is also God's incomparable Gift of love to the world. Through the ages these divine gifts were able to resist the onslaught of the Evil One, and have never been overcome by it.

Golgotha was Satan's most ardent effort to destroy God's love and peace. The worst thing Satan could do could not withstand our victorious and triumphant Christ. His love overcame the world and He once again brought peace into the heart of man.

Christ overcame death and He is alive! If you invite Him into your life, you will experience the peace of God that passes all understanding. Then you will also discover in a very special way that God's perfect love casts out all fear (see John 4:18).

May God grant this peace to you abundantly as an individual, to His church to our beloved country.

Lord, God of peace, please give us Your peace and Your love in these troubled times. Amen.

SEPTEMBER

THE BEAUTY OF CREATION

The earth is the LORD's, and everything in it, the world, and all who live in it; for He founded it upon the seas and established it upon the waters (Psalm 24:1-2).

Spring awakens in all its beauty after the dreariness of winter; hesitantly at first, but then in all its glory of color, luscious greenery and birdsong and involuntarily one becomes astonished by the beauty of God's Creation. What was dead and dull becomes an abundance of color. The birds that migrated during the winter months return and warm the hearts of all who want to listen to their joyful singing.

When you look around at that time of year, you cannot help but prayerfully sing the words of that immortal song, "How great Thou art!"

In a world where everybody seems intent on self-destruction; a world of violence and anarchy, pollution and extinction, the replacement of natural resources with artificial aids, spring arrives and hope flares up again. There is also a revival of faith. If you have any feelings at all, you cannot escape the inspiration that forces you to make your contribution towards conserving the beauty of nature, because it is part of your precious inheritance from our Creator.

Always remember that God assigned you to help preserve and protect this earth. He left it in your care. Therefore, look after it well, it is very precious and without the beauty of Creation, it would practically be impossible to live on this planet. The responsibility is yours. Practice your stewardship with responsibility, love and care.

Thank You, Lord, for countless blessings which are visible in nature all around me. Amen.

How Do You React to Life?

"I have come that they may have life, and have it to the full" (John 10:10).

People react differently to the various stresses and strains of life. Some people regard life as a never-ending struggle and become aggressive as a result. Others are indifferent and insensitive and accept what happens to them neither complaining nor being thankful. Most people react emotionally and are ruled by their feelings.

Your reaction to what happens in your life can either be a blessing or a curse. When something upsetting happens, you can sustain spiritual and emotional wounds that can have a devastating effect. On the other hand, with God's help, you can control your reactions and your faith while patience and endurance grow and become stronger. Resist reactions of self-pity, frustration, impatience, anger and other negative character traits.

People of different ages also react differently. It seems as if the younger generation manages to react with naive calm. Older people often react with remorse or depression. However, each individual has his own reaction towards life's experiences.

As a Christian you undoubtedly know that you were created in God's image and are therefore very precious to Him. If you maintain an intimate relationship with Him, you will be filled with humble self-confidence, be at peace with God and your fellow men while living in harmony with your inner self. By His grace you will have confidence and because you are spiritually balanced, you will have the strength to handle every situation in life through the wisdom and power of the Holy Spirit. Christ offers you an abundant life if only you would put all your trust in Him.

I praise You, most holy God, because I am able to cope with life through the power of Your Son and Your Spirit. Amen.

ENFOLDED BY HIS LOVE

Blessed is he whose transgressions are forgiven, whose sins are covered (Psalm 32:1).

Forgiveness of sin is necessary for a new spiritual life of growth and fruitfulness. Unforgiven sin is a very heavy burden to bear. Often people break down under its load and feel as if they cannot go one step further. This can cause both physical and mental illness. It can even lead to suicide.

Christ came to deliver us from sin. His birth was a deed of divine omnipotence. God sent His Son to be born on earth, to live and work among ordinary human beings, to die, to rise again and ascend to heaven – so that you and I could be saved from sin and enjoy the wonderful privilege of eternal life.

If you desire a life of rest and peace of mind, it is possible by acknowledging Jesus Christ as your Savior and Redeemer and by committing your life to Him unconditionally.

When you have done that, you need never feel ashamed to confess any sin that you have committed. In 1 John 1:9 we have His invitation to do just that, "If we confess our sins, He is faithful and just and will forgive us our sins and purify us from all unrighteousness." You, however, have to take the first step in this process.

If you know for sure that Jesus is eagerly waiting to forgive your sins and comfort you with His unfailing love, why don't you decide right now to go to Him with the burdens of your sin and your guilt? He will bring rest, peace of mind and tranquility into your life.

Have you noticed what is said in Psalm 32:10, "Many are the woes of the wicked, but the Lord's unfailing love surrounds the man who trusts in Him."

Just as I am, You are calling me: forgive, cleanse and free me Lord.
I rely on Your promise – O Lamb of God, I come! Amen.

CULTIVATE AN INNER LIFE

"Remain in Me, and I will remain in you. No branch can bear fruit by itself; it must remain in the vine. Neither can you bear fruit unless you remain in Me" (John 15:4).

Hard work in spring time holds the promise of a rich harvest in summer. Cultivating a dynamic inner life is imperative if you wish to become mature in Christ. To really know Him is the most rewarding experience of your life. People may experience it differently but getting to know God is undoubtedly a reality.

Unfortunately there are those people who boast about their spiritual maturity. They have sadly lost touch with the reality of life the way it is experienced every day by "ordinary" people. In their efforts to take hold of the hand of God, they let go of life's realities altogether. When this happens, their faith repels those who do not know God because they regard these people as haughty and loveless.

The life of Jesus Christ on earth was characterized by a great love and true concern for the most humble person. In this He was very practical: He not only taught deep spiritual truths, but also took care of people's physical needs. He taught His followers that it is impossible to love God without loving your neighbor and that love is not real unless you give of yourself, serving those you love.

Along the path of spiritual growth there needs to be the practical expression of inspired service. What value does your spirituality have for God or your fellow man if it is not coupled with the practical expression of love? Reflect your love for Christ in creative service so that ordinary men and women will praise God that you are a living branch grafted onto the True Vine!

Lord, let Your beauty fill my life so that it becomes a reflection of Your love. Amen.

A DESIRE TO GROW SPIRITUALLY

For He satisfies the thirsty and fills the hungry with good things
(Psalm 107:9).

A feeling of spiritual discontent can be a blessing in disguise. It is only when a person becomes discontented with himself that he can or wants to improve. Only then can he become the person God intended him to be.

Spiritual discontent can lead to a greater understanding of God as well as a more intimate relationship with Him. You might have been satisfied with your spiritual state for a long time, but now something has happened to make you aware of the poor state of your spiritual life.

You suddenly become deeply aware of a desire for a more realistic experience with God. There is a deep hunger in your heart to know God more intimately and your eyes are opened to your spiritual needs.

When you become aware of this desire, it is your responsibility to do something about it. God has already done everything possible from His side by giving Himself in the person of Jesus Christ.

The first step to satisfy your spiritual hunger and to set your spirit free is to return to the basic elements of your faith. You have to set aside all the unnecessary frills that suffocate your faith or force you into a rut. When you do that, you regain a simple childlike faith in Christ.

When He is the source of your life, your spirit is nourished and you become inspired by a divine power that knows no spiritual hunger or thirst. "I am the Bread of Life. He who comes to Me will never go hungry, and he who believes in Me will never be thirsty" (John 6:35).

Source of abundance, I praise Your name because You satisfy my hunger and thirst daily through Jesus Christ, my living Redeemer. Amen.

SPIRITUAL GREATNESS

"Put out into deep water, and let down the nets for a catch" (Luke 5:4).

Perhaps you have been wading in shallow spiritual waters for too long. Perhaps you have been fulfilling your spiritual responsibilities carelessly. Although you might have been satisfied to a certain extent, you instinctively knew that there was more to Christianity than what you were experiencing.

The fundamental truth of the matter is that the strength of your faith depends on the quality of your commitment to Christ. If Christ is merely a side issue in your life instead of the motivating force, you must expect your faith to be weak and insufficient.

Christ has done everything possible for you. He came to earth to reveal God to us. He suffered and died on the cross for us. After His resurrection and ascension, He gave His Spirit to all who accept and love Him. He makes sure that His living presence is with us at all times. There was nothing more that He could do.

How does your life, your faith and the quality of your commitment compare with these biblical truths? The answer does not depend on the master, but entirely on you.

If you are feeling spiritually dissatisfied and are longing for a deeper, more realistic relationship with God, simply turn to Him in simple, remorseful confession and faith.

Confess your spiritual lethargy and your neglect of the things of God. Commit yourself unconditionally to Him. He is waiting with arms wide open to receive you. It is wonderful to live and work for God, while being nourished from the depths of His love and grace.

O Spirit of God, fan the flame of my love and faith into a mighty fire so that I may live to the glory of my Savior. Amen.

YOUR TRUE SELF

"Flesh gives birth to flesh, but the Spirit gives birth to spirit" (John 3:6).

A person's physical birth is an irrefutable fact. Without being born you would not have existed and while on earth, you are very much aware of the fact that you are alive. Because physical existence can be seen and managed every effort is made to make it as attractive as possible. Money, time and energy are spent on taking care of all our physical needs. People without a spiritual awareness make this the object of their lives.

In these cases the human spirit is neglected and even ignored. Some people even deny the existence of the spirit and focus all their energy on what can be seen and felt.

Jesus made a statement regarding this in John 6:63, "The Spirit gives life, the flesh counts for nothing." If a person's spirit is strong and healthy, it will be revealed in his body; if the spirit is attractive, it will be reflected in the body – even if that person is not physically very attractive. In the final analysis it is the quality of one's spirit that radiates from the body, and nothing can conceal that.

Christ teaches us that man's spirit should be top priority and He promises His disciples His indwelling Spirit to assist them in this. To allow the Spirit of Christ to dwell in you is an experience that will change your life. It is like being born again (see John 3).

Your values change completely; you become spiritually sensitive; your relationships with people change; God becomes a living reality – and you become what God intended you to be. Your true self!

Renew my heart, Lord, to suit Your requirements. Transform me so that I can achieve Your goal for my life. Amen.

Rock of Ages, Cleft for Me!

The Lord is my rock, my fortress and my deliverer; my God is my rock, in whom I take refuge (Psalm 18:2).

Every person needs a safe haven. It may be the security of your own home or just a simple shelter against wind and rain. During times of war refuge is sought from enemy bombings. In times of social unrest, people hide from their assailants.

Bombs, natural disasters and other dangerous situations are, however, not restricted to our physical existence. The truth is that our spirits and minds are more often the targets of life's storms. To find refuge from this and to prevent emotional wounds, we need a refuge that is steadfast and safe so that we can run to it, totally confident that we will be safe there.

In spite of what is happening in your life, regardless of the seriousness of your present situation, place your confidence in the Almighty God through faith in Christ Jesus at all times. Even when everything seems to be lost and it feels as if your whole world is falling apart, put yourself in the loving care of the Lord Jesus Christ.

God promised never to leave you nor forsake you (see Heb. 13:5-6). Christ promised to be with you always until the end of time (see Matt. 28:20). With this assurance you can face life confidently because the Holy Spirit will guide you into all truth (see John 16:13). You have an invincible refuge where you can take shelter. Praise the Lord, O my soul!

Rock of ages, cleft for me, I hide in You, my refuge and shelter. Amen.

WE BELIEVE WITHOUT SEEING

Therefore we are always confident. We live by faith, not by sight
(2 Corinthians 5:6-7).

When you struggle with problems, difficulties and disappointments, or when you have to make crucial decisions, do you trust God to the extent that you are willing to put your life unconditionally in His hands? Are you absolutely confident that whatever He allows to happen to you will work out for your good? Or are you struggling ahead in your own strength until you feel totally defeated?

Jesus Christ came to confirm that God loves you without a shadow of doubt. Nobody can argue about His care, help and compassion for you. You are precious in His sight!

If this is true, then it is also true that Christ will not allow anything to happen that could hurt you. On the contrary, He wants only what is best for you. When you have this assurance in your heart, you cannot do anything but trust God unconditionally in everything that you undertake.

To ensure that you have peace of mind, you have to place yourself, your plans and your problems in the hands of your Savior. Discuss your problems and secret fears with Him in prayer; talk to Him about the important decisions you have to make. Remember at all times that you are talking to someone who graciously calls you His friend.

You will experience the living presence of Christ in every situation of life. He will lead you through His Spirit and guide you to find rest and peace of mind. Even if you cannot see the way clearly, your faith will carry you through.

Heavenly Father, lead me every step of the way. Amen.

WHERE THERE IS WATER, THERE IS LIFE!

He turned the desert into pools of water and the parched ground into flowing springs (Psalm 107:35).

Water is absolutely crucial for survival. Man, plants and animals suffering from drought will pine away and eventually die. The severe droughts that have been experienced in many parts of the world are living proof of this fact. Water is crucial to man's prosperity and survival.

Your spiritual life can suffer in the same way, unless you drink of the water that Jesus offers you. There is no human substitute for that. Christ offers you something which only God can give, and through that He changes the barren desert of your life into a fertile paradise and the burning sand into bubbling springs – an unmistakable sign that God has touched your life.

If you want your life to have purpose and meaning, take deep draughts from the fountain of living water that Christ offers you, "Whoever drinks the water I give him will never thirst" (John 4:14).

Get to know Christ through the revelation of His character in Scripture; through the dedication of your life to Him; through daily conversation with Him in prayer and by submitting yourself to His authority.

Keep in touch with the Source through prayer and meditation. Then you will grow spiritually. He invites you, "If anyone is thirsty, let him come to Me and drink" (John 7:37). Where there is water, there is life!

My soul thirsts after You, O God. Thank You for the life-giving water in Jesus Christ that quenches my thirst. Amen.

THE GREATEST TEST OF CHRISTIANITY

Whoever claims to live in Him must walk as Jesus did (1 John 2:6).

Today people are probably talking more about their faith than at any other point in time. It is common to hear someone publicly delivering his personal testimony, or confessing that he is a born-again child of the Lord. People are questioned openly whether their lives are committed to Christ. Many people find it confusing, unless they understand what it means to be a Christian.

If you want to let the world know that your life belongs to Jesus Christ your Redeemer, words alone will never be enough – even though you speak in the tongue of an angel. You might possess a deep knowledge of the Bible, or have theological insight, yet it will only reveal that you are a person with good qualifications or great intellectual abilities.

In the eyes of the world, the final test of Christianity will depend on the way you express the qualities and character of Jesus in your everyday life. It will depend on your attitude and actions towards other people. If you look at your fellow men with the eyes of Jesus and if you love them with a love that is born of Christ, you will not need to prove anything. Jesus Christ will be revealed in everything you do and say.

Commit yourself fully to the grace of Christ, so that He can transform and renew you to His glory. In this the Holy Spirit is indispensable.

Perform only Your will in my life Lord, until my whole life is committed to You. Make my heart Your throne. Amen.

AGGRESSIVE CHRISTIANITY?

Be devoted to one another in brotherly love. Honor one another above yourselves (Romans 12:10).

Aggressive Christianity can do immeasurable harm and damage to the very cause that we have such a passion for. It is a sad fact that aggression in people can prevent others from experiencing the most wonderful, most inspiring power in the world. In some cases it actually makes a mockery of the Christian religion.

It is a tragedy that many well-meaning Christians try to force their faith on others in such a crude way, that they alienate those people instead of attracting them. They put sensitive people off in an attempt to enforce what they propagate. They do this without consulting the Holy Spirit for guidance or studying the methods that the Master used in treating the people.

Religion that is founded on a personal encounter with Jesus Christ is powerful. Man does not have to be presumptuous or aggressive to propagate these truths. They are, first and foremost, perceived in the lives of those who are controlled by the Spirit of Christ. Such faith results in love for your neighbor as well as respect and consideration for others and their viewpoints.

The quiet influence of a committed life that does not shy away from propagating the challenges, comfort and deliverance offered by Christ is more effective and lasting than that of someone who is always overbearing and aggressive.

Savior and Lord, help me to live in such a way that it will motivate others to love and respect You. Amen.

Prayer: Respiration of the Soul

Hear my prayer, O Lord; let my cry for help come to You (Psalm 102:1).

Many Christians regret the fact that they don't spend more time in prayer. They are intensely aware of the poor state of their quiet time and yet, when they seriously try to improve on it, they find their thoughts wandering, their spirit restless and few of their lofty intentions realized.

However, prayer is the most natural need of the human spirit. In the depths of your being there is a need that cannot be explained if God is left out of it. When you meditate on the purpose and mystery of life you can never find a meaningful answer without God.

Prayer is the heartbeat of the soul. You may probably not understand anything about the various theological schools of prayer, but every time you think of God, you feel a deep desire that you cannot explain or describe. That is your searching mind and hungry heart, reaching out to God in the most elementary form of prayer.

Though prescribed prayers and orthodox methods of prayer may help you enter into God's presence, it is the cry of distress from a broken spirit, often expressed in confusion and despair, that moves the heart of God.

Every time you call on the name of the Lord, He is already waiting to meet you. Every time your thoughts focus on Him, you are praying. Therefore, don't despair or become despondent if your prayers seem to be insufficient and ineffective. Every thought about God is a prayer that unites you with a compassionate Father who wants to give you life. And in this life Christ is the source and prayer the breathing.

O Holy Spirit of God, I don't always know how or what I should pray. I praise You for conveying my unspoken prayers to the Father. Amen.

TRUE GODLINESS

Create in me a pure heart, O God, and renew a steadfast spirit within me (Psalm 51:10).

Many people have the wrong idea that godliness is something unattainable to the ordinary human being. For them it is a dignified lifestyle that is elevated above a normal way of life. Therefore, to be called pious, is not really complimentary. Piety is popularly associated with long-windedness, tedious prayers and strict discipline that is forced on you in order to prepare you for heaven – while in the meantime you are of no earthly use!

However, acquiring godliness involves much more than strict obedience to religious laws that are adhered to only by those who have the time and desire to apply them.

True godliness means opening up your life to the Holy Spirit and allowing Him to express Himself through your life. It involves asking Christ to come into your life and to take full control. When you become conscious of His indwelling presence, you start experiencing a feeling of tremendous liberty and relief. He grants you freedom and a new appreciation of the real essence of life when you confess your sins.

Godliness asks total commitment to the will of God and total dedication of spirit, soul and body in obedience to Christ. True godliness can only be experienced if you have the assurance that God has forgiven all your sins and that you are serving Him with a pure heart, guided by the indwelling Holy Spirit. Then godliness unconsciously becomes your most precious possession.

Holy God, please grant me the faith that will make my piety true and real. Amen.

THE MASTER POTTER

"You must follow Me" (John 21:22).

It will be worthwhile to meditate today on the marvelous way in which the Master Potter changed the life of Peter!

Outwardly Peter was a great success. He was well-built, had a sound knowledge of the sea and fishing, and had great influence amongst the fishermen of Capernaum.

But in the school of the Master he had to learn that inner strength was of greater importance than physical power; if inner life failed, no physical strength could help.

Peter also had to learn that the knowledge he thought he possessed was restricted to one area and that he could not fix his own broken life in the way that he fixed torn fishing nets. Only the great Artist of Life could mend his life. His leadership qualities and pride had to be changed and he had to learn to wash others' feet. Peter used to be a leader but he had to become a follower.

Despite his great physical strength, Peter was actually a man of great inner weakness. When Christ mentioned pain, suffering and death, Peter recoiled. When he wanted to walk on the water, his faith deserted him and the Lord had to save him. Then at the gate of Gethsemane he fled with the other disciples and to crown it all, he denied Jesus three times.

Therefore, take courage poor sinner! God anticipated great possibilities for Peter. After confessing his love for the Lord Jesus he received the command, "Follow Me." Hesitantly, but obediently, he started walking the path of true discipleship. Peter obeyed His marching orders, fulfilling God's purpose for his life. What about you and me? How are we going to react?

Thank You, gracious Lord, that You are holding my hand. I will follow willingly and prayerfully through the guidance of Your Holy Spirit. Amen.

GROWTH THROUGH PAIN

"I will refine them like silver and test them like gold. They will call on My name and I will answer them" (Zechariah 13:9).

The same fire that consumes coal also refines gold. Both are minerals, but gold has certain qualities that are not found in coal and that make gold more precious than coal.

People who go through the fiery furnace of testing react differently from one another. Those who trust the Lord steadfastly and unconditionally are refined and strengthened. They receive grace to accept and handle the emotional demands that are made on them. Those people who do not trust God are consumed by bitterness and rebellion.

Believers who go through God's fire with dignity are strengthened and their characters are molded according to the will of God and eventually they experience victory. The people who doubt experience confusion and depression and head for total destruction. Testing from God will never harm us unless we become callous, bitter or skeptical.

How you react to tragedies and trials in your life is vitally important. Some blame God and turn away from Him. Others draw closer to God and accept the full measure of His comfort and grace. When we become angry, frustrated and bitter, we are only wounding our own hearts. When we pursue His love in prayer, the pain is relieved, the wounds healed and we grow in joy and acceptance. Then gold flows from the fiery furnace.

For those who love and trust God, times of trials and testing become times of purification and growth with spiritual maturity as a result.

May the testing that I go through draw me closer to You, O Heavenly Melter, so that I can reflect the image of Christ in my life. Amen.

Prayer Cultivates Insight

If any of you lacks wisdom, he should ask God who gives generously to all without finding fault (James 1:5).

Some people regard prayer as a spiritual exercise required only by those who either doubt their own abilities or don't have the courage to accept the challenges of life.

It is true that God gives confidence to those who lack it and that He helps the helpless. True prayer, however, is much more than pressing the emergency button when we find ourselves with our backs to the wall.

Prayer provides a rich blessing for those who make it an essential part of their daily lives. To wait patiently and quietly in the presence of God makes it possible for us to experience something of His Holy Spirit. Then, instead of displaying our wish-list before God, our times of prayer become periods during which we restore our equilibrium and receive strength, wisdom and peace.

When we look at life through the eyes of prayer, it takes on a whole new dimension. Instead of judging situations hurriedly and shortsighted, we calmly start understanding God's plan for our lives more clearly.

It is an undeniable fact that God provides clear guidance to those who turn to Him in prayer when they listen to what He tells them through His Holy Spirit. Whether in doubt or confusion, insecurity or fear – the person who prays receives wisdom and insight from God. This in turn cultivates a certainty concerning God's love for us and insight into life with all its challenges. God is the Source of all love and if you don't approach Him regularly, you will never be able to understand the essence of life.

Holy Father, let Your Spirit guide me into all truth about myself. Thank You for the gift of prayer to assist me in this. Amen.

PEACE AND QUIET AMIDST THE STORM

In repentance and rest is your salvation, in quietness and trust is your strength (Isaiah 30:15).

One especially gets to know God in silence. In the midst of the deafening noise that characterizes our times, it is good to remember this. The rushing madness of modern life contributes little towards an emotional equilibrium. Appointments, agendas and scores of other activities determine the quality of our lives that make it increasingly difficult to become still.

This agitating hustle and bustle has probably also invaded our spiritual activities in varying degrees. We become too busy to worship, for fellowship with other believers, to read the Bible and too busy to spend time in prayer. Being too busy will eventually threaten our spiritual growth causing it to become totally meaningless. The faster we run, the more overwhelmed and impoverished we become. Then our spiritual lives deteriorate and our relationship with the Lord, the Source of our strength, weakens.

In these circumstances, remember that with God there is always a place of peace and calm. There you can be alone, yet never lonely because He is there! The wonder of His grace is that He is already waiting for us to draw near to Him, to fill us with renewed strength if life's burdens become too heavy, to regenerate us to meet all the demands of life in His glorious name.

In this also, Christ was our Perfect Example. In spite of His very full schedule, He regularly made time to spend with His Father – even if it had to be in the still of the night. That was the reason why He could handle His workload calmly and in a balanced way.

Good Shepherd, bring me to the quietness of green pastures and waters of rest to draw strength from You and meet the demands of life. Amen.

THE BLESSINGS OF A GRATEFUL HEART

"He who sacrifices thank offerings honors Me" (Psalm 50:23).

There are many people who complain incessantly. Sometimes their complaints are valid, but often they complain merely because they are dissatisfied with life. Constant complaining can become a lifestyle. Eventually you forget that there are more things to be grateful for than to complain about. If you are currently complaining more often than expressing gratitude, you are living an inferior life.

It is impossible to have a grateful heart without also possessing an appreciative spirit. Such a spirit makes getting along with others easier and more rewarding while it deepens your understanding of life and makes those who live and work with you happier as well. Never let a day go by without consciously expressing your gratitude.

Open your eyes to what is beautiful around you and praise God for what you see or experience. Such an attitude not only enriches your life but also adds joy and satisfaction to it. God's treasures are then at your disposal because praise and thanksgiving are the keys to God's storehouse of treasures.

It is very difficult, almost impossible, to find someone who praises and thanks God constantly yet remains depressed. Human experience has proved over and over again that when you start thanking God for His gifts of grace, He is already planning the next blessing for you.

If you concentrate on practicing the art of praise and thanksgiving, you have discovered the secret of a creative, inspired life.

Praise the LORD, O my soul; all my inmost being, praise His holy name (Ps. 103:1). Amen.

GROWTH IN CHRIST

I pray that out of His glorious riches He may strengthen you with power through His Spirit in your inner being (Ephesians 3:16).

We live in a world of instant needs and instant solutions. Instant food, instant cash and many other items must be produced instantly otherwise they lose their value. Those things that have true value for man cannot be conjured up instantly with a magic wand. Trees grow tall and strong because they do so slowly and purposefully.

When you decided to follow Christ, you entered into a new relationship with the Father. You knew your sins were forgiven and that the Holy Spirit was now living in you. Yet even at that point you knew that you had a long way to go before you would be the person God intended you to be. Although redemption is appropriated immediately, there is no such thing as instant holiness or godliness.

As a Christian disciple you are expected to grow so that you can become strong in Jesus Christ. Without this growth there is nothing but spiritual backsliding. It is possible to maintain an outward form of piety for some time, but the inner power and strength that are the signs of a dynamic spiritual life will eventually die.

Growing in Christ influences your life very positively. You approach life differently. Instead of judging others, you see their potential in Christ – what they can be once Christ takes control of their lives. Love becomes the motivational force in your life and you are delivered from pettiness and hatred.

Growing in Christ is an exciting daily experience that enriches your life in a meaningful way.

Dear Lord Jesus, keep the desire to grow constantly burning in my heart through the ministry of the Holy Spirit. Amen.

THE REVELATION OF GOD'S LOVE

Then some of the Pharisees and teachers of the law said to Him, "Teacher, we want to see a miraculous sign from You" (Matthew 12:38).

Many people are skeptical about the Christian faith. If a dying person is not healed miraculously, the very existence of God is questioned. God is blamed for wars, droughts and famine. He is held responsible for disasters everywhere. Often we hear people scornfully ask, "Why didn't God prevent that?" These people dramatically claim visible proof of God's love and concern. They will only believe if they have seen a crooked arm go straight, the cripple walk or the blind man see.

The whole world around us witnesses God's power to perform miracles every day. If it had not been for God's omnipotence and love, we would not have experienced the seasons – each with its own charm and beauty. Without God there would have been no trees, flowers, rain, sunshine or any beauty of nature.

Study the history of the human race and you will perceive God's grace and power. He blessed man with gifts of knowledge and art. He also gives you the faith that carries you through times of testing and trials. He heals you in times of sorrow. He gives tolerance, patience, understanding and love.

But much, much more than all this He gave you the greatest Gift – Jesus Christ (see 2 Cor. 9:15). His love was made visible in His Son, our Savior and Redeemer. Could man have asked for a greater miracle from God?

In the miracle of the love of Christ, my Lord, do I find You my God and King. Amen.

THE PRESENCE OF CHRIST

"And surely I am with you always, to the very end of the age" (Matthew 28:20).

There are people who speak of Christ in theological terms, and interpret His message on a social level. No matter how they try to explain Him, they cannot do Him justice unless they have a personal encounter with Him. It is impossible to speak of His saving grace if you don't know Him. It is also impossible to know Him and not develop a better understanding of life.

To some people, knowing Christ is a deep mystical experience. There are sincere, dedicated people who claim to have received a vision from the risen, glorified Savior. Because the average person hasn't had such extraordinary experiences, he feels that experiencing the living presence of God is only for a chosen few – not for him.

Experience has taught that the awareness of Christ's presence comes to those who have a personal relationship with Him. This takes time, commitment and spiritual discipline. It is true that Christ gives Himself to a person, but it is the person's responsibility to nurture the relationship. You can only experience His presence if you have accepted Him unconditionally as your Savior and constant Companion.

This intimacy does not minimize the reverence and awe that you have for Him. On the contrary, it increases your love so that every aspect of your life is in harmony with Him. Always bear Christ in your heart and mind and you will become wonderfully conscious of His constant presence in your life.

I praise You, Lord Jesus, that I may know You as a living reality in everyday life. Amen.

You Must Make a Choice

"He who is not with Me is against Me, and he who does not gather with Me scatters" (Matthew 12:30).

A person who refuses to take sides where Jesus is involved, has already chosen against Him. Scripture clearly indicates what Christ expects from His followers. He set the perfect example of what life for a Christian involves, and anything less is unacceptable to Him. During the time of Jesus' ministry on earth there were those who felt they could not meet His requirements. Yet He never forced them to submit to Him nor did He compromise to win them over.

Then there were those who decided to follow Him but disappointed Him at times. He loved them sufficiently to forgive them and offer them a second chance, but without ever lowering His standards.

Unfortunately it has become obvious through the years that many people – including prominent Christian leaders within the church – are trying to compromise with the world. Sometimes the compromise is only implied in order to be popular or acceptable to the world, but nevertheless, the lowering of Christ's standards is not rejected or despised as it should be.

Christ's command to you as His follower is to maintain the teachings and lifestyle that He exemplified. If you find yourself in a situation that is contrary to the life and teachings of our Lord, distance yourself from it. You may become most unpopular in social and business circles – and even in your church! Remember, however, it is your duty and privilege to please God and not people through your life and work.

Faithful Lord, please make me faithful in following Your example and obeying Your commands. Amen.

KNOW WHEN TO LET GO

David also said to Solomon his son, "Be strong and courageous, and do the work" (1 Chronicles 28:20).

The zeal and commitment displayed by some people is praiseworthy: the director of a company, the principal and the teacher, the brilliant surgeon, the Sunday school teacher, the football player and referee and many more. But there comes a time when it is absolutely crucial to stop and give other, younger people the opportunity to utilize their talents and abilities to the benefit of society.

The fact that you know your job is important is no guarantee that you are the only one who can fill that position – even if you do it with love and dedication. Some people cling to their positions far too long, refusing to accept the possibility that someone else could take their place. A reputation of excellent service is often nullified because jealously guarded a person's position for too long.

David received the grace to accept the fact that he would not be the one to build the temple (see 1 Chron. 28-29). In the first chapters God showed him that Solomon was the one to build the temple. There was no jealousy or resistance in David. Solomon must have appreciated this encouragement – not only because he was chosen to do this work for God, but to have David give him sound advice as well.

The Chinese say that when you think of yourself as indispensable, you should do the following: fill a bucket with water; put your arm into the water and then take it out again – the hole you left in the water is an indication of how much you will be missed. Through God's grace and guidance you will know when to step down.

Gracious Lord, please help me to be sensitive to the Holy Spirit so that I will know exactly when it is time for someone else to take over. Amen.

THE SPIRIT SETS FREE

"I will ask the Father and He will give you another Counselor to be with you for ever – the Spirit of truth" (John 14:16-17).

Freedom is a very popular word. Prisoners longingly think about it. Some who are under the impression that they are being oppressed make it a lifestyle – only to experience a different kind of oppression. Many people consider freedom as permission to do whatever they want to, and if anybody dares to disagree he is immediately branded as the "oppressor". Every form of discipline is rejected with intense bitterness.

True freedom, however, submits to the law and involves much, much more than any political or social aspirations. It is a spiritual experience that is expressed through moral obligations. You do what you know you have to do – not what you want to. You become what God expects you to be and not some image that you conjured up yourself.

You can only be truly free when you joyfully accept the responsibilities of being a child of God. To avoid your responsibilities means that you are actually confined in a self-made prison. Eventually you are tortured by feelings of reproach, insecurity and confusion.

Freedom is a relationship with life. When Christ Jesus becomes the Lord of your life, you experience the immense joy of being set free from your sins. Fear is replaced by faith, hatred by love and demoralizing attitudes and thoughts are replaced by freedom inspired by Christ. When He controls your life through His Holy Spirit, sin no longer has control over your mind or actions any more and you are free to love and serve God. Then your heritage becomes a reality and you take Jesus up on His promise in John 14:27 where He said, "Peace I leave with you."

Lord, I exult in the freedom that You bring into my life. My Redeemer and Friend, keep me from the bondage of sin. Amen.

GET OFF THE GRANDSTAND

"If anyone would come after Me, he must deny himself and take up his cross and follow Me" (Mark 8:34).

Paul had most probably often watched the Isthmus Games in Corinth. This was the precursor to the Olympic Games. He probably also looked on as unarmed Christians fought for their lives against wild animals in the Coliseum in Rome. While a few were fighting in the arena, thousands sat on the grandstand, cheering loudly.

In the same way many of us have become spectators on the sidelines of life. Thousands upon thousands are sitting on the grandstand while a handful are fighting courageously. Many people call themselves Christians, but never think of getting involved, or of sacrificing anything for their convictions. Often our priorities are wrong. When our Christian duties need to be weighed up against other things the demands of Christianity always come second.

And how do the spectators react when their team's achievements do not live up to their expectations? They are jeered and criticized. When someone in the arena puts a foot wrong, the tongues start wagging.

People who do things for God's Kingdom are certainly not perfect. Someone was once heard saying, "I've got nothing against Jesus Christ, but it's His ground staff that bothers me." We may not, however, remain neutral because we know that we are not perfect.

In this world a never-ending feud is raging between good and evil, right and wrong, truth and lie, light and darkness, life and death. That is why God's children dare not remain on the grandstand. Jesus Himself never remained neutral – even though it cost Him His life. He expects us to follow suit. Christianity involves dynamic action in life's arena!

Take my life O Lord, let it glorify You more and more. Amen.

DO NOT RESENT BUT LOVE

Do not repay evil with evil or insult with insult, but with blessing because to this you were called (1 Peter 3:9).

If someone causes you hurt or suffering, the natural human reaction is to take revenge. A Christian is expected to forgive and forget. It is human to harbor grievances or revenge until it causes total enmity or leads to broken relationships. In many instances it also creates warped personalities.

While suffering injustice or undeserved pain, it is not easy to turn the other cheek. Your natural reaction is self-protection and self-preservation. Forgiveness never even enters your mind when you bear a grudge or try to protect yourself from being hurt again by someone who has wronged you.

The outcome of such an attitude is a drawn-out feud while the relationship between the two people gradually deteriorates.

To obey the command of Christ Jesus and to forgive is never easy. But if the love of God can be discerned in your life, it is always possible. If you think that it is too much to ask of you, consider for a moment the wonderful blessings you experience because of Jesus' forgiveness. His love for you was so great that He took your place on the cross – in spite of your recurrent transgressions.

In the light of all this you dare not refuse to forgive others. If you refuse to forgive others, you are burning the very bridge that you have to cross to receive deliverance.

O Holy Spirit of God, please help me to rise above my own pettiness and to love my fellow man at all times. Amen.

PERPLEXED, BUT NOT DESPERATE

We are hard pressed on every side, but not crushed; perplexed, but not in despair; persecuted, but not abandoned; struck down, but not destroyed (2 Corinthians 4:8-9).

Sometimes the course of life is disturbed very suddenly when problems appear from nowhere. Nobody on earth is safeguarded against problems. Nowhere in the Scripture has God promised the Christian pilgrimage to be plain sailing.

While a ship is still anchored in the harbor, it is safe. However, ships cannot remain there. They have to go out to the open sea, weathering storms and dangers to deliver their cargo. It is when we go out in life that we should tackle problems courageously in faith.

When we approach our problems positively, we find that God uses them to motivate us to serve Him more effectively and to treat our fellow man with compassion.

When you go through a difficult time, don't break down or double up under the burden. Wait quietly on the Lord and determine through prayer whether He is trying to teach you something. Don't allow your problems to dominate your life. Do not become panic-stricken however bad things may seem. Remember, God is greater than any problem you could ever have.

Each problem and attack on your spirit differs. It might be very dramatic and unexpected, or it might be very subtle and almost unnoticed.

Without a living faith that enables you to triumph over your problems, the road will become impossibly steep. Faith in God's goodness and the certainty that He has a wonderful plan for your life will equip you to approach the future with hope and courage.

Heavenly Master, I praise You that nothing can separate me from the love of God that is in Christ Jesus my Lord. Amen.

LIFE IS BOTH SPIRITUAL AND PRACTICAL

I pray also that the eyes of your heart may be enlightened in order that you may know the hope to which He has called you, the riches of His glorious inheritance in the saints (Ephesians 1:18).

Many people have a very distorted idea of what it means to live a spiritual life. They think it refers to living in a mystical world that is totally detached from the realities of everyday life – that the practical things in life are to be ignored and forgotten; that all our energy is to be directed towards developing an ethereal way of living.

While our Lord was walking this earth His teachings were deeply spiritual, but at the same time essentially practical. It is impossible to draw a dividing line between what Jesus regarded as secular and what He regarded as spiritual. To Him every form of life, every thought, every deed, was an expression of His relationship with His Father in heaven. That is why those who are really God's children can also not divide their lives into two watertight compartments. Life on earth is practical, but we must give expression to the spiritual.

Faith that paralyses the mind to such an extent that the realities of this earth are of no value cannot be inspired by the Spirit of Christ. His Spirit sharpens the mind and makes it alert to God's divine will.

The highly regarded Swedish doctor and writer Paul Tournier wrote, "I wait for God to renew and stimulate my mind to such an extent that I become creative instead of being the clanging cymbal that Paul speaks of."

The spiritual expression of life always involves reality and enables you to a certain extent to look at people's problems the way God does. In this way practical and spiritual issues merge while life becomes balanced and whole.

My Lord and my Example, I praise You for the privilege that I may express my spiritual life daily to Your glory. Amen.

GOD IS FAITHFUL

What if some did not have faith? Will their lack of faith nullify God's faithfulness? (Romans 3:3).

Let us end this month with the wonderful and comforting truth: God *is* faithful. When you trusted someone and he disappointed you, you feel deeply hurt and disillusioned.

You probably then also declared publicly that you would never trust anybody again. At the time you meant every word, but you can seldom persist, because our whole life is based on trust. Your family life, friendships, business associations and social relations, yes, even politics require an element of trust. Without trust society would fall apart.

Because man's nature is so fragile and unreliable, people are easily disappointed. Disappointing someone is not always intentional and sometimes it is unavoidable, but because of our imperfect and sinful nature, it is something we have to accept.

The only Unchangeable One in a changing world is God! He is forever the same. His promises in the Scripture are certain and unfailing. People have been confirming His faithfulness from time immemorial. Even though He did not always act according to their plans and desires, He did prove in His own, unique way that He is faithful and true. He brings His plans to pass in the lives of those who trust Him unconditionally.

God expects your unqualified trust. When clouds of doubt and sorrow threaten and when it seems as if everybody has disappointed you, then hold on tightly to God's trustworthiness. The clouds will disappear and you will be able to rejoice in God's faithfulness once more.

My Lord and my God, I may not always understand everything, but I trust You unconditionally. Amen.

OCTOBER

THE OMNIPRESENT CHRIST

OCTOBER 1

Jesus Christ is the same yesterday and today and forever (Hebrews 13:8).

The image you have of Christ will determine the depth and quality of the faith that you have in Him. If you only think of Him as a good man who lived about two thousand years ago you will honor His memory.

If you regard Him as the most prominent religious Teacher of all time you will marvel at His wisdom. If you believe that He enables you to live a rich, meaningful life through His indwelling Spirit you will thank and praise Him and will try to glorify Him by the quality of your life.

You may only know Him as a good man, a wonderful Teacher, the One living in you through His indwelling Spirit, yet there is another aspect which reveals His magnificence: He is eternal. He says of Himself in John 10:30, "I and the Father are one," and in John 8:58, "Before Abraham was born, I am!" The living Christ is the Eternal Being who came to earth to reveal God in human form.

This amazing truth is actually too sublime for the human mind to grasp. It would have remained this way if it had not been for Christ's wonderful simplicity. He did not make His entry into this world accompanied by hosts of angels – no, He was a baby in a manger. He became a carpenter who made friends with fishermen and tax collectors. Yet His eternal nature is not obscure to the sensitive follower who is willing to accept His divine authority.

And as He was with those people in His eternal image, so He is with you today. At the beginning of a new month, this is a source of great comfort. He is still the same, loving, healing, helping Lord, who gives Himself to all who seek Him and love Him.

Omnipresent Savior, I praise You for Your Spirit that dwells in me to teach, guide and comfort me. Amen.

FEELINGS OF GUILT

I write to you, dear children, because your sins have been forgiven
(1 John 2:12).

Many people lead negative, miserable lives because they allow feelings of guilt to oppress and wear them down until they break. Things that happened in the past still embarrass them. Perhaps they gravely disappointed some-one and it still lies on their conscience. There are many examples, but the outcome is always the same – a destructive feeling of guilt.

Scripture tells us very clearly that we are all sinners and that Jesus came to save us. It was an act of grace that culminated in His crucifixion on Golgotha where the Son of God sacrificed His life so that we could be forgiven and redeemed from sin.

If you are constantly haunted by guilt it is an indication that you find it difficult, even perhaps impossible, to accept that Christ died for you. Your attitude then borders on a denial of the foundation of the Christian faith.

Liberate yourself from the chains of guilt and self-condemnation. Turn to Christ in heartfelt remorse and true confession. Accept His redeeming love and grace with a grateful heart. That will enable you to live life to the full as a liberated person. Make the following your sincere prayer:

Emptied of all except my sin, I cling to Your redemptive work.
I pray for forgiveness because You took my guilt upon You!
Lord, You who are the Rock that was cleft for me,
please cleanse and purify me.

Thank You, Lord and Savior, that I can live life to the full, knowing that You have forgiven my sins and enable me to live according to Your will. Amen.

Jesus Transforms Anxiety into Joy

OCTOBER 3

In this you greatly rejoice, though now for a little while you may have had to suffer grief in all kinds of trials. These have come so that your faith may be proved genuine (1 Peter 1:6, 7).

There are times in life when everything seems empty, dismal and dreary. Your business may not be going according to plan; there may be much tension within your family; sickness, loneliness or the death of a loved one may be the cause of the deep sorrow you are suffering.

The good news of the Christian faith is that you are never alone in sadness, sorrow and suffering. Whatever the circumstances never forget Paul's encouraging words, "I consider that our present sufferings are not worth comparing with the glory that will be revealed in us" (Rom. 8:18).

There is one condition – you must believe that Christ is your Savior and fully trust in Him. Then you have the glorious assurance that you need never struggle with your problems and anxieties alone. He promised to be with you always – never to leave you nor forsake you. With the comforting assurance of this promise to support you, it is unavoidable that you turn to Christ as your Guide and Companion. Then the road you follow can never become too difficult.

If you adhere to this simple condition, you will experience the peace that surpasses all understanding. It will support you and keep you on your feet even under the most difficult circumstances. It is through the wonder of God's grace that you can already taste the joy of heaven on earth.

How often, O Lord, did You not turn my anxiety into joy! I will never be able to thank You enough for that! Amen.

PARENTAL RESPONSIBILITIES

He walked in the ways of his father Asa and did not stray from them; he did what was right in the eyes of the Lord (2 Chronicles 20:32).

Very often good or bad character traits can be traced back to parents who either stressed or ignored the Christian principles in the upbringing of their children.

This statement is verified by numerous examples in the Bible. Consider Jehoshaphat who was obedient to the teachings of his godly father Asa. He was also obedient to the will of God, taught people the law and sought God's guidance in establishing the administration of justice.

There are, however, also examples of parents who did not raise their children according to God's standards. The high priest Eli and his sons are examples. Although Eli was fully aware of the scandalous way in which his sons dishonored their office as priests, he never tried to stop them. The result was that Eli's office as priest was taken away from him and his sons died unnatural deaths.

To have a good start in life your family life should be founded on Christ's principles as set out in His Word. It is not enough to leave a child's spiritual development in the hands of the church. As a parent you are your child's role model and it is vitally important that you should live according to your Christian principles.

If you express Christian virtues verbally and through your actions; if prayer and worship as family form an integral part of your life; if Christ is a living reality in your home, then you have done much to set a standard which will help your children through life.

Jesus, Friend of children, please help me to raise my children in such a way that their lives will bring glory to Your name. Amen.

OCTOBER

4

LIVING CONFIDENTLY

OCTOBER 5

I have learned to be content whatever the circumstances. I know what it is to be in need, and I know what it is to have plenty (Philippians 4:11-12).

Some people are so timid that they allow themselves to be treated like slaves. Such people agree with any viewpoint and are afraid to voice their opinion. They prefer not to be noticed and lose confidence in God and in themselves. Their life becomes increasingly confusing and complicated because they are frantically trying to always please everybody around them.

As a follower of Jesus Christ there are powers at your disposal that enable you to tackle life positively and constructively. These powers can only be effective if you use them.

You have to accept the fact that dynamic discipleship is based on faith that finds expression in deeds – not on your feelings. Your emotions have to give way to your convictions. Confirm again and again that God loves you, even though you might be experiencing the darkest time of your life. Acknowledge His presence consciously, even though initially you may not be aware of it. As your thoughts are increasingly controlled by your obedience to Christ, your self-confidence will develop and grow strong.

If your life is based on your faith in Christ, your confidence will gradually increase and you will overcome feelings of inferiority. There will be nothing that you will not be able to handle through Christ's wisdom and power. Then you agree with Paul when he says, "I can do everything through Him who gives me strength" (Phil. 4:13).

I thank You, Lord Jesus, that I can start every day with confidence because You will give me strength. Amen.

SOMETHING TO GET EXCITED ABOUT

"Go, stand in the temple courts," he said, "and tell the people the full message of this new life" (Acts 5:20).

People love to talk! They enjoy reasoning about matters, have discussions and conferences, talk about other people or chat about matters of common interest. To communicate is a pleasant pastime and without it our lives would be less exciting.

Unfortunately there are many people who talk without thinking. Sometimes it causes serious misunderstandings. Words uttered carelessly can ruin friendships. It is very difficult to consider every word before you utter it because sometimes you don't have time to think before you speak. We all know how we regret saying something wrong or hurtful.

Your attitude towards life determines your words. They reveal the person you are deep down inside. If you are an embittered person, it will be impossible for you to keep up a pretence of unselfish love. Very soon your words will expose your true self.

A prerequisite for constructive, positive conversation is a spirit that is in harmony with the Holy Spirit. You will understand and forgive and will be sincerely interested in others. Such an attitude will make your conversations interesting and constructive. You will then express your love for Christ your Savior and you will know what the apostle meant in Acts 5:29, "We must obey God rather than men!"

Your testimony will cause joy and excitement for you and those who listen to you.

Holy Spirit, Teacher of the Truth, please make me excited about God's miracles so that I can testify enthusiastically to a lost world. Amen.

DIVINE HEART TRANSPLANTS

OCTOBER 7

"I will give you a new heart and put a new spirit in you; I will remove from you your heart of stone and give you a heart of flesh" (Ezekiel 36:26).

Dr. Chris Barnard performed the first heart transplant on Louis Washkansky on December 3 1967 in the Groote Schuur Hospital in Cape Town.

Receiving a new heart was already mentioned in Old Testament times. Since Jesus Christ came into the world, millions of people have received new hearts.

Mr. Washkansky lived for only eighteen days with his new heart, but those who undergo heavenly heart transplants will live forever.

Mr. Washkansky received a new heart because Miss Denise Darvall died in a car accident and was the donor. We receive new hearts because a Man aged 33 died on a rugged cross on Golgotha!

The medical profession dreamed of doing heart transplants for many years. But God longed to save man's sin-shattered heart from eternal death.

When performing a heart transplant not just any heart will do. Certain attributes and characteristics are required. Only the Son of God had the right qualities.

There is great joy when a sinner receives new life. All of heaven rejoices, the angels sing songs of praise and the heart of the Father is glad! The recipients of new hearts are immeasurably grateful towards the Donor who died so that we may live.

After eighteen days Mr. Washkansky's body rejected the new heart and he died. We can also reject Christ, the One who can heal broken hearts, but this would be disastrous and lead to eternal death.

Create in me a pure heart, O God, renew my spirit and make me steadfast in faith. Amen.

THE HOLY SPIRIT CREATES LIFE

That is why many among you are weak and sick, and a number of you have fallen asleep (1 Corinthians 11:30).

One often hears people complain that they belong to a church that is dead and has no vision. They feel empty and frustrated and they complain that they leave the worship services without having received anything worthwhile.

These people eventually drift away from the church and the congregation. Church members are decreasing in number and the church is losing its power. People ask why so many churches are empty.

The Christian can never become passive. Jesus expects dynamic action from His followers. You dare not remain on the sidelines, lounging in your comfy chair while criticizing the church. Every person has a function in the fellowship of believers. It may be administration, manual labor, pastoral care or spiritual leadership.

If you feel that you don't fit into any of these categories one other – perhaps the most important – option remains: prayer!

If you are serious about your faith, you will pray for the Holy Spirit to dwell in your life. Ask Him to assist you on your pilgrimage on earth. Be sensitive to His soft voice and instructions. Open up your heart and mind to His divine influence. He will not only lead you, but He will equip you to serve God effectively where He needs you the most.

When you obey the Spirit, you will experience new, vibrant life. Admitting the living Christ into your life will add a new dimension to your worship. When you start living for Christ, the church will be revived.

Create new life, Holy Spirit, and lead us to a place of worship. Amen.

A PRAYER FOR COUPLES

May the God of peace ... equip you with everything good for doing His will, and may He work in us what is pleasing to Him, through Jesus Christ (Hebrews 13:20-21).

James D. Freedman wrote a striking benediction for married couples that contains deep scriptural truths. Read and meditate on this paraphrase when you kneel together before God to pray for your marriage:

May you experience the ultimate excitement expected from matrimony. May life grant you patience, tolerance and understanding. May you always need each other – not so much to fill emptiness but rather to share completeness. For a mountain to be perfect, a valley is required. The valley does not make the mountain less of a mountain, but more so and in the process the valley becomes more perfect because of the mountain towering above it. Let it be the same with each of you.

May you need each other, but not because of weakness. May you desire each other, but not because of want. May you attract each other, yet never feel forced. May you hold each other, yet never feel imprisoned. May you achieve success in all the important ways, yet never disappoint each other with insignificant matters. May you look for something to praise in the other and often say, "I love you," without noticing the minor shortcomings. Should arguments force you apart, may you both have enough wisdom to take the first step towards reconciliation.

May you become conscious of each other's presence, physically as well as spiritually so that you can experience warmth and intimacy when you are close, and even when you are in separate rooms or cities. May you find abundant happiness and find it in making each other happy. May you know love and find it in loving each other.

Father God, Source of all love, bless our marriage with Your presence every day. Amen.

MAKE TODAY WONDERFUL

This is the day the LORD has made; let us rejoice and be glad in it (Psalm 118:24).

Regardless of how things may seem, you are greater than any circumstances or situation that you may find yourself in. You might doubt this truth and as a result your life will be filled with fear and insecurity and every new day will become an unbearable burden. You start the day more conscious of your heavy burdens than of the One who offered to bear them for you (see 1 Pet. 5:7).

Every new day is a unique gift to you from God. What you make of it is your responsibility. You may be influenced by your past and be filled with hope for the future. How you welcome each new day will depend on your mood and attitude towards life.

Fortunately as a Christian you don't have to leave your mood in the hands of fate or coincidence. You don't allow it to descend upon you without channeling it into a creative, constructive power. You were never meant to be the victim of changing emotions or fluctuating circumstances. God has given you the ability to determine your mood as well as the pace of your life. Therefore, you can live a happy, victorious life!

When you wake up in the morning it is important to start the day on a positive note by praising God for His presence and His goodness. Then you will approach the day with joy and expectation.

Father, I experience Your presence every moment of the day. Teach me to number my days in such a way that I will become wise. Amen.

THE GREATEST GIFTS OF ALL

O
C
T
O
B
E
R

11

There are different kinds of gifts, but the same Spirit. There are different kinds of service, but the same Lord (1 Corinthians 12:4-5).

The Christian faith finds expression in many ways. It changes people's lives radically; it alters attitudes; it brings healing for the sick; in more than one way it makes God a reality and it proves that the teachings of Jesus Christ are more than a neat philosophy – in short, it is a practical way of life.

Because you as a Christian love and serve the risen Lord, you may perhaps continually be looking for signs to confirm your faith. Perhaps you desire one of God's extraordinary gifts to be able to do mighty things in His name.

The gift of tongues, healing, teaching, performing miracles and discernment are but a few of God's fantastic gifts. You probably think that if you had only one of these gifts, you could reach the pinnacle of all spiritual experiences.

However, Paul calls upon us to strive for the most excellent gift (1 Cor. 12:31) when he says, "Now I will show you the most excellent way." Then he reveals to us that love is the greatest of all God's gifts. Therefore, we can say that the climax of all spiritual experiences is to love God above all else and to love our neighbor as ourselves. Whatever other gifts you may possess, if the love of God does not find expression in your life, they don't mean a thing.

Love changes ordinary things into something divine and causes the most humble gift of the Spirit to reveal the living Lord. That is our calling in this world.

Grant me, Lord, a greater awareness of Your love, so that my life may reflect Your glory every day. Amen.

THE RIGHT PERSPECTIVE ON SORROW

Those who sow in tears will reap with songs of joy. He who goes out weeping, carrying seed to sow, will return with songs of joy, carrying sheaves with him (Psalm 126:5-6).

If we are sure of the fact that we are children of God, we have the guarantee that no measure of sorrow or pain will break us. God does not expect us to not feel sad when the darkness of loss descends on us. On the contrary, Christ grieved at the grave of His friend Lazarus. God, however, expects us to see sadness and sorrow in perspective. "Brothers, we do not want you to ... grieve like the rest of the men, who have no hope" (1 Thess. 4:13).

God does not guarantee that His children will be exempt from suffering and loss. It is only in heaven that our tears will be dried. Nevertheless, God has repeatedly promised us His loving and comforting assistance.

In spite of our sadness, we have to confirm our faith in life. Faith is not an insurance policy against sorrow. Faith is the grace that God grants us to bear those sorrows. We never have to bear our pain alone. Christ gives us the strength to face any kind of disaster with dignity. All we have to ask is, "What can I do (and become) with this pain in my life?" Then yesterday's pain seems to fade and we need not fear tomorrow any more.

The most precious experiences in life are not found in times of superficial pleasure, but in the hour of our most painful sorrow. We see God much more clearly through tear-filled eyes than when we are experiencing elation.

That's why we experience sorrow and loss as a prelude to the better things in life. "I consider that our present sufferings are not worth comparing with the glory that will be revealed in us" (Rom. 8:18).

Dear Father You taught us to find strength in being quiet and in trusting You. Please give me strength in this dark hour. Amen.

GROWTH THROUGH FAITH

OCTOBER 13

"If a man remains in Me and I in him, he will bear much fruit; apart from Me you can do nothing" (John 15:5).

If your faith costs you nothing or does not demand anything from you, it is most probably weak and ineffective. To be satisfied with a superficial spiritual life is a sad indication of self-satisfaction and increasing worldliness. It is only through prayer, Bible study and meditation that you can create a new hunger to find and do the will of God in your life.

A Christian must hunger for spiritual food and continually desire to have a deeper experience with God through Jesus Christ. When a Christian stops growing it signals danger; it sounds the death-knell of spiritual progress. That is why Paul pleads with his readers, "I pray that out of His glorious riches He may strengthen you with power through His Spirit in your inner being" (Eph. 3:16).

It is true that God's gift in Christ Jesus is a free gift to all. We cannot beg, borrow, steal or earn it. Yet it does not exempt us from the responsibility to stay close to Him always and to do all we can to get to know Him better. Christ says emphatically, "Apart from Me you can do nothing" (John 15:5). Spiritual growth is an ongoing process to which we should dedicate ourselves wholeheartedly.

A living faith requires effort from our side and it is a real challenge to become like Jesus. However, Christ would not have required us to become like Him if it were impossible or unattainable.

He always meets us in our honest efforts and strengthens us through His Spirit. If you are a Spirit-filled follower, you will obediently follow wherever He leads. Your life will be elevated to a new level of spiritual power and joy.

Holy God, help me to abide in Christ so that I may grow consistently and bear abundant fruit. Amen.

YOUR GUIDE TO CHRIST

No one can say, "Jesus is Lord," except by the Holy Spirit (1 Corinthians 12:3).

There is no doubt that Jesus is King! Confirming that Jesus is King of your life is a testimony of your commitment and faithfulness to Him. It implies that you have submitted to Him unconditionally, that you trust Him without reservation, that you obey Him implicitly and that you live in faith.

Having Jesus as King of your life does not guarantee that you won't be tempted or experience failure. One moment you might be overjoyed at the quality of your relationship with Him and the next you might experience the scorching flame of fiery temptation. You will often be flung about between the two opposite poles of your sinful nature and the wonder of God's healing grace.

When Christ reigns in your life, He not only expects absolute loyalty and faithfulness, but He guarantees to live in you through His Holy Spirit. This knowledge is most humbling. He promises to dwell in us and to renew us, and to live and work through us to establish His sovereignty on earth. He is King, Lord and Master, but also Friend, Redeemer and Counselor – what grace! Indeed He said in John 15:14, "You are My friends if you do what I command."

This divine acceptance that follows your submission and dedication to God generates a steadfast assurance of His love and presence in your everyday life.

The Holy Spirit leads you to an increasing consciousness of God's presence and authority in your life. This glorious reality is the foundation of your life every day.

Holy Spirit of God, I praise You that You guided me to Christ and still guide me to His glory every day. Amen.

SERVING OTHERS

Love must be sincere. Hate what is evil; cling to what is good (Romans 12:9).

Sometimes we have a hidden and rather unflattering agenda when we do good to others. We all know people who selflessly do as much good to as many people as they possibly can. They play an important role in the community, and without them this world would definitely have been a worse place. The motive behind their kindheartedness is reflected in the quality of their good deeds.

Then there are those people who will only do good while they are inspired by applause and excessive gratitude. They only function while they are praised. As appreciation wanes, so does their enthusiasm.

Others serve their fellow men only to boost their own ego. The more committees they serve on, especially as chairperson, the more important they feel. If they fill an executive position, they are very impressed with themselves.

The benefactors, and even those whose hidden motives are to derive personal satisfaction should never be mocked. They do bring sunshine and light into the lives of others.

The Christian believer's only incentive for good deeds should be pure, honest Christian love – love for Christ and love for people. Because love is the motivation for Christian service, it is always constructive for both the receiver and the giver. Self-glorification is overcome by the desire to glorify God.

It is important to be guided by the Holy Spirit and to allow Him to work, serve and love through you if you want to experience the type of Christian love that finds expression in practical service. Only then do you render inspired service to your fellow men.

Merciful Master, may my service to my fellow man be totally motivated by Your divine love. Amen.

INNER CONFLICT

For what I do is not the good I want to do; no, the evil I do not want to do – this I keep on doing (Romans 7:19).

Everybody knows, to a greater or lesser extent, about the inner conflict caused by our "dual personality". There are times when you experience an overwhelming desire to live an honorable life without having to compromise. At such times spiritual values appeal to you in such a way that God's presence becomes a tangible reality in your life.

It is, however, possible that even while you are rejoicing in the certainty of your faith, your spiritual defenses weaken and spiritual pride starts undermining your faith. Eventually your spiritual fitness declines and all of a sudden the spiritual strength that you once had is just not there any longer. It also becomes increasingly difficult to maintain spiritual enthusiasm.

You know what is expected of you and what you have to do, but you are just not able to do it. Your weaker nature is in conflict with your mind and you become a slave to sin.

The constant battle between good and evil in your spirit can only result in victory if Christ is in total control of your life. If you are totally committed to Him and enjoy the assurance of His living presence, then His omnipotence is at your disposal and you become whole. Without the assistance of the Holy Spirit this is impossible.

Somebody once asked St. Francis of Assisi how it was possible for him to do so much for the Lord. He answered, "The Lord God looked down from heaven and asked, 'Where can I find the weakest and most insignificant person on earth?' Then God saw me and said, 'I'll work through him; he will never become proud because he will know that I'm using him because of his insignificance.'"

Gracious Lord, please heal me from my sin that, as Your child, I can be whole. Amen.

BE PATIENT

OCTOBER 17

For a thousand years in Your sight are like a day that has just gone by, or like a watch in the night (Psalm 90:4).

Hasty decisions made impulsively and impatiently are often regretted later on. Many people rush into ventures blindly – only to fail hopelessly. They decided on a certain action that proved to be wrong afterwards. Adversity and sorrow followed all because they acted in haste.

It requires discipline to accept God's will, to trust Him unconditionally and to submit to His will for your life. Yet this should be your attitude when you have to make an important decision. Many people maintain that the matters that they are involved in always need to be completed in a hurry and therefore they don't have the time to lay things before the Lord first.

Others again trust their own initiative and follow their own instincts. If this is your attitude it will be impossible for you to escape tension and worry. Neither will you ever be sure that the decision you make is right.

Jesus is the ultimate example of Someone who, in spite of a full life, trusted God the Father completely and waited on Him in everything He planned and did. He knew that in a demanding and fast-moving world, God's timing was always perfect. He is the only One who knows the future and who knows what is waiting for each one of us.

Place yourself and your plans for the future in the loving hands of God and then rest assured that you will not make the wrong decision. God knows what is best for you. Cultivate the Christian virtue of patience so that you can live within God's will for you and experience the joy of having peace of mind under all circumstances.

Lord, please protect me from making impulsive decisions. I trust You with my life and therefore also with my decisions. Amen.

An Illusion of Success

God said to him, "You fool! This very night your life will be demanded from you. Then who will get what you have prepared for yourself?" (Luke 12:20).

Success means different things to different people. Some regard success as the acquisition of social status and an accumulation of great riches and treasures. Others think success is building an empire out of nothing. Then there are those who define success as the complete expression of the personality and the development of hidden talents.

Depending on your viewpoint, you will try to achieve success in your own unique way. Yet no matter how honest your motives may be success is only achieved when every facet of your life is being completely satisfied.

Society evaluates us according to our achievements. Did you win or lose? Did your business show a profit or a loss? The most important question to ask is if your success measures up to God's standards of success. Can you honestly and truthfully say, "I have lived my life to the full and it has meaning and purpose?"

Many precious hours are wasted because people are under the illusion that riches, pleasure and status determine success. Real success is being able to stand before God with a pure heart knowing that in His name you have contributed positively towards the world that you live in.

The living Christ challenges you to return to your own true self by accepting Him as your Savior and Teacher. When He is the focal point in your life, everything else falls into place. Your faithfulness towards Him brings a type of success that is not only rewarding to you, but is also acceptable to your Lord and Master.

By serving and loving You, gracious Master, I find life rich and rewarding. Amen.

QUIETNESS AND TRUST

In repentance and rest is your salvation, in quietness and trust is your strength (Isaiah 30:15).

OCTOBER

19

We live in a world of increasing noise, unrest and tension. How should one manage the stress that involuntarily builds up inside you? Start with the past. We all need inner healing because tension normally has an awful history. Don't carry the past around like an unbearable burden. Christ has promised to make everything "new". He has also cast your past into the depths of the ocean.

Don't bottle up your feelings. Discuss your problems in a mature way with your spouse, a trusted friend or a pastoral counselor. If need be, don't hesitate to seek professional help. Beware of isolating yourself behind a wall of silence or bottled up anger.

Look for a haven of peace and tranquility for your spirit, a place where you can spend time with God and get a new perspective on life. You will feel the tension draining from your spirit. There are many channels through which you can unburden your soul: friendships, sport, poetry, music, literature, art and especially quiet times spent with God.

Let go and let God. Don't bang your head against the same wall all the time. Do not overestimate your own abilities. Hold on to God's glorious promises. It is when we don't know how to carry on that God steps in because He knows what is best (see Isa. 41:10).

Do not become despondent. Start doing something positive. Go out into the world and see the needs of others. It is then that your own needs fall into perspective.

Learn to live within your limits. Be honest with yourself. Share everything with God and He will give you peace.

Thank You, Lord, for the knowledge that in the midst of pressure that sometimes reaches hurricane strength, I can find a quiet place of rest. Amen.

In Christ's Company

They asked each other, "Were not our hearts burning within us while He talked with us on the road and opened the Scriptures to us?" (Luke 24:32).

You may be knowledgeable about the Christian message and intensely interested in Bible study – but it is only when you spend your days in the company of the living Christ that you become conscious of His divine presence and your faith becomes a wonderful reality and a creative power.

Nothing can compare with those quiet moments of fellowship that you spend alone with God. During those times you can give Him your undivided attention. Knowing that His Spirit desires a deeper unity with your spirit creates an inner strength.

As years go by, this fruitful and enriching experience becomes more and more precious and meaningful.

However, your whole life cannot be spent in seclusion with the Master. You have to make a living through your business, your trade or profession. Busy times that consume your energy will force you to cut short the time spent alone with Him.

If you have a meaningful encounter with God in those quiet moments, you will not find it difficult to concentrate on Him later, even during those very busy times of the day. Use the quiet moments in your day to become conscious of His presence and you will experience the unspeakable joy of being in His company all day long. Your heart will become strangely warm like the hearts of the two men on their way to Emmaus.

Help me, Lord Jesus, to utilize every moment to strengthen the bond between us. Amen.

CHEERFUL IN THE FACE OF ADVERSITY

OCTOBER 21

All the days of the oppressed are wretched, but a cheerful heart has a continual feast (Proverbs 15:15).

Paul was sitting in a cold cell of a Roman jail when he encouraged the Philippian Christians to be cheerful, "Rejoice in the Lord always. I will say it again: Rejoice!" (Phil. 4:4).

One of the most valuable gifts that the Holy Spirit has bestowed upon God's children is the gift of contagious gladness and joy. There are those who are convinced that joyfulness is the most important fruit of their faith. They even regard it as a denial of their faith if they become downhearted or depressed.

Yet even the Christian's life is subject to tides of ever-changing emotions. The life of our Lord is an excellent example of this as He also experienced the heights and depths of the spirit. It is impossible for a Christian to always smile and if he tries to do this, his appearance becomes false.

The joy that Christ brings into our lives is much more than just a smile. There are times when you would much rather cry. However, when we set our minds on Christ, a peaceful spirit is established and this generates real joy and gladness. You live in the assurance that God is in control even in the most confusing times of your life. This blessed assurance is worth more than a mere smile or passing emotions.

Christian joy does not depend on emotions, but on the unchanging Lord. That is why you can say:

When wild, wild storms were raging
I found a steadfast Rock deep down:
The Word that saved me from disaster –
God is my Father; I His child!

I praise and thank You, Lord my God, that I can live joyfully and trustingly because Your Spirit dwells in me. Amen.

Hang in There!

"I have told you these things, so that in Me you may have peace. In this world you will have trouble. But take heart! I have overcome the world" (John 16:33).

Perseverance, persistence, courage – these are anchors that we should grab hold of in the storms of life. At times we are flung to and fro by the waves of deep, deep emotions. But even in the worst storm, God has supplied a lifebelt: faith! Your tenacious spirit enables you to cling to that lifebelt. Even though the hope may be very slim at first it grows during each period of testing until by the grace of God, it becomes strong and powerful.

If you are looking for something to help you overcome the circumstances that are threatening to overwhelm you, if you are feeling restless and insecure today, then my advice to you is the same I would give to the drowning person: do not struggle or fight against the waves in your own strength. Just lay your life quietly in God's omnipotent, saving hands. That will give you peace amidst the storm and peace always creates power which is the starting point of courage and perseverance. Perseverance is courage without bitterness and long-suffering without pity.

If we gradually learn to accept our circumstances rather than rebel against them, we discover a new strength within ourselves. We also approach our problems differently. If on the other hand, we give our emotions free reign, it is easy to allow fear and doubt to move into our hearts. If we allow that, we hesitate and our newly found courage disappears.

Faith can be used as a bridge: faith in life, in yourself and especially in God. Decisiveness is a fruit of faith and it ignites the fire of perseverance to live victoriously!

Faithful Companion, thank You, that in the dark days of confusion, sorrow and doubt, You are always there to encourage me. Amen.

THE COURAGE OF YOUR CONVICTIONS

OCTOBER 23

It is written: "I believed; therefore I have spoken." With that same spirit of faith we also believe and therefore speak (2 Corinthians 4:13).

If people had really lived their lives according to what they confessed, the world would indeed have been a better place. There are many people whose lives contradict their confessions.

Our lives should complement our confessions of faith in a meaningful way otherwise we are destroying our own testimony.

Some people say that they believe in God, yet they always worry. Others again say they are members of a certain congregation, yet they seldom attend services. Then there are those who say they believe in the power of prayer; yet they never pray.

Superficial faith can never grow into a strong conviction. To be able to live a successful Christian life, there are certain convictions that you must regard as inviolable as life itself. A strong conviction does not mean that you are stubborn, narrow-minded or fanatical. What it does mean is that you hold on to Christian principles even when the winds of adversity and doubt rage around you.

What then are the basic principles of such a steadfast conviction? Basically every disciple of the Master should cling to the fact that, "God was reconciling the world to Himself in Christ" (2 Cor. 5:19).

This truth is non-negotiable to any Christian. It is the foundation of his faith, because it testifies of his submission to the divinity of Jesus Christ. If this message is your honest conviction, you will spread the news and convince others because your life will confirm your testimony.

Lord, my God, help me to have the courage of my convictions without becoming petty or fanatical. Amen.

JOB SATISFACTION

Whatever your hand finds to do, do it with all your might (Ecclesiastes 9:10).

Many people are inclined to bring a spirit of servility into their job situation. They drag themselves from one boring day to the next and hate every moment at work. They question the reason for working and even for living.

They are convinced that God is definitely not interested in them. From time to time they manage to escape from their slavery for a little while, usually during weekends or during their annual leave. The majority of their time is spent on a job they absolutely hate.

To be able to appreciate life, you must find joy in the little things you do. To spend your life stuck in a groove just to acquire riches, makes a mockery of the precious time that God has granted you. Unfortunately it is possible that you have been trapped in your current situation for so long that you cannot think of any other alternative.

If it is not possible for you to change your job, it is necessary to change your attitude towards your job. If you are rebellious or disapproving, your human relations will be tense and unhappy. In order to find a way out or to change your attitude, you have to free yourself from the power of tormenting emotions and start thinking and acting positively even in the most negative circumstances.

As a follower of Jesus Christ you will not be excused from performing unpleasant tasks. But because the Holy Spirit is at work in you, it will be possible for you to do so with pride and joy. Because you know and serve Christ, you can apply His principles at work as well. That is what makes the difference between monotonous servility and joyful commitment.

O Holy Spirit of God, through You I am able to complete even the most boring and menial task to Your glory. Amen.

THE TRUE MEANING OF LOVE

Keep on loving each other as brothers (Hebrews 13:1).

Love is one of the most misused and misunderstood words. Perhaps it is because we only have one word in our language to express the various kinds of love: love for God; erotic love; love for family; love among friends; love for a fellow man. Through the years the word has been used to describe various experiences and different objects. However, when you consider the bitterness, hatred and violence rampant in the world today, it becomes evident that man does not understand the meaning of love.

Jesus was unequivocal about this topic when He commanded us to love one another as He loves us. One does not need a very high level of intelligence or much effort to be able to describe or explain this because Jesus demonstrated the meaning of the word practically and very clearly in all His daily actions. He gave His life so that we could be saved from sin and its devastating effects. He Himself said, "Greater love has no one than this, that he lay down his life for his friends" (John 15:13).

Christian love presupposes tolerance and understanding. It implies compassion, grace and forgiveness and it requires that you rise above pettiness, pride and prejudice.

You have to reach out to others, showing them the same care and compassion that Christ has shown you. Finally it means that you will open up your life to the influence of the Holy Spirit so that Jesus Christ will become visible in your every thought, word and deed.

Is that asking too much of those who bear the name of Christ?

I really love You, O Lord. Help me to prove this practically in my everyday attitudes and actions towards those I meet. Amen.

CONSISTENT PRAYER

Pray continually (1 Thessalonians 5:17).

People have spent a lot of time studying the art of prayer in an effort to explain it to people. Numerous books have been written on the topic. Certain disciplinary measures are prescribed to capture wandering thoughts and bring them into prayerful submission. Some people have found these guidelines very helpful. To others they are a source of frustration because they cannot comply with them.

Whatever method you may be using to cultivate a meaningful and fruitful prayer life in order to have a purer and more profound relationship with God, be careful not to spoil spontaneous, unsophisticated communication between you and God. To have a set time for prayer is fine, but it should never become a deadly routine that causes you to complain, "It is time for me to go and pray – again!" Joy and power will disappear from your prayers. There will be no inspiration or enthusiasm and your prayers will become meaningless.

Purposeful prayer depends on your attitude towards God. Your longing to spend time with God is something that the Holy Spirit evokes. However, your fellowship with God can be just as real and vibrant in the monotony of everyday life as when you are with Him in private.

Make a habit of talking to God in a natural way – as you would to a good, trusted friend. Share your life with Him: Your joys and sorrows; your prosperity and disappointments; the good and the bad. Always ask God's support, help and guidance. Very soon prayer will become an inseparable and very natural part of your life. Then you will start understanding Paul's call to, "Pray without ceasing."

Thank You, God, that I am not restricted to time or place when it comes to praying. Thank You that I can pray anywhere. Amen.

GROWTH IN THE LATE AFTERNOON

They will still bear fruit in old age, they will stay fresh and green (Psalm 92:14).

In our day and age commerce, industry and technology have but one message: "It's a young person's world!" You are expected to be a manager at the age of thirty, a director at forty and when you are fifty you are considered too old for anything and you are pushed aside. In Scripture, however, there are numerous examples of encouragement for those over fifty that are substantiated by real life.

It is true that having turned fifty you should be able to offer a better quality of workmanship and expertise. This is so because experience has shaped your abilities into a fine art. You never need to be ashamed of the quality of your work. Quality achieved through tranquility and experience now distinguishes your work.

You also no longer find disappointment so traumatic. Experience has taught you that these things point the way to greater achievements. You do not get carried away by emotional zeal. You have come to realize that life is built with bricks of reality through hard work and not by raging emotions. You now have strength and understanding only obtainable through experiencing the battles of life.

You have also learnt to handle the adversities of life and to turn them into opportunities. Therefore, you are not so easily discouraged any more. You know that you have a contribution to make towards society because there is just no substitute for experience.

You have also learnt to trust God, because He has proved Himself faithful over so many years. He promises that those who live righteously will bear much fruit.

Thank You, heavenly Father, that You never reject those who get older but that You prove Yourself faithful to the very end. Amen.

ARE YOU A WORKAHOLIC?

In vain you rise early and stay up late, toiling for food to eat – for He grants sleep to those He loves (Psalm 127:2).

There are many people who are incurably addicted to their work. They may be involved either in spiritual or secular work but, due to a number of reasons, they allow their work to control every area of their lives. The inevitable result is that they have little or no time for their families or to relax.

The motive for their addiction, whether it be a desire for achievement, to establish security or to accumulate great riches is of little importance. The inevitable outcome will be a total breakdown in their health, disintegration of family life or a distorted outlook on life.

Yes, God expects the Christian to perform his daily task with dedication and in honesty and also to glorify Him. He also expects you to spend time away from your work, resting and relaxing so that you can return to your job refreshed and strengthened to reach your full potential.

This can only be achieved if you maintain a healthy balance between work and leisure. To be able to do this, Christ needs to be an inseparable part of your life. You must be sensitive to the voice of the Holy Spirit. Only then will you be able to give work and rest their rightful place in your daily routine, knowing that God will abundantly supply all your needs as long as you obey Him and organize your life according to His will.

Take a look at your life and make sure what it is you want from life and where you are heading.

Make me reliable in my daily tasks, O Lord. Let me follow Jesus' example, and make time to rest and become quiet before You. Amen.

HAPPINESS WITHIN YOURSELF

OCTOBER 29

Whoever gives heed to instruction prospers, and blessed is he who trusts in the LORD (Proverbs 16:20).

Happiness is an inner state. It originates in the heart and mind of the person who lives in harmony with God and finds fulfillment in serving others. Due to this elementary principle it is possible to experience constant happiness even under the most adverse circumstances.

If you want to experience real joy, your priorities must be in order. Unfortunately this is where many people are found wanting. In their search for happiness they think material things will provide happiness. Others feel they need the freedom of self-expression to ensure happiness.

Then they throw all forms of convention overboard and indulge in extravagance, only to discover that it leads to frustration and eventually to spiritual bankruptcy.

Then there are people whose addiction is to collect things. They find consolation in being surrounded by items they can count and handle. However, before they know it they have to admit that they don't possess these things, but are in fact possessed by them. Others have the philosophy that life was made especially for them and owes them something. They take from life whatever they possibly can. Unfortunately their selfishness and covetousness isolate them from others, while their self-centeredness causes their lives to end in immeasurable loneliness.

The happiness that people are striving for so desperately is only to be found in the life where God is in control. It requires the discipline of obedience to God's will. With this discipline and obedience comes an immeasurable, deep peace and joy which have their origin in total commitment. That is real joy!

Gracious God, thank You that I may enjoy the happiness which comes to those who really love, serve and obey You. Amen.

How Do I Discern God's Will?

"What shall I do, Lord?" I asked (Acts 22:10).

God no longer appears to us in the middle of the night to reveal His will like in Samuel's case. Neither does He send the angels from heaven with a message, or send letters falling from heaven to let us know what He expects from us. How can I possibly know what God's will is?

First of all your heart must be in a condition where it knows no will of its own in any matter. When we are willing to obey God's will, we have already solved nine-tenths of the problem. Once you have reached that stage, you are not very far from finding out what God wants you to do. You don't allow yourself to be led by your feelings or emotions because you know it is easy to be deceived.

Search the Scriptures to find God's will because the Spirit and the Word must work closely together in this process. If you listen only to the Spirit and disregard the Word, you are deceiving yourself. When the Holy Spirit leads and guides you, He always does so according to the Scripture and its basic principles – never contrary to this!

You must be sensitive to God's guidance in all circumstances, because He will sometimes show you the way in conjunction with the Word and the Spirit. Kneel down and ask God to reveal His perfect will to you. Through prayer and the study of God's Word, through meditation and the guidance of the Holy Spirit you will be able to make a decision which, to the best of your knowledge, will be God's will for you.

When you have peace of mind and heart, continue to pray. When the conviction grows that you are acting according to God's will, move forward in faith.

Father, thank You for enabling me to discern Your will through the Holy Spirit, Your Word and prayer. Make me willing to obey. Amen.

ACCEPT THE CHALLENGE

OCTOBER 31

"If anyone would come after Me, he must deny himself and take up his cross and follow Me" (Mark 8:34).

Let us conclude this month with the challenge in our Scripture verse for today. Life is filled with many challenges. You might hear a sermon that challenges you to a new life in Jesus Christ. A serious medical condition might challenge you to react in a certain way. There might be tension in the relationships within your circle of friends and you might feel challenged to intervene and restore harmony.

When you refuse to accept a challenge, you're actually turning your back on an opportunity to develop your intellectual and spiritual abilities. Accepting the challenge might have such far-reaching effects that you instinctively wish to turn away from it, convinced that it is far above your ability to do anything constructive about it. You should, however, always remember that God often reveals His will to us through challenges.

As a Christian you should never turn away from a challenge praying to the Lord. Seriously consider the situation in His presence. Be prepared for any idea that He might inspire you with and make sure that your spirit is sensitive to His guidance. When challenges are prayerfully considered, they can develop into glorious opportunities.

The joy of accepting a challenge and successfully completing it is a joy that must be earned. The one who persistently sidesteps the challenges in his life will never know the inner satisfaction derived from victory.

Don't be scared of challenges, they bring meaning and purpose to your life. Accept the challenge from the Master to take up and carry your cross, but always remember that He is there with you, carrying the heaviest load.

Holy Lord, give me the courage and the grace to handle every challenge that comes my way wisely and courageously. Amen.

NOVEMBER

How Do I Find God?

But if from there you seek the LORD your God, you will find Him if you look for Him with all your heart and with all your soul (Deuteronomy 4:29).

How often do we hear people complain that they find it difficult to establish an intimate relationship with God? They lack something in their lives because they feel that they have lost contact with the Master. They become spiritually despondent, their faith becomes weak and they stumble.

You must remember that your life as a Christian will have its ups and downs. To keep your faith consistent requires a special measure of self-discipline, self-control and persistence.

There will be times when you will desire to enter into God's presence during your quiet times, but will feel frustrated when your thoughts wander. Your attempts to work for the Lord where He needs you may be thwarted by obstacles over which you have no control. Keep in mind that disappointment and disillusionment are Satan's favorite weapons.

You should learn to turn to the Holy Spirit under all circumstances for help and support and for the grace you need to act according to the will of Jesus, your Redeemer.

An iron will and steely determination will enable you to become more and more conscious of God's presence in your life at all times!

This means that prayer is of primary importance in your honest search for God. When you invest your time and energy in serious prayer, the dividends are surprising and immeasurable. Put Him to the test.

Blessed Redeemer, I seek You with all my heart. Thank You for the gift of prayer! Amen.

FEAR OF GROWING OLD

We do not lose heart. Though outwardly we are wasting away, yet inwardly we are being renewed day by day (2 Corinthians 4:16).

Fear of growing old influences one's attitude towards life negatively and makes you grumpy. When you have reached the point where you no longer appreciate any beauty around you; when all humor has gone from your life; when friendship means very little to you because old friends have passed away, or if you are constantly dreading the fact that you are growing older – then indeed you are someone to be pitied. Meeting such people, or just hearing about them makes one sad.

An effective way to combat the ageing process is to develop an attitude of love. Aged people who have a youthful attitude towards life are people who are in love with life itself. They appreciate all friendliness shown to them and never regard it as their right. They have a grateful spirit and they keep in mind that old and young have different priorities and interests in life. Above all, they continually praise God for the gift of life.

However, one cannot deny the fact that advancing years leave their mark on a person's physical abilities and can restrict certain activities. As a disciple of Christ Jesus, it is imperative that your spirit should mature and become more like Christ. As you grow older, your gentleness, compassion and courtesy towards others should also increase. Then there will be no room for depression.

Growing older is unavoidable and when it is accepted as a gift from God, it becomes His finishing school in your life.

Thank You, dear Lord, for the wonderful privilege to be Your witness even in old age. Amen.

LIVE VICTORIOUSLY

I can do everything through Him who gives me strength (Philippians 4:13).

People react differently when confronted with problems, adversities or hardships. Many people seem to break down at the mere idea of hardship and they convince themselves that they will never be able to triumph over adversities. They will never admit that they are incapable of facing challenges, but always blame other people or circumstances for their failures.

On the other hand we find those people who are stimulated by challenges. When they have to face dark, difficult situations, it seems as if they have inner reserves to draw from to lead and support them. Thoughts of defeat, frustration or failure never even occur to them because they are constantly planning constructively for a better future.

A Christian should never complain because that will show a lack of confidence in the abilities of our heavenly Father. Regardless of how difficult or demoralizing the situation might seem; regardless of how ominous the depression or disappointment may be, always hold on to God's promise, "Never will I leave you; never will I forsake you" (Heb. 13:5).

The greater the threats in your life, the closer you should live to God. In the consciousness of His living presence you will understand what Paul meant when he said, "I can do everything through Him who gives me strength" (Phil. 4:13).

O Holy Spirit of God, teach me to trust You unconditionally so that I can live triumphantly in the midst of sorrow and discouragement. Amen.

Exam Time!

Then He said to him, "Follow Me" (John 21:19).

For three years Peter was enrolled in the school of the greatest Teacher of all times. While he was taking classes, he had to write a test every now and then. Some he failed miserably and others he scraped through.

He failed geography: the "rock" crumbled. He failed seamanship: he wasted time in shallow waters when he was supposed to be out in the deep-sea. He wanted to walk on the water but sank because of unbelief. He failed agriculture: he couldn't distinguish between wheat and chaff. He failed human relations: he followed his best Friend from afar and denied Him, thus siding with the enemy. He even failed theology, for when he had to grow spiritually, his Teacher had to reprimand him, "Get behind Me, Satan!" (Matt. 16:23).

But praise God, Peter passed the test of faithfulness because when everybody else wanted to desert Jesus, Peter asked, "Where else can we go?" He also passed the most difficult test of faith with his testimony, "You are the Christ, the Son of the living God." Then with tears of remorse and confession of guilt, Peter passed the important test of conversion.

For the final exam he had to answer one question only, "Simon son of John, do you truly love Me?" Jesus repeated the question three times and all three times Peter answered correctly.

He passed the examination of Christian discipleship with distinction and was ready to obey when Christ commanded, "Follow Me."

Gracious Teacher, thank You for the training I receive in Your classes of love. Keep me diligent. Amen.

DISCIPLESHIP REQUIRES DISCIPLINE

If anyone is in Christ, he is a new creation; the old has gone, the new has come! All this is from God (2 Corinthians 5:17-18).

There are people who want a religion to suit their personal lifestyle without requiring any sacrifice from them. They look for an "enlightened" church that demands little from them regarding their spiritual life. As a result these people never experience the impact of a vibrant faith.

For discipleship to be really effective, one should accept the challenge of discipline. You should be aware of the flaws in your character, acknowledge your guilt and failures and admit and confess your dependence on Christ.

Your whole life should bear testimony that the Spirit of Christ dwells in you. Acknowledging your helplessness and need then indicates the turning point in your pilgrimage.

When you feel incapable of complying with the demands set by the Master or that your spiritual life is falling apart, you need to share this with Him and ask His help. Nobody who honestly trusts the Master for help, has ever been disappointed.

To accept Christ's help involves the responsibility of voluntary discipline. It is important to place your spirit, soul and mind under the total control of the Holy Spirit. Your thoughts will become constructive and your character strong so that you can do the will of God eagerly.

Only then do you, as His disciple, answer to your high calling because you have taken your place in a new dispensation in Christ's Kingdom, under His sovereignty.

Holy Master, I praise You that You enable me through Your Holy Spirit, to submit myself to the discipline of Your loving will. Amen.

Do Not Be Afraid

The LORD is my light and my salvation – whom shall I fear? The LORD is the stronghold of my life – of whom shall I be afraid? (Psalm 27:1).

Fear is one of the most destructive forces at work in man's emotional life. It can blur your judgment, affect your intellectual abilities, create deep emotional stress and undermine your health. Many people, paralyzed by the power of fear, have found themselves saying and doing things that are not in keeping with their personalities at all. Under normal circumstances they would never even have considered thinking or saying certain things.

How you handle fear is mostly a personal decision. Jesus, however, invites you to come to Him with all your fears and problems. He offers you the relief and strength of His loving care. This invitation from the Lord is anything but meaningless.

While on earth, the Lord Jesus Christ experienced every conceivable human emotion. Everything He offers and promises you, is based on an intimate, first-hand knowledge of your deepest feelings and sorrows. He experienced it all in His own life here on earth.

When your time of testing comes; when fear threatens to overwhelm you and tear your life apart, when you want to flee in anguish from the blows of life, then it is time to remember the invitation Jesus offered and to react to it in faith and trust. He will lift the unbearable burden from your shoulders. Your path will be illuminated with the light of His love, and He will lead you into His land of peace of mind and tranquility. Remember, the Lord is your Light, your Savior and your Refuge!

Savior and Redeemer, thank You that You set me free from the power of fear. Amen.

WARFARE BEFORE VICTORY

Thanks be to God! He gives us the victory through our Lord Jesus Christ (1 Corinthians 15:57).

The Christian's life is often compared to warfare or battle. The battle between good and evil, right and wrong, light and darkness is part of the lives of each of God's children. To deny the existence of such conflict will not let it vanish. Evil with all its vile extensions is present for all to see.

Christians need not fear evil powers, provided they fight them in the name of Christ. Tragically many people, in the face of overwhelming temptation and struggle, attempt the battle in their own strength. It is therefore inevitable that they will suffer shameful defeat.

To be able to overcome the Evil One, it is important to call upon a power greater than yourself. Because your resources are insufficient it is imperative that you call upon the omnipotence of God and the protection of the living Christ. He has made His unlimited power available to every disciple who calls on Him in faith.

Accept this divine omnipotence in faith. When your struggle against the Evil One is at its most intense and you find your spiritual defenses weakening, then turn to the Lord, allowing an awareness of His living presence to possess you. Then Evil will let go of you and you will live in victory through the power of the Holy Spirit.

However, to "turn to Jesus" involves much more than the panicky welling up of emotions. It is an act of faith that enables you to testify triumphantly, "No, in all these things we are more than conquerors through Him who loved us" (Rom. 8:37). Without a spiritual battle there can be no victory.

By Your power and grace, holy Lord, even I am able to live triumphantly. Amen.

MAGNIFICENCE THROUGH PRAYER

After Job had prayed for his friends, the LORD made him prosperous again and gave him twice as much as he had before (Job 42:10).

It is not difficult to make enemies. All you need to do is say something wrong by mistake. It does not always pay to do an autopsy on a deceased friendship. However, to talk matters through with the honest intention of reviving such a friendship, is often successful. On the other hand, if this honest intention is lacking, such a conversation can make matters worse.

Nobody likes to make enemies and it is important to remember that there is always a possibility of transforming enmity into friendship. This is not easy because it requires someone with a humble and pure spirit to be able to forgive, forget and persist in sincerity. You will have to know how to handle false pride, avert secret fears and deal with the thoughtlessness of false friends.

Only somebody who stands strong in his faith in Jesus Christ is equipped to change enemies into friends. Some people keep the smoldering ashes of hostility glowing through their deeds, words and attitudes. It does not promote human relations or long-standing friendships.

One method of changing an enemy into a friend is to start praying sincerely. Many might find this a strange suggestion, but in actual fact it is the only way to form a constructive basis for friendship. Prayer changes your attitude towards people and events. When this has happened, half the battle is won.

Faithful Friend, teach me to live in You so that I will develop a forgiving spirit. Amen.

UNAVOIDABLE RESPONSIBILITY

So they are no longer two, but one. Therefore, what God has joined together, let man not separate (Matthew 19:6).

One of the tragic aspects of modern life is the insignificant value that many people attach to the sanctity of marriage. Unfaithfulness in marriage is regarded so lightly that it is accepted as the rule rather than the exception.

It also seems as if divorce is taking on endemic proportions. Then there are unmarried couples who live together as man and wife who are not willing to make a commitment to each other and even try to raise a family born out of wedlock.

There are a great number of people who propagate compromise and reduce marriage to a "piece of paper". This argument is without any foundation. Failure in marriage or refusing to enter into marriage can be ascribed to the fact that one or both parties refuse to accept responsibility.

No marriage can be permanent without the ongoing touch of God's grace. This enables marriage partners to make, and keep, seemingly super-human vows to each other and to God.

Remember that God instituted marriage and that is why it is holy. It is an inseparable union to which both husband and wife agree before God. They vow to live before Him in faithfulness, to build a family life and to handle life's problems and joys together as one. Refusal or failure to accept this reveals complete unwillingness to accept responsibility towards each other and towards God.

Do you find the road of matrimony hard? Get help from Jesus Christ who will strengthen and support you to do what is right in His eyes.

Lord of our marriage, give us grace to accept the responsibilities of married life and do what is right in Your eyes. Amen.

THE PURE SPIRIT OF PRAYER

Praise awaits You, O God, in Zion; to You our vows will be fulfilled. O You who hear prayer (Psalm 65:1-2).

Some people find prayer something dull that they feel they have to do. These people miss the real meaning and true purpose of prayer. If they happen to have the time they will quickly ask God to bless and keep them and their loved ones. Having done that they feel convinced that they have done their duty and then feverishly rush along life's hectic stream of activities.

This restricted use of the mighty weapon of prayer renders it powerless. Prayer is much more than a selfish S.O.S. or a wish-list presented to God. It is a dynamic action that can enrich every area of your life.

When you enter into God's presence, you should spontaneously praise Him, regardless of your emotional state. You should learn to focus on Him and praise Him with a grateful heart.

Joy and gratitude will then become a part of every aspect and situation in your life. You will stop complaining about all your problems and you will start considering the innumerable blessings to thank God for.

This attitude will make it easy for you to handle the difficult part of prayer: to pray for your enemies and to forgive those who trespass against you. It will bring about a new freedom and liberation in your prayers. You will become a disciple who cannot stop singing God's praises.

When all the obstacles have been overcome, the purifying power of the Holy Spirit can flow into your life, creating a powerful, meaningful life of prayer where you praise the Lord unceasingly.

Eternal Father, I praise You for teaching me to pray in a spirit of gratitude. You cause my heart to sing for joy. Amen.

RESIST TEMPTATION

Be self-controlled and alert. Your enemy the devil prowls around like a roaring lion for someone to devour (1 Peter 5:8).

Nobody is immune to temptation. Even Jesus experienced the subtle attacks of Satan's cunning lies. When temptation presents itself, it is always with great conviction and the promise of enrichment and satisfaction.

If you acknowledge and accept Christ's authority in your life, you are ensured of protection against temptation. While you are confronted with temptation, you become aware of warning lights that start flickering in your spirit. If you are wise you will heed these warnings and stop looking for reasons to give in to these harmful temptations.

If you are struggling with some very powerful temptations at the moment, there are a lot you can do to overcome it. You will find that the Bible is always a source of wisdom, power and inspiration. That is why you must get to know the Word in times free from temptation. Jesus used the Word to resist Satan every time he tried to tempt Him.

The highest authority you can appeal to for assistance against temptation is the name of Jesus Christ. When you experience those fiery temptations or find yourself in great need, just whisper His name. Power and tranquility will be given to your struggling spirit. Never underestimate the power of the name of Christ: Satan trembles at the mention of His name!

We also have the Holy Spirit. When God's Spirit fills you, you can live a victorious, triumphant life.

Master, in Your holy name and through the Holy Spirit I will triumph over temptation. Amen.

HEALTHY HUMAN RELATIONS

If it is possible, as far as it depends on you, live at peace with everyone (Romans 12:18).

Life in the fast lane necessarily causes nerves to be on edge and tempers to flare up. The demands made on people put them under great pressure. As a result, we often find that peace-loving people snarl at each other because they are experiencing unbearable stress. It causes ill feelings and ultimately warped human relations.

As is the case with everything else that is worthwhile, you need a high level of self-control, discipline and the right attitude to work and live with others. It is imperative to respect the right of others to have their own opinions and viewpoints. You are compelled to accommodate these, even though you may not always agree.

Every person has the right to a fair hearing. Anything short of it implies bad manners and a lack of consideration for the other person's fundamental human rights.

To obtain this goal, you must follow the example of our Lord Jesus Christ. His revelation of selfless love, compassion and humility drew people to Him, yet did nothing to minimize the authority He had or the respect that even His enemies treated Him with.

Make Christ your role model regarding your attitudes and conduct and then you will enjoy healthy relationships with the people He sends across your path.

Living Lord and Redeemer, I follow Your example so that I can live in peace with myself and others. Amen.

ADVICE FOR DEPRESSION

Why are you downcast, O my soul? Why so disturbed within me? Put your hope in God, for I will yet praise Him, my Savior and my God (Psalm 42:5-6).

When your spirit is downcast and it seems as if everything you touch is doomed to fail, it is difficult to maintain a spirit of hope and expectation. The situation becomes worse because you cannot hide this depression. Few people understand what it feels like when this morbid spirit descends on your life.

There are, however, very definite ways to fight this situation:

- Firmly believe that God is greater than your circumstances or problems that are weighing you down and accept victory in His name. Say with Paul, "In all these things we are more than conquerors through Him who loved us" (Rom. 8:37).
- Lay your problems and tensions before your heavenly Father in prayer. Don't use vain, meaningless words. Communicate with God without ceasing. Pray about your current needs and expose every private problem to Him. The results will uplift and gladden your spirit.
- Believe that God can and wants to achieve something through this dark period of your life. "We know that in all things God works for the good of those who love Him" (Rom. 8:28).
- Identify the cause of the state you are in. If you are sick, consult a doctor. Visit people. Go out and meet life – even if it means to struggle at first.
- Turn your eyes away from yourself and your problems and see the world in need out there. See God's purpose with the world. The world belongs to God and you are His child and He loves you!

Eternal and unchanging God, in Your presence my depression is driven away and my downcast spirit strengthened. Amen.

THE TITUS-MINISTRY

God, who comforts the downcast, comforted us by the coming of Titus, and not only by his coming, but also by the comfort you had given him (2 Corinthians 7:6-7).

The world is teeming with people who are downcast. And with it prophets of doom – people who take a morbid delight in spreading disturbing prophecies and rumors. They are never happier than when they can upset others with their idle gossip.

When people are at their lowest, they need the company of someone who can encourage them. You might be aware of the cause of a person's depression or despondency and you might know about something that could worsen the desperate situation. As an encourager, you should always find something positive to comment on.

A true follower of Jesus Christ will always try to have a stabilizing influence on a disturbing situation. Even though prophets of doom predict disasters, you can bring confidence and encouragement into the lives of those who are insecure and fearful of the future.

If you want to practice the Titus-ministry of encouragement and convey a spirit of stability to insecure, discouraged people, you need inner spiritual qualities that can only be obtained through continuous fellowship with the living Christ in your daily life.

If you live and work in the presence of Jesus Christ, your life will not only be enriched, but will also bring comfort and blessings into the lives of those you meet. This is a glorious but important ministry, because by God's grace you have the ability to encourage, inspire and stabilize.

Through the strength I receive by Your grace, Lord Jesus, I will also try to inspire and encourage others. Amen.

GOD IS ON YOUR SIDE!

So we say with confidence, "The Lord is my helper; I will not be afraid. What can man do to me?" (Hebrews 13:6).

All of us experience situations at some time or another where we feel extremely uncomfortable. You might be called upon to perform a task that you are not equipped for or feel incapable of doing. The situation you are in may create a feeling of fear or worry in you. The unknown and insecure future might cause you to become deeply anxious or concerned. Not one of us is totally exempt from similar feelings and sensations.

One of God's most comforting promises is found in Hebrews 13:5 where He assures us, "Never will I leave you; never will I forsake you." Christ also says in Matthew 28:20, "And surely I am with you always, to the very end of the age."

God lovingly invites you to turn to Him and to leave all your worries and cares with Jesus Christ. He cares for you; He is on your side; He loves you because you are His child. Jesus gave us the blessed assurance that nobody who comes to the Father through Him, will ever be turned away – and that nothing can take us from His hand!

When you are battling with a difficult situation, do not try to solve it in your own strength. If you do, you will experience the torture of stress and tension and find yourself sinking into a swamp of doubt and despondency.

Go to Christ in prayer with your problem and allow Him to guide you through difficult times. Also remember that there is nothing in the whole wide world that can ever separate you from His love.

My Guide and Lord, only You can enable me to tackle life with all its problems and to live victoriously. Amen.

FAITH IS NECESSARY FOR SUCCESS

Have faith in the LORD your God and you will be upheld and you will be successful (2 Chronicles 20:20).

Steadfast faith is essential if you wish to live a pure life. If your life is focused on God through Jesus Christ, you have the kind of faith that continuously inspires you and will inevitably lead to success.

Once you have achieved success it does not mean you can leave it at that. Success is an ongoing process which is forever revealing experiences which encourage you to live a fuller, richer life. If you should ever reach the stage where you feel you have achieved all that life has to offer and that there is nothing more to strive for, you will make the shocking discovery that you have lost something priceless.

You should always set goals for yourself and you must believe that you are able to achieve them. Always look ahead and conquer new horizons in His name. Your life should never be without a challenge.

Through the ages people have been searching for greater knowledge of God and a deeper experience with Him. A child of God's purpose should always be "to know Christ and the power of His resurrection and the fellowship of sharing in His sufferings" (Phil. 3:10). Only then does one experience a new awareness of God's presence and a taste of the inner joy brought about by the desire to reach greater spiritual heights.

While you practically apply your faith and it gains depth, you will succeed in enriching your spiritual life. That is real success. To achieve it faith is essential!

Through my faith in You, Lord, I understand life and the real meaning of success better. Amen.

WORD OF GOD: WORD OF LIFE

I want you to know, brothers, that the gospel I preached is not something that man made up (Galatians 1:11).

Since the beginning of man's existence on earth, he has been developing certain theories concerning various topics. Some are based on religious convictions or philosophical hypotheses; others represent the product of man's brain-power or imagination; and others are the result of academic research.

Many of these people regard the Bible with skepticism. Others apply their scientific principles in an effort to analyze the Bible in such a way that it will satisfy their reason. All these methods lead to conflicting views that do nothing else but confuse the whole issue of the authority of the Bible. They make the Bible as clear as muddy water.

In spite of being subjected to harsh criticism throughout the ages, the Bible has remained steadfast and intact. Theories have differed from one another; scientific formulae have changed; viewpoints have varied, but the Word of the eternal God, based on His wisdom and truth remains unalterable. First Peter 1:25 says, "The word of the Lord stands forever."

God Himself inspired the message of the Bible. The Gospels set a pattern for daily living that has stood the test of time. Hold on to the teachings of the Bible. It will be a source of never-ending inspiration, stability and peace to you.

O Word that became flesh, I build on Your foundation and I trust in the salvation that You bring. Even if mountains should crumble, You never will. Amen.

DOES CHRIST CONTROL YOUR LIFE?

Now I know that you fear God, because you have not withheld from me your son, your only son (Genesis 22:12).

There are many important matters that demand our attention every day. Our business, studies, taking care of our families, the aged or the sick are only a few of the justifiable and urgent demands made on our time and energy. Considering all this, one can certainly ask, "Is there still time for God in our lives?"

You would have preferred God to take up the supreme position as Ruler in your life and you would have liked Him to be top priority in every aspect of your life. But unfortunately that is impossible because you do have a very hectic life with many responsibilities.

Because God Himself lived among people, He fully understands the pressures we experience in our lives and how easily we become confused over our values. He nevertheless claims top position in your life. He is worthy of that position, and He knows that when He is placed first, He can influence you to live your life to His glory and to your immeasurable advantage.

When your heavenly Father is placed at the bottom of your priority list, you rob Him of His privilege to guide and accompany you and to do His will through you.

Honor Him with your time, talents and possessions. Lay your plans before Him in prayer and allow His Holy Spirit to permeate your thoughts. Then you will discover that, if He occupies the throne of your life, everything else falls into perspective.

Grant me the ability, O Lord, to put You first in everything so that Your Holy Spirit can control my entire life. Amen.

THE INFLUENCE OF AVOIDANCE

Where can I go from Your Spirit? Where can I flee from Your presence? (Psalm 139:7).

Many people bluntly refuse to face harsh realities and rather choose to follow an escape route instead of accepting reality. This is especially true of our spiritual lives. We sidestep the challenges of Jesus Christ.

When the Master calls you to do a specific task, you don't refuse openly, but you suddenly become very busy with something completely different. You think that you are still serving God, but you are not serving Him the way He expects you to.

Many earnest disciples of Jesus despise themselves when they realize they have turned away from the challenges of the Master because they feel too weak and incompetent to do what they know He requires of them. Therefore, make sure that in serving the Master you are pleasing Him and not yourself.

Turn your attention away from yourself, stop worrying about what people will think or say, and focus your love and commitment on the Master. When He holds top priority in your life, you will discover new strength and confidence at work. This will enable you to accept every challenge or task He sets before you.

To sidestep or avoid the duty you have to perform, will paralyze your moral and spiritual life. Accept the challenges of life in the strength and power of Christ. Then you will develop the spiritual strength that keeps you on God's predetermined course for your life.

Lord of my life, give me the courage to persevere on the road You have planned for me. Amen.

The Blessing of Positive Thinking

Pleasant words are a honeycomb, sweet to the soul and healing to the bones (Proverbs 16:24).

Old age is not so much a matter of years, but more of an attitude and outlook on life. Your thoughts must be positive and constructive and it is imperative to strive for physical and spiritual health. We don't have answers to the secret of happiness in life yet, but there are a few things that we do know.

- It is possible to be happy, satisfied and productive even in old age. People who are creative reveal fewer signs of stagnation and degeneration than their inactive peers.
- A healthy love for the life God has granted you is not something that can be switched on and off like a program on TV. It is a lifestyle and attitude built up over many years.
- Cheerfulness is a treasured possession. It doesn't safeguard you against depression but makes us acceptable companions and friends. A sense of humor is a great asset in old age. The writer of Proverbs rightly said, "A cheerful heart is good medicine, but a crushed spirit dries up the bones" (Prov. 17:22).
- An anonymous author wrote the following prayer on growing older, "Master, teach me the valuable lesson that it is possible for me to be wrong at times. Keep me reasonably pleasant. I do not want to be a saint because some of them are difficult to get along with and an aged person who has turned surly is one of Satan's masterpieces. Make me thoughtful, but not moody, helpful but not bossy. It seems like a tragedy not to use the vast stock of wisdom that I have built up, but You know, O Lord, that after all, I still wish to keep a few good friends."

Lord of my life, make my words and actions pleasant and help me to be the bearer of Your joy and love. Amen.

THE SPIRIT GLORIFIES CHRIST

"He will bring glory to Me by taking from what is Mine and making it known to you" (John 16:14).

We cannot fully understand and appreciate the work of the Holy Spirit unless we understand His relationship with Christ. Christ promised that the Holy Spirit would come to comfort His followers when He left them. The Spirit would reveal Christ to their hearts in His triumphant, heavenly glory.

The disciples longed to have Christ with them continually and permanently. Because He was fully aware of this longing, He promised them that the Holy Spirit would reveal Himself to them in a special way.

It was a glorious gift of grace – and it is still available to every follower of Jesus Christ. Everything that the Spirit would receive from Christ, He would reveal to God's children: His love, peace, joy. Everything that could be a blessing to them, the Spirit would reveal and bestow.

In the life of the dedicated disciple, the Holy Spirit ensures the strengthening presence of Jesus Christ! The Spirit helps us to remain in constant fellowship with Jesus; to get to know and serve Him better.

The Holy Spirit quietly works inside us with dynamic power. The fruit of the Spirit grows in our hearts imperceptibly and is revealed by our lives, "The fruit of the Spirit is love, joy, peace, patience, kindness, goodness, faithfulness, gentleness and self-control" (Gal. 5:22).

In this way, God, through Jesus Christ, is glorified in us by the help of the Holy Spirit. This is what we have to watch, pray and work for.

O Holy Spirit, let Christ live in me and strengthen me against evil powers. Thank You, O God, that You love me with eternal love. Amen.

ACCEPT THE TRUTH

The man of integrity walks securely, but he who takes crooked paths will be found out (Proverbs 10:9).

It is often easier to ignore a weakness than to try and overcome it. If you are an introvert and don't like getting involved in arguments with other people, you will probably go to great lengths to avoid any form of conflict, even when you don't agree with something. To ignore a mistake won't make it disappear, but rather make you the victim.

To keep quiet about something that is wrong, causes you to brood on it only to have it expressed in unexpected and strange ways. If you are bottling up intense emotion, you will soon find that it is released in short-temperedness and irritation. You will get upset easily and soon your emotional stress will manifest itself in physical disorders.

When you become aware of something that is wrong, do everything within your power to set matters straight. Once you have identified the problem, ask God to help you deal with it wisely and in love. If you experience inner conflict and tension, seek deliverance by asking the Father's assistance. Allow His love to cast out all hatred and pride. Always maintain a spirit of forgiveness as it will neutralize the negative effect of stress and tension.

In your attempts to set matters straight, you must spend much time in prayer before expressing an opinion or passing judgment. Make sure your advice is born of love and wisdom and that it will help solve the problem. Allow God to work through you because then you will be serving the truth in love, and mistakes will be rectified in a constructive way.

I confess my mistakes and pray that You will help me overcome them. Guide me through Your Spirit to handle others' mistakes in love. Amen.

BEING WEAK IS NOT A SHAME

But God chose the foolish things of the world to shame the wise
(1 Corinthians 1:27).

Never despise yourself because you think you are weak. You may admire the great works that others do and desire to do the same deep down in your heart. Perhaps you did make an effort in the past, but failed so miserably that you decided never to try again. You accepted the weakness as a flaw in your character and decided that it formed such an integral part of your individuality that you could not do anything to change it.

The only shameful thing about a weakness is when you stop trying to overcome it. You were born helpless, but you were not meant to stay that way. You have the opportunity to develop power and strength through the grace of the almighty God.

It is God's will for you to be strong and therefore He supplies the power through the ministry of the Holy Spirit. He Himself promised that, "You will receive power when the Holy Spirit comes on you" (Acts 1:8). This power will enable and strengthen you to become the person God intended you to be.

Eventually every weakness can be overcome when you become aware of the fact that God's Spirit can dwell and work in your spirit. Through His ministry as the Spirit of grace, you discover that you have God-given talents and strength which give purpose and inspiration to your daily existence.

It is utter folly to be satisfied with weakness while you could be strong if you allow the Holy Spirit to work in you. Test God in this and you will find Him faithful!

O Holy Spirit of God, dwell in me so that I can overcome my weaknesses and become strong by the grace of God. Amen.

THE GRACE OF A NEW BEGINNING

He who was seated on the throne said, "I am making everything new!" (Revelation 21:5).

God's immeasurable grace makes it possible for a person never to reach a stage in life where he cannot start over. Every day is a new beginning! Our God is a God of "second chances" – even if you are a murderer on a cross! It is your privilege and responsibility to use every opportunity as you think best.

Due to failures of the past, you may have lost the spirit of hope and expectation. However, this can only happen if you allow it to. Whatever happened in the past may never cause you to lose sight of what the future may hold.

If you wish to experience a fresh start there are certain things you have to accept. First you have to decide that you want to lay down your old life once and for all. The new and the old cannot merge. Christ said, "Neither do men pour new wine into old wineskins. If they do, the skins will burst, the wine will run out and the wineskins will be ruined. No, they pour new wine into new wineskins, and both are preserved" (Matt. 9:17).

Secondly it is important to admit and realize that all new life comes from God, the Source and Creator of all life. Without this confession you will never get to know the dynamics of the Holy Spirit that flows through you with renewing power.

A new life that is based on a spiritual foundation requires an intellectual effort. You continually have to confirm that the new life that flows through you is the result of God's grace. A new life in Christ will then become your inheritance.

Praise the Lord for He is good! By His grace I am a new person! Amen.

REAL PEACE

Yet when I surveyed all that my hands had done and what I had toiled to achieve, everything was meaningless, a chasing after wind; nothing was gained under the sun (Ecclesiastes 2:11).

Different people have different values in life. Some people will give everything they have to obtain riches and earthly possessions. Others desire power and authority over people. There are those who strive for academic achievements while yet others withdraw themselves from society to live in total seclusion. The world is full of people who are striving to obtain a variety of goals and objectives, yet statistics prove that relatively few people find true peace of mind.

It is undoubtedly true that the above-mentioned people will experience a sense of satisfaction for some time when they have achieved another goal in their search for happiness and peace. Eventually feelings of dissatisfaction, unhappiness and frustration will replace their peace and their search for happiness will start all over again.

Jesus gave His disciples – including us – the following advice, "But seek first His kingdom and His righteousness and all these things will be given to you as well" (Matt. 6:33). If submission, dedication and obedience to God are of primary importance to you, God will make sure that you receive everything you need for your well-being.

Pope John Paul once said, "Peace is not established when treaties are signed in boardrooms. Peace is what comes from the heart of men." Follow Jesus' example in every situation and you will experience tranquility and peace that surpass all understanding. Only then will you find something in life that truly satisfies!

Peace, real peace You give when the burdens of life weigh us down. The way You show me, is the way to true happiness. Amen.

BE YOURSELF!

The voice is the voice of Jacob, but the hands are the hands of Esau
(Genesis 27:22).

It is surprising how many people try to be someone else. Often it is done subconsciously when in the company of important people.

Opinions, language and attitudes easily conform to the company that you keep at a specific stage. If the mood is rowdy and boisterous, you become equally loud. When the conversation is serious and intellectual, you try to do the same, sometimes with disastrous results. There are a variety of ways in which we try to adapt to people when we find ourselves in a given situation. Often we are scared to be "different".

Remember that God created you to be a unique, one-only individual. He does not make duplicates. He gave you your very own personality and mind as well as the ability to utilize and develop these. He is also gracious enough to give each of us a free will that determines our behavior.

You should never allow people to influence you negatively in the use of your God-given talents. Maintain an intimate relationship with Jesus Christ and allow His Holy Spirit to control your mind and attitude. Then you will act with new-found confidence. You will earn the respect of others and peace of mind will become an integral part of your life as you trust in Jesus.

Always remember that Jesus said, "If a man remains in Me and I in him, he will bear much fruit; apart from Me you can do nothing" (John 15:5).

With the help of Your Holy Spirit, dear Lord, I will try to be the person that You intend for me to be. Amen.

Spiritual Bankruptcy

"What good will it be for a man if he gains the whole world, yet forfeits his soul? Or what can a man give in exchange for his soul?" (Matthew 16:26).

The average person wants to achieve something in life and wants to know that he did not live in vain. To be able to experience this satisfaction, he keeps on setting goals for himself and then tries to achieve what he feels is imperative for his success. He surrounds himself with everything that status and riches can offer: a large income that will ensure a sense of security; friends who will help him reach his goals and introduce him to the "right" people.

Often when people have gained everything they could ever have hoped for they still feel dissatisfied and empty. They get a vague impression that they missed out on something of cardinal importance.

Anybody who has neglected his spiritual life is foolish and short-sighted however successful he may be in worldly matters. He has mistakenly convinced himself that gold is more important than God; that the visible is more important than the invisible; that a forged balance sheet is more important than honesty and integrity.

Nobody who disregards God can be successful. When your spiritual life is in harmony with God and when you keep on growing until you reach spiritual maturity – only then do you understand the meaning and purpose of life.

Not to acknowledge the indwelling Spirit of Christ is a recipe for disaster. Then you only "exist" without living the vibrant, abundant life that Christ promised us. That is spiritual bankruptcy that is much worse than financial bankruptcy.

Lord Jesus, I realize the importance of my spiritual life. Help me to understand the true meaning and purpose of life. Amen.

Spot Potential

I press on toward the goal to win the prize for which God has called me heavenward in Christ Jesus (Philippians 3:14).

It does not matter where you come from, but it does matter where you are going. In every lost sinner there is, by the grace of God, a potential saint.

Unfortunately most people regard the person who has fallen by the wayside as a sinner and a failure. Consider for one moment what that life can become through the omnipotence of Christ.

To condemn a person in advance or to give up on him is dangerous and unfair. It restricts your view on his real potential, especially if he has already been branded as a moral failure. It also creates a feeling of doubt and incompetence in that person who is keen to try and accept life's challenges.

To believe in someone's potential is a tremendous inspiration for that specific person. It encourages him to try even harder and to aim at even loftier objectives.

One of the most encouraging characteristics of Jesus' conduct towards ordinary people was the way in which He dealt with their past. He did not condemn the adulteress, but said to her, "Go now and leave your life of sin" (John 8:11). We find various cases in the Bible where He was confronted with people's sin and weaknesses and saw their potential instead of their past failures.

When you want to help someone who has come to a fall, you have to forget the past with all its miserable failures and encourage the person to accept help from the living Lord.

Loving and merciful Father, enable me to see each sinner as potentially saved because You saved me. Amen.

I KNOW FROM EXPERIENCE

I know that my Redeemer lives, and that in the end He will stand upon the earth (Job 19:25).

This is a glorious testimony, because it speaks of a steadfast certainty of God. It speaks of a heart that is at peace and a spirit that rises triumphantly above all situations and circumstances.

To say these words in faith is to approach life with total confidence. Nobody can know and trust his Lord and still go through life full of fear and anxiety. To know Him is to know life in its fullness. If one has experienced the fullness of life in Jesus Christ, it is no longer a rich promise only, but a glorious reality.

The person who thinks that faith in Jesus Christ robs one of all purpose, joy and beauty in life, lives according to a religious code not to be found in God's Word. Such a "faith" is definitely not based on the teachings of the Master. Because our Lord lives triumphantly and gloriously, those who follow Him will experience the same.

His power enables you to do the seemingly impossible and to live triumphantly. His love becomes a dynamic force in your life that enables you to live life to the full. Your life becomes balanced and calm and your joy originates from the very special relationship that you have with your heavenly Father.

This faith that is founded on experience, leads to an intimate, personal relationship between you and God. Your faith is no longer based on hearsay, but on firsthand knowledge gained from experience. Then you also find that everything else in your life falls into place with Jesus at the center.

Christ, my personal relationship with You will stand the test of eternity because Your grace is inexplicably great. Amen.

GLORY IN HIS GRACE

The grace of the Lord Jesus be with God's people. Amen (Revelation 22:21).

The benediction quoted above is the final words of the Bible. How soothing and comforting it is to leave this busy month of November behind with these words.

Most of us suffer torment at some or other time. We are not sure what to do then, because of our human weaknesses and shortsightedness. Some try to handle every situation in their own strength while others give up before they have even started because the problems seem insurmountable.

Then you find those who emanate self-confidence and who are exceptionally proud of their achievements. They claim all the credit for themselves and they proudly boast that they rely only on their own abilities.

Everybody, however, should be sure that the only way out of a problem, or the only reason for success, originates solely from the compassionate love and grace of our heavenly Father. Because He loves you, He blesses you with His grace.

If you are going through a tough time or trying to find relief for your heavily burdened heart, submit yourself unconditionally to the grace of our Lord Jesus Christ and pray for the strength to see you through these bad times. He promised never to leave you nor forsake you.

When you consider your achievements and successes of the past year, always remember that without the grace of God nothing would have been possible.

O Lord, I glory in Your grace. You saved me and You are my heart's desire. Amen.

DECEMBER

IMMANUEL! GOD WITH US!

The Word became flesh and made His dwelling among us. We have seen His glory, the glory of the One and Only, who came from the Father, full of grace and truth (John 1:14).

Few people were aware of the fact that the Child was born in Bethlehem. That this Child could be the long-awaited Messiah did not even cross their minds. Very few people had the spiritual insight to appreciate this miracle. Those who did expect the Messiah were looking for something radically different, as He would be the "Wonderful Counselor, Mighty God, Everlasting Father, Prince of Peace" (Isa. 9:6).

They expected a successor to the throne of David. Therefore, it was quite unthinkable that He would come in such utter poverty, without the pomp and ceremony that usually accompanied a royal birth.

Nevertheless, this was the Child who had come to influence the history of mankind like nobody before or after Him.

Even in the twenty-first century this Child has an immeasurable influence on all mankind. He is loved and hated; respected and despised; accepted or rejected. He still inspires the humble at heart and still changes cowards into heroes. This can only happen because He is and will remain a living reality in this world.

May you experience the presence of the risen, living Christ every day of this Christmas season and may this fill your heart with great joy.

Thank You, Jesus, that You are Immanuel! Make this Christmas season joyous and meaningful because You are the Center. Amen.

IMPROBABLE GROWTH

A shoot will come up from the stump of Jesse; from his roots a Branch will bear fruit (Isaiah 11:1).

Who would be interested in a tree trunk that was chopped down and left to rot? It is a sign that all growth and beauty has come to an end, regardless of how majestic that tree might once have been.

This was the case with the house of David. This royal family once grew strong like a tall tree in the center of the nation. But in time it was stripped of its splendor. Only ruins were left and all the former glory was gone. The only one who remained of this noble lineage was Mary, but she had such little status that she could not believe that God had chosen her to be the earthly mother of His Son.

Yet by God's power, from this poor remnant of the once mighty kingdom of David grew a shoot of unexpected, exciting new life. The shoot that Isaiah prophesied about is none other than Jesus Christ Himself!

A shoot can grow and develop into an independent, majestic tree. Christ has become an indestructible trunk. The Child became the Way, the Truth and the Life. Forever He will reign supreme over all the earth!

With Christmas drawing near, we have to evaluate our personal relationship with Christ once again. We must humble ourselves before Him because of our spiritual decay. From the stump of Jesse God brought forth new life.

In the same way He is able to make new, vibrant life spring forth from a spiritual life that has degenerated. He makes our lives a true feast in Christ.

Child of Bethlehem, I give my life into Your hands. You alone can make new life spring forth from a dried, half-dead trunk. Please do this for me Lord! Amen.

GLORY TO GOD!

"I will do whatever you ask in My name, so that the Son may bring glory to the Father" (John 14:13).

In the four gospels we find numerous accounts of the sensational miracles that Jesus performed. In the book of Acts we have proof of God's healing power working through the apostles to heal the sick, lame and blind. The apostles operated in the power of the Holy Spirit who took control of their lives on the day of Pentecost. Yet at every occasion they gave God all the glory.

After Christ's ascension divine healing was not mentioned that often in the early church. At that time there was an awakening regarding the powerful working of the Holy Spirit. Today we also find a growing revival in the church through the power of the Holy Spirit, with the emphasis on physical and spiritual healing.

Two important facts need to be mentioned with regard to this gracious ministry of God: First, it is common knowledge that healing includes the restoration of body, spirit and mind. A perfect body that houses a wounded spirit has little value. On the other hand it is true that a person who has a healthy mind and spiritual depth has the inner strength to cope with physical shortcomings.

Secondly, God, through Jesus Christ, is the great Physician. A ministry of healing that emphasizes anybody but God cannot be from God and must be regarded as false.

During this time of rest, come to God with your tattered life and give Him all the glory for healing and rejuvenation. Soli Deo Gloria!

I praise You, Father, that I can come to You with my sickness. Thank You for not only healing my body, but also my soul and spirit. Amen.

LIVE AN EXEMPLARY LIFE

May the favor of the Lord our God rest upon us (Psalm 90:17).

Others judge our lives daily and it influences them to a greater or lesser extent. If you are self-centered and selfish, petty and bigoted, people will only tolerate your company when they are forced to, otherwise they will try to avoid you at all cost.

Such an unfortunate situation reflects spiritual and mental immaturity. Some people boast that they don't care what others think of them or say about them. With such an attitude they avoid the challenge to develop an exemplary life as a Christian that will be acceptable to their fellow man.

An exemplary life originates in man's inner being. That is where divine qualities enter a person's life. You become conscious of your union with your Creator as well as of everything else that is good and perfect. True exemplary conduct has a spiritual quality that can only become part of your life if you live in harmony with God through Christ and the Holy Spirit. Such harmony is an ever-deepening experience of growth into better understanding of the Father and His will for your life.

In this way you develop a nobility of character that is greater and more real than anything which can be obtained cosmetically. It involves a noble character that bears testimony of strength, understanding and Christian love.

While your personality is developing under the guidance of the Holy Spirit, your character will become pure, strong and exemplary. Because you know God, you will understand life and will also have compassionate understanding for your fellow man.

Holy Lord, may my humble and insignificant life reflect the beauty of Your character. Amen.

BE A PRACTICAL CHRISTIAN

In the same way, faith by itself, if it is not accompanied by action, is dead (James 2:17).

Many of us are preparing to go on holiday at this time of the year. We will find ourselves in a totally different environment, among totally different people who will be watching our behavior and thereby judge our Christianity.

Unfortunately there are many Christian disciples who don't always live creatively or constructively. They practice religion and are considered dedicated, but unfortunately their lives don't reveal Christ at all. Such people are often quite outspoken when it comes to certain dogmatic issues, but they lack a spirit of love and understanding except perhaps when they are in the company of like-minded people.

If you are a Christian who is filled with the attitude of your Master, you will be self-confident and enthusiastic. You will know that all things work together for your good because you love Him. You may still experience trials, testing and conflict, but you will be able to handle them, knowing that your Master is sufficient for you.

Your faith in Christ flows from your life as a blessing to those who come into contact with you. The depressed will be uplifted; those who feel defeated will receive a vision of victory; the weary will discover a new zest for life – all because something of your contagious faith has touched their lives.

A Christian is above all someone whom God can use – especially during the holiday season. He promised, "You will receive power when the Holy Spirit comes on you; and you will be My witnesses" (Acts 1:8).

My Guide and Lord, may I walk so close to You that others may see something of You in my life. Amen.

COMPASSIONATE CARE

"Whatever you did for the least of these brothers of Mine, you did for Me" (Matthew 25:40).

During the Christmas season we find more intensity of emotion than at any other time. The joy of those who can be with their loved ones is doubled because it is the festive season. For those who are alone because they have lost a loved one, the loneliness is doubled, because it is the festive season!

During the festive season there are joyful people in cheerful homes, but there are also tramps on the streets, prisoners in cells, sick people in hospitals, the lonely in apartments … and where Christmas brings so much joy to the privileged, it increases total desolation for others on a day that was meant to be so different.

Are you one of the privileged? If so, look around you and pray that your eyes may be opened to the pain and sorrow of so many others. Look for an opportunity to spread the peace of Christmas with a friendly smile, a visit, an invitation or a friendly gesture to those who need it. There are so many dark skies that you can help brighten up, so many heavy hearts whose burdens you can help carry, so much sorrow you can help alleviate. All that is required is an eye that sees the misery; an ear that hears a plea for help; a helping hand; a heart that reaches out in compassion to those in need.

Don't you want to enlarge your tent and make room for others? Joy is sure to follow because you cannot give someone roses without their fragrance clinging to your hand as well. "Whatever you did for one of the least of these brothers of Mine, you did for Me " (Matt. 25:40).

O Christ, make me an instrument of Your joy and peace this Christmas season. Amen.

STRENGTH IN LIVING WATER

God opened the hollow place at Lehi, and water came out of it. When Samson drank, his strength returned and he revived (Judges 15:19).

After his glorious victory over the Philistines, Samson was exhausted and thirsty. It is not unusual for people to feel drained of all strength towards the end of the year. Mental and physical exhaustion can cause this. You can also feel weak and worn out after you have received bad news and experienced trauma. Spiritual and emotional emptiness or confusion drains your energy and strength.

If you merely succumb to your emotions and meekly accept the situation, you are in danger of suffering a total breakdown both mentally and physically. The results can be as destructive as they are far-reaching. There is, however, a way of getting out of this vast, dismal desert.

Turn to Jesus Christ in the moment of intense weakness. He is the Water of Life. He is waiting to strengthen you with living water – that wonderful, refreshing gift from God. Make sure you reach the Fountain of living water like Samson did. The Lord is offering Himself to you. In and through Him you will be revived, refreshed and renewed in spirit and in mind. You need not suffer weakness and insecurity any longer because in Christ you become a new creation. Being filled with His Holy Spirit will revive you and your life will have new meaning and purpose.

Ask God to fill you with His Holy Spirit at all times but especially when you are experiencing a low in your life. He will enable you to triumph in times of spiritual barrenness. Drink deep draughts from the fountain of faith and overcome your weakness in His strength.

As the deer pants for the water, so I thirst for You, O God! Amen.

NIGHT OF ALL NIGHTS

There were shepherds living out in the fields nearby, keeping watch over their flocks at night (Luke 2:8).

In the Bible we read about a number of special nights. Some of them are laden with tragedy while others are ablaze with bright hopes and expectations.

The night that God's angel of death visited Egyptian homes was a night of terror and dread. Yet that same night brought liberation for the Israelites. The blood of the Lamb on the door posts protected them. This foreshadowed the redemption that God's children would enjoy in Jesus Christ.

The night Jacob slept under the starry sky and dreamt about the ladder that reached heaven was wonderful. At Bethel, he built an altar to the glory of God who appeared to him and made him wonderful promises.

Then there was the night in king Belshazzar's palace when a burning finger wrote on the wall, "You have been weighed on the scales and found wanting" (Dan. 5:27). It must have been a frightening experience. That same night Belshazzar died.

Yet another memorable night was when Jesus taught Nicodemus the eternal truth concerning the rebirth of man.

It was a night of fear when Jesus prayed in Gethsemane, "Yet not as I will, but as You will" (Matt. 26:39).

Then there was the dark, dark night when Peter denied Jesus – and Judas betrayed Him. But the greatest and most glorious of all nights was the one in which Jesus Christ our Lord was born. There were stars, angels, shepherds and magi, a stable and a crib – Joseph and Mary and the Child were there too! Praise the Lord!

Thank You, Lord Jesus, for that glorious night when You came to us so that we could come to God. Amen.

LIGHT IN THE DARKNESS!

The people walking in darkness have seen a great light; on those living in the land of the shadow of death a light has dawned (Isaiah 9:2).

Christmas announces the Advent or coming of Christ to drive back all darkness with His glorious light. The aged Simeon also calls the Child of Bethlehem, "a light for revelation to the Gentiles" (Luke 2:32).

There is appalling darkness in this world: thousands plod along in the darkness of unbelief, superstition and ignorance. The heathen, he that has become alienated from the church and the atheist live in spiritual darkness. They are all lost in the dark dungeons of their sin and are tortured by their own wickedness and disillusionment. Like Judas, who walked out into the dark night after betraying Jesus, they are often driven to suicide as a result of their evil deeds. Or they merely exist, living lives without any meaning.

This is quite unnecessary and it dishonors God. Christmas fulfilled Isaiah's prophecy, "The people walking in darkness have seen a great light" (Isa. 9:2).

This is a liberating message that expels all fear of the darkness of life and of death. The Child of Bethlehem came to conquer all darkness, to overcome death, to ensure that the grave would not be the end but only the bright doorway through which we enter into that brilliant glory that we call heaven. "Even though I walk through the valley of the shadow of death, I will fear no evil, for You are with me" (Ps. 23:4).

On that first Christmas day the Light of the world came to transform the darkness in our lives into bright, heavenly, glorious light that drives away the night!

Lord, my God, You are my Light and Redeemer. Whom shall I fear? Amen.

ENCOURAGEMENT

The Sovereign LORD has given me an instructed tongue, to know the word that sustains the weary (Isaiah 50:4).

Words have immeasurable power and influence. Because the effect of the spoken word can be so far-reaching, it is vitally important how we use words. Cynical adults have destroyed the enthusiasm of many young, dedicated Christians by proclaiming that their spiritual experiences would not last long. This leads to intense discouragement.

In every area of life you will find people who regard it their duty to discourage others. Unfortunately most of the time they themselves did not achieve anything worthwhile and deep inside they begrudge others their successes.

As followers of the Master who strive to follow His example, we must consciously try to say things that inspire and encourage. This does not imply that you must agree with everything, but that you speak a word of wisdom and encouragement to those who require help and guidance.

Sometimes it might be necessary to criticize, but this should never be done in an unfriendly or harsh manner. Let it always be in love, constructive and with Christ's attitude. To be a person who encourages makes you a blessing in the community where you live and work.

When you start treating people in this manner, you will find your own spirit inspired and you will become gloriously conscious of the Lord's presence in your life. Therefore, start practicing the ministry of encouragement in His name. It is most unlikely that you will experience despair yourself while encouraging others, especially if it is done in the attitude and love of the great Comforter.

Gracious Lord, You have encouraged me so often. Make me willing to be a source of encouragement to others. Amen.

ALL ROADS LEAD TO THE CHILD

"This will be a sign to you: You will find a baby wrapped in cloths and lying in a manger" (Luke 2:12).

There are people who keep on demanding concrete proof of God's existence. Although they are living in a world of miracles, they refuse to notice or acknowledge it. It is difficult to establish what proof will satisfy their searching minds, because the great universe speaks clearly of God's power to work miracles.

God uses various ways to speak to man: through nature and through Scripture and also through the Word that became flesh. God's ways differ so much from man's ways. Scripture explains this in 1 Corinthians 1:27-29, "But God chose the foolish things of the world to shame the wise … He chose the lowly things of the world and the despised things – and the things that are not – to nullify the things that are, so that no one may boast before Him."

God revealed Himself to the humble shepherds as well as the magi by showing them the Baby in the manger. That confirmed their faith. Together, in spite of their diversity they worshiped the Child.

God has given man ample proof of His greatness and goodness. It is your duty to recognize Him in the miracles that happen around you daily. See Him in the vastness of the expanse, but also in small, simple things.

God reveals Himself to you in your private world. Whatever road you have taken to the crib, your worship of Him unites with that of all those who each followed their own road to reach Him. True worship transcends human differences and makes us one before God.

Immanuel, thank You that I may worship You in unity with all believers in a spirit of love and understanding during this season. Amen.

FROM CRIB TO CROSS AND CROWN

"Look, the Lamb of God, who takes away the sin of the world!"
(John 1:29).

It is a wonderful privilege to kneel at the crib with the shepherds and the magi but the person who does not look beyond the crib has not even begun to understand the true meaning of Christmas.

Jesus was born to die and we must already see the shadow of the cross on Golgotha. We must see the Child suffering and hear Him cry out, "My God, My God, why have You forsaken Me?" (Matt. 27:46) before we can understand the real meaning of Immanuel – God with us.

The American author Frederick Beuchner gives us an interpretation of the nativity scene through the eyes of one of the magi,

> We weren't there long, but let me tell you, we already saw it on His face, there, that evening … death, His death. It was like a crown on His head – this death that He would die. And we knew, that night, that to stay with Him would mean looking for trouble. It would mean being willing to share His death. Perhaps that is why we left so soon.
>
> "But now, after many years I'm asking you, brothers, and God knows, I'm asking myself first of all: Isn't it the truth perhaps – a truth greater than any other truth, greater than the stars we studied – that to try and live without Him is a death that is far worse than to die with Him?

We look beyond the crib and the cross and see the crown He wears because He overcame death and rose triumphantly. And He promised, "Be faithful, even to the point of death, and I will give you the crown of life" (Rev. 2:10).

Blessed Child, Jesus, crucified and risen Lord, thank You for the new life that I found in You by dying to myself. Amen.

A KING WITHOUT AN ADDRESS

He came to that which was His own, but His own did not receive Him (John 1:11).

We know that the omnipotent God is the Creator of the universe and that everything in heaven and on earth belongs to Christ through God the Father. He prepared a special place for Himself in the universe where He would stay when He descended to earth in the flesh.

For this purpose the nation of Israel was elected. God established a gracious covenant with them. With words of love He prepared them for His coming. Through the words of Micah and other prophets He portrayed both the humiliation and elevation of the Messiah for them. When the King of kings was born as a man, He came to a nation that was His own in a very special sense.

Though He came to His own, His own did not accept Him. It was as if all of creation was holding its breath for this great moment. One would expect Him to find a door wide open into the house of Israel, especially among the servants in His temple.

How disappointing the reception was that they prepared for Him. He came to His own, only to be rejected by His own – a King who came to bless and bring forgiveness, righteousness, sanctification, and eternal life to His people. But the palace door was locked. A king without an address, not even the inn had a place for Him.

And this is how Christmas becomes part of the suffering of our Lord. Beyond the wooden crib we see the wooden cross and hear the violent cry of His own people, "Crucify Him! Crucify Him!" When the Son of Man came to His own, He was met with unbelief and rejection. If He had to come again today – would it be any different?

O Holy Child, I beg You to make my heart and life a fit dwelling-place for You. Amen.

FOLLOW YOUR GUIDING STARS

The star they had seen in the east went ahead of them until it stopped over the place where the Child was. When they saw the star, they were overjoyed (Matthew 2:9-10).

The magi went to Jerusalem in search of the King. They were received as honored guests at the court of King Herod and also discussed their search with theologians. But neither the royal hospitality nor their shared knowledge brought them any closer to their goal. That was why they left the palace and the bright city lights. Only then were they able to see the brightness of the star that guided them to Bethlehem.

God supplies guiding stars to guide people along the path of life. You are no exception. Perhaps you do not fully appreciate the value of this truth because you might be wasting your time on petty matters that blind you to the reality of this privilege. Your own achievements might satisfy you, yet God has prepared much, much more for you.

Risk breaking away from distracting influences and insignificant matters and start seeking the glory of God through the guidance of the Holy Spirit. Your whole approach towards life would change radically. Second-best will no longer satisfy you because you will desire to really know God and to serve and worship Him above all.

Acknowledge His authority and accept the guidance of the Holy Spirit. This requires time spent in reading the Scripture, prayer and meditation. Your obedience will result in positive, creative actions. Like the magi, your heart will be overjoyed.

Loving Savior, guide me through Your Holy Spirit into a deeper, more fruitful spiritual life in fellowship with You. Amen.

WHAT IS REALLY IMPORTANT?

This is my prayer: that your love may abound more and more in knowledge and depth of insight, so that you may be able to discern what is best (Philippians 1:9-10).

Christ was the center of everything that first Christmas. God meant it to be that way. Very subtly, however, He was pushed to the background to accommodate other things. For us to rectify that, there are a few matters that should be put in their right perspective.

We should not take part in commercializing Christmas. We must guard against becoming absorbed by all the accessories of Christmas and to push Christ aside. Always remember that Christmas is meant to celebrate Christ.

Celebrate Christmas with your family. On that first holy Christmas night, father, mother and Child were inextricably together in the stable. Christmas elevated the family to a divine unity.

Every Christmas card you send must be your personal confession of faith that testifies that Christ is the important factor, not human sentiments. We must experience the glory of Christmas in our hearts because this Child is also our Lord. We defy God's divine purpose with Christmas by seeking superficial happiness in senseless festivities, drinking sprees and dances.

At Christmas the world must see to whom we belong: the cards we send must be Christ-centric; our Christmas tree should symbolize the cross and our sacrifices must testify that we have sacrificed our lives to the Child of Bethlehem.

Father, guide me beyond the outward signs of Christmas to find true inner joy that can only be found in the Christ Child. Amen.

God's Glorious Guidance

Blessed is the nation whose God is the LORD (Psalm 33:12).

Every day should be a day of thanksgiving that proclaims God's omnipotence; that He controls history; that He answers prayer; that He lives eternally.

We must call to mind the "great and glorious deeds that the Lord has done." When the sun stood still for Joshua in the valley of Aijalon; when Christ changed water into wine; when He raised Lazarus from the dead; when He Himself triumphantly rose from the dead. The great wonder is that these were all acts of God – man had no part in any of them.

We should remember that God answers prayer. "God is our refuge and strength, an ever-present help in trouble" (Ps. 46:1). What a privilege it is to have a God who answers prayers in times of crisis! Prayer is not a form of escapism; it is the power that results in victory. Prayer is the concrete proof of our steadfast faith in a God who helps us to help ourselves.

At Christmas time we should also confirm the truth of Psalm 50:15, "Call upon Me in the day of trouble; I will deliver you, and you will honor Me." Our greatest danger does not come from the outside, but from within: not honoring God by submitting our lives to Him. That is why Christmas also calls us to turn back to God because without Him, history has no value or meaning.

If we are God's people and we are people of faith and prayer, then God will transform the crisis of our time into a glorious opportunity in which to proclaim His omnipotent power. Then we will experience peace.

Thank You, Almighty God, that I belong to You completely and am protected by Your omnipotence. Amen.

FILLED WITH PEACE

May the God of hope fill you with all joy and peace as you trust in Him, so that you may overflow with hope by the power of the Holy Spirit (Romans 15:13).

The God we worship is a God of peace! Whoever denies this fact is doomed to a never-ending struggle and eventual destruction. That is why God sent His Son to earth as the Prince of Peace.

Peace of mind is a gift from God. It is a spiritual state in which a person can confirm with David, "I will lie down and sleep in peace, for you alone, O Lord, make me dwell in safety" (Ps. 4:8).

How many sleepless hours do we spend in anxiety because we try to find peace without God? How we chastise ourselves unnecessarily because we look for calm and acquiescence somewhere else!

Peace of mind is that quiet, certain knowledge that I am safe and secure in God's care. Therefore, I realize that the opportunities life offers are greater than its worries and cares. When I accept God as the Source of my peace and joy and when I am bound to Him in faith, then I have taken the first step on the road to peace of mind and serenity.

Because my spirit is in harmony with God, I also live in harmony with my fellow man. Not being at peace with God makes it impossible to have healthy relationships with others and few things can destroy our peace of mind as easily as discord.

God's peace is a by-product of a life that is submitted to Him and in which He guides us to quiet waters of rest where there is peace. This happens on condition that we have a living, practical faith in our Savior, Jesus Christ.

God of Peace, protect us from our enemies, give us peace in our land so that we may experience prosperity as a gift from You. Amen.

In Quietness and Trust

In quietness and trust is your strength (Isaiah 30:15).

In this busy Christmas holiday season, it is good to come to a standstill for a while and to restore strength of body, soul and spirit. This can only happen if we take our battered body and spirit to God to become revitalized and empowered by Him. An anonymous writer blessed us with the following striking message and prayer:

Slow me down, O Lord.
Calm the anxious beating of my heart
with the peace that only You can give.
Check my hasty tread with a vision
of the eternal vastness of time.
Grant me, in the midst of days of confusion,
calmness not bound by time.
Break the tension of my nerves and muscles
with the soothing music of murmuring streams.
Allow me to understand the restorative power of sleep.
Teach me the art of one-minute-vacations:
to walk slower and enjoy the beauty of flowers;
to communicate with a friend,
to read a few lines of the Good News.
Remind me daily that the race is not always won by the swiftest;
that there is more to life than acceleration.
Let me look up through the branches
of towering trees and understand that they grow
strong and high because they grow slowly and well.

Lord, my God, You also rested from Your work. Teach me to relax meaningfully and creatively. Amen.

A GIFT FOR THE CHILD

They opened their treasures and presented Him with gifts of gold and of incense and of myrrh (Matthew 2:11).

It is a glorious mystery that God, the Giver of every good and perfect gift, finds pleasure in receiving gifts from those who love Him. Of course everything we own belongs to Him – we only manage all His treasures. This makes the wonder even greater and more glorious.

There is, however, one thing that the Master finds more precious than anything else: the love of your heart. Whatever we offer Him, whether it is time or service, has very little value unless it has been sanctified by our love for Him. Love is the total sacrifice that we can offer the Child of Bethlehem as a gift.

This gift makes all people equal in the eyes of God. There are those who are able to give Him pure gold, shining silver or precious myrrh; others again can only give Him a lamb ... yet others not even that. The Master looks beyond the gift to the quality of the love that inspired the offering. The love that sanctifies the gift is more important than the gift itself.

How can we bring Jesus gifts that are inspired by love? The practical application of our love for Jesus is to find another human being in need. These days you need not look very far. Then offer to help that person in the name of the great compassionate One. Do this in honor of His birth. Become a friend to the lonely; comfort those who mourn; feed the hungry; smile at the desperate. Then in the quietness of your heart, you will hear the voice of the Master saying, "Well done."

Above all give yourself anew to Him as a gift of gratitude.

May the love that I have in my heart towards You, O Lord, find expression in deeds of love towards people in need. Amen.

IF CHRIST HAD NOT COME

"If I had not come and spoken to them, they would not be guilty of sin. Now, however, they have no excuse for their sin" (John 15:22).

Isn't it true that one only appreciates something once it is no longer there? It is like that with your parents, your health, and your friends. What a touching thought when Christ Himself says, "If I had not come ..."

First of all we would not have experienced Christmas: no Christmas carols, presents, family get-togethers or Christmas blessings. It is difficult to picture such a situation without the shepherds and the angels; the magi and the star; Joseph and Mary ... the Child!

A real danger exists today for us to celebrate Christmas without Christ because we have pushed Him to the background of all our activities.

If Christ had not come we would have lived in a world without the message of love. Because that is the good news of Christmas: God loves us and we love God and one another – and this is possible only because Christ came!

If Christ had not come we would not have had the gospel. There would have been no Christian church. We would not have experienced prayer, baptism or Holy Communion. We would not have had the New Testament!

It would have been a world without redemption. We would have carried the burden of our own sin because the cross of reconciliation with God would not have been there. We would have lived under the cruel authority of Satan.

If Christ had not come, we would not have had any hope for the future. But, praise God, Christ came!

O Christ, I long for You who brought redemption for me! I praise and thank You for Your immeasurable love. Amen.

Do Not Fear!

"Do not be afraid. I bring you good news of great joy that will be for all the people" (Luke 2:10).

This world has become a labyrinth of fear. We are plagued by a thousand fears. We fear for what is going to happen to the world, we fear for our finances and our health, our children and our country, old age and loneliness, the past and the future, life … and death.

Where did this fear originate? It started in paradise at the time of the fall, "I heard You in the garden, and I was afraid" (Gen. 3:10). Sin is the root of all our fears and as long as man continues in sin, he will not be able to rid himself of fear.

Where do we go with our fear? Christmas proclaims, "Immanuel – God with us" God Himself says, "Do not be afraid" Therefore, the only place to go with our fear, is to Christ. A Savior was born so that He could free us from the bonds of fear. He removes God's judgment; He overcomes sin; He enables us to face the future fearlessly, because He promised, "Never will I leave you; never will I forsake you." (Heb. 13:5).

Love is the antidote for all our fears. John the apostle of love says, "There is no fear in love. But perfect love drives out fear" (1 John 4:18). On Christmas day God demonstrated His love for us, "For God so loved the world that He gave His one and only son" (John 3:16).

On Christmas day we can confess our love for Him afresh and prove our love for Him by loving our fellow men. Then we can face the future without fear.

Redeemer and Friend, thank You for setting me free from my fears. Even when I go through deep darkness, I will not fear for You are with me. Amen.

LIGHT IN THE DARKNESS

The light shines in the darkness, but the darkness has not understood it (John 1:5).

It is a tragic reflection on modern society that we have to be reminded every year of the true meaning of Christmas. For weeks and even months a commercial campaign gains momentum, and culminates in a shopping frenzy. This feverish commercial spirit leads to over-spending and wastefulness that is erroneously referred to as "the Christmas spirit". In actual fact it is a blatant denial of Christ's birth and life on earth.

This conflict between religious theory and actual religious practice is nothing new. Ever since the godly Light came to shine on earth in the person of Jesus Christ, people have failed miserably to appreciate its real value. At Christmas they stand in awe of the divine revelation and bring glory and honor to the Child of Bethlehem. But then they turn around and follow their previous superficial way of life again.

The light of Christ the Lord is still shining, but only those who choose to look beyond the superficial commercial Christmas celebrations can see it. To experience the light of Christ in your heart, you have to rid yourself of all powers that break you down and that are secretly at work in your personality. Pettiness caused by a lack of understanding; bitterness caused by a lack of love; jealousy cultivated by a feeling of inferiority as well as many other destructive forces can all be overcome when placed under Christ's scrutiny.

Before the light of Christ can shine into your heart, your heart and mind must be open to the influence of the Holy Spirit.

Jesus, Light of the world, shine freely in my life this Christmas so that I can reflect the light of Your love. Amen.

GOD VISITS US THROUGH CHRIST

God was reconciling the world to Himself in Christ, not counting men's sins against them (2 Corinthians 5:19).

The coming of our Lord Jesus Christ into this world is the single most important event in the history of mankind. Wise men and prophets foretold this event. He came to deliver man from the power of sin and evil and to reveal the person of God to all who would believe in Him.

No wonder that people looked forward to His coming, expecting Him to have all the nobility and royalty one would expect a king to have. Yet it was only the humble, like the shepherds at Ephrata and the magi from the East, who were able to recognize His divinity.

He came to save man with His sacrificial love. He first of all reached out to mankind by fully identifying with their suffering and imperfection. He did not condemn them for the sins they had committed, but offered them a positive, liberating alternative. There were, however, the spiritually blind and they rejected the light He offered and placed obstacles in the way of those who wanted to follow Him.

Christ comes to those who need Him and He requires total submission of themselves and their lives. When He owns your life, He fills it with praiseworthy qualities. He also guarantees God's presence so that His followers are able to accept the challenges and trials of life with the certain knowledge that "God is with me in every situation."

Christ's incarnation brings fulfillment, purpose, peace, power and everything else that is required to live a meaningful Christian life. Then God's coming in the person of Jesus Christ was not in vain.

Lord and Savior, thank You that I have been reconciled with You and can now live to glorify You. Amen.

IN THE FULLNESS OF TIME

After Jesus was born in Bethlehem in Judea, during the time of King Herod, Magi from the east came to Jerusalem (Matthew 2:1).

When the eternal Lord stepped into time, God's time reached its fullness. It happened at a very particular point in history and at a specific place. There is something final and complete regarding Christ's incarnation. From that moment on the world has never been the same, because it was confronted with holiness and righteousness in its purest form. Man now not only perceived his deepest humiliation, but also the dazzling heights that he could reach when inspired by Jesus Christ.

One of the outstanding results of the incarnation of Jesus is that a holy, sanctified life became a practical reality for the ordinary person. In every generation we find pious people who isolated themselves from the hurly-burly of everyday life to meditate on spiritual truths. They undoubtedly enriched society through their priceless contributions.

But the Carpenter of Nazareth lived among the people in the most humble circumstances. His life was totally submitted and dedicated to God.

Every time that you consciously enter His presence, you will be able to overcome even the most stubborn problems, triumph over temptations and live the mundane everyday life with dignity and courage.

When Christ enters your world, an unbelievable change occurs in your situation. Your life can never be the same again because in your life God's fullness of time becomes a reality and the Child of Bethlehem is born triumphantly into your life.

Faithful and eternal God, I praise and thank You that my times are in Your hands. Amen.

God's Saving Grace!

For the grace of God that brings salvation has appeared to all men (Titus 2:11).

On that first Christmas Day our heavenly Father stepped out of heaven to come and stay with us. "The virgin will be with child and will give birth to a Son, and they will call Him Immanuel – which means, "God with us" (Matt. 1:23).

On Christmas Day the saving grace of God becomes available to us through His Son, Jesus Christ. On Christmas Day Isaiah's words spoken many years before become a reality, "Your eyes will see the King in His beauty" (Isa. 33:17).

God revealed Himself as Father on Christmas Day. He stretched out His hands to bless mankind and to lead us along green pastures and beside quiet waters where there is peace. With caring hands He comforts us (see Isa. 66:13). With His artist's hands He re-creates our lives into masterpieces.

On Christmas Day God reveals Himself as the Son of Man who becomes flesh like man but remains without sin. He came to bear the curse of our sin so that we could be set free from it and so become His very own. He brings us victory – even over death – and gives us eternal life.

God's appearance on earth through Jesus Christ that first Christmas already had the latent promise of the Holy Spirit who would come to empower us; to equip us; to teach, guide and comfort us; to enlighten our minds, warm our hearts and lift our spirits in worship.

I wish you and your loved ones abundant Christmas blessings on this very special day – the day God's saving grace appeared!

Father, Son and Holy Spirit, I commit myself to You anew on this joyful Christmas Day. Amen.

To Live like Christmas Children

"I will set out and go back to my Father" (Luke 15:18).

This Christmas teaches us certain truths afresh – truths we must apply in our lives in the year that lies ahead.

We know that Jesus did not remain in the crib. For many people this never becomes real enough so that they follow Christ as He leaves the crib and the stable behind and stands firmly in practical everyday reality.

If Christ had remained a child we would never have received the Sermon on the Mount with the Beatitudes to satisfy man's needy heart. He would not have been able to carry the cross to Golgotha. He had to leave the stable and become a Man to fulfill the will of God.

Faith that remains in the stable is not sufficient: we must have faith based on the cross, Resurrection and Pentecost. Only then can God send us into the world to do His will.

If we really meet the Child of Bethlehem during the Christmas season, He will show us the way to the Father's house. Like the prodigal son, man also left his Father's house and was stuck in the land of sin. In his deepest need he found out that there is a Way back to the Father's house and heart.

That is the guarantee that Christmas gives us for the future. The Child became a Man and says to us, "I am the Way" We must undertake this journey and follow the Way from the crib to the cross and eventually into the Father's house and heart.

Father, I want to move beyond the crib. Help me to grow spiritually because I have experienced yet another Christmas through Your grace. Amen.

JOYFUL CHRISTIANITY

"My soul glorifies the Lord and my spirit rejoices in God my Savior" (Luke 1:46-47).

There are many people who regard their religion as a somewhat heavy and even unbearable burden. This dampens their enthusiasm and they are quick to frown on the slightest hint of light-heartedness in spiritual matters. They become very somber when they bend under the heavy burden of their religious conscience. God definitely did not intend it this way!

For a Christian his faith in God should be a joyful experience. Through Jesus Christ you are enabled to live in constant fellowship with the Father. He takes great interest in every aspect of your life. When you are happy, He is glad; He comforts you in your sorrow and sadness; He supports you when the burden becomes too heavy; He helps you to get up when you have stumbled over the obstacles in your spiritual life; He enjoys your successes just as much as you do.

Christianity does not remove joy and happiness from your life. On the contrary, Christianity restores your gladness and joy. Through your intimate fellowship with Christ you realize what a blessing His presence is every day. The more you thank and praise Him, the more joy you experience, knowing that He is with you always.

Joy is a fruit of the Holy Spirit (see Gal. 5:22). Your Christian submission and dedication should reveal the joy of the Lord in every aspect of your life. While you live daily for Christ, you must rejoice in the fact that He lives in you. His love and joy must be reflected in your life as a testimony for Him. Then, every day will be Christmas Day!

Dear Lord Jesus, I rejoice in the fact that You are with me always. Amen.

THANK GOD FOR FRIENDSHIP

Jonathan my brother; you were very dear to me. Your love for me was wonderful, more wonderful than that of women (2 Samuel 1:26).

This is the season when God enriches our lives as we reaffirm old friendships and establish new ones.

A friend is someone you can turn to without thinking twice when you go through hard times and who will sincerely share in your joy and good fortune.

You seek your friend's advice when you are worried, and welcome his good wishes once the problem is solved. You can share a secret with him, but he will never search your heart, looking for secrets that should not be revealed. You lean on him when your heart wants to break yet he never exploits it. He goes down on his knees with you when life has dealt you a blow.

You can cry on his shoulder when you are sad and laugh freely with him when you are happy. He will have tears on his cheeks when you suffer and a twinkle in the eye when the sun is shining for you again. He marvels at your good qualities and loves you in spite of your weaknesses.

He laughs at your moods without getting angry. He is proud when you excel, but is not ashamed of you when you fail. He is satisfied when you please him, yet does not blame you when you disappoint him. He will tell you the truth, even if it might hurt you and you can tell him the truth without fear of offending him.

He will not hesitate to prove his friendship, even at the risk of it being abused. He helps without expecting anything in return.

Redeemer and Friend, help me to be a faithful friend. Thank You that You want to be my best Friend. Amen.

DRAWING UP A BALANCE SHEET

Search me, O God, and know my heart; test me and know my anxious thoughts (Psalm 139:23).

The dying days of the year are days of stock taking and self-examination. That is why this prayer is also our prayer during these sacred moments. Some of our prayers do not challenge us at all. We only say the prayer to soothe our conscience, but when a prayer is honest and soul-searching it is also liberating.

Praying that God will search and know your heart can create a total revolution. It strips one of all superficiality and hypocrisy. You see yourself as God sees you. It is a humbling experience but at the same time loaded with a rich measure of blessing and grace.

It is important to test and evaluate your life from time to time for unless we pass God's test, He cannot use us. Under the guidance of the Holy Spirit we become instruments in His hand and are used to His glory.

If our introspection leads us to a better understanding of our own weaknesses, unworthiness, sinfulness and insufficiency, it should never drive us to despair. We should then cling to Him more tightly as the unchanging, gracious, eternal Father. Christ promised us in 1 John 1:9, "If we confess our sins, He is faithful and just and will forgive us our sins and purify us from all unrighteousness."

Examination then brings us to the eternal grace of God. When you appeal to that grace, you will never be disappointed. Even though you might have to sigh with Paul, "What a wretched man I am! Who will rescue me from this body of death?" Then the Holy Spirit answers in your inner being, "Thanks be to God – through Jesus Christ our Lord!" (Rom. 7:24-25).

You have shown me indescribable grace! Praise the Lord for His loving kindness endures forever and ever. Amen.

MEDITATION

When anxiety was great within me, Your consolation brought joy to my soul (Psalm 94:19).

We are left with the burnt-out ashes of the old year while the New Year is only a weak, dim glimmer ahead of us. While the year is experiencing its dying hours, we are tempted to look back. Unfortunately many people then dwell and concentrate on failures, disappointment and other misfortunes. It causes them to fear the future.

To meditate on the past certainly has its rightful place in your life, but then it should always be done constructively. You should learn from past mistakes, but not be weighed down by their burden. Also guard against excessive feelings of guilt.

At the same time you should be careful not to rest proudly on your laurels, congratulating yourself on the successes achieved during the past year. They should only serve as inspiration to strive for more in future and to work even harder in the year that lies ahead. They are but landmarks of God's eternal grace at work in your life.

When you prayerfully review experiences of the past year, you should be determined to enter the New Year in the company of Christ and under His guidance. Let Christ be your Example and your Guide. Let your mind become sensitive to the voice of the Holy Spirit, and make a decision to obey His will under all circumstances.

By employing balanced meditation, you will face the future with confidence, assurance and peace in spite of what may have happened in the past. You will only be able to do so when you live close to God, obeying His will. Then you will become aware how His consolation calms your soul.

You, who have always protected us, our God in whom we trust, You are our refuge when storms rage. We rest in You. Amen.

ALL'S WELL THAT ENDS WELL

Give thanks to the Lord, for He is good; His love endures forever
(Psalm 106:1).

I know in whom I trust,
even when day turns to darkness;
I know the Rock on whom I have built,
He is my salvation.
When I reach the end of my life,
totally free from all my cares and sorrow,
I will praise You with a purer song of praise
for every day of grace You granted me."

With these words we can leave the old year behind us and enter the new year. But more than that: we can approach our deathbed with them on our lips and enter eternity with them in our hearts.

Now, in the final moments of the year, we recall the entire path on which God has led us. We thank Him for every step of the way because He loved us through it all.

There is much for which we have to beg forgiveness: wasted time; love not spent; prayers that weren't uttered; missed opportunities.

There is an endless list for which we have to thank God: protection, healing, support and our daily bread.

May we be inspired by Marie Louise Haskins's words, "I asked the Man at the gate for a light for the dark road that lay ahead. He said to us, 'Place your weak hand in the almighty hand of God and walk courageously into the darkness. It would be better for you than a light and safer than a well-known path.' And so I walked holding God's hand towards the breaking of a new day in the East."

O Lord, we thank You abundantly for the past year and we enter the future holding Your almighty, loving hand. Amen.